# Lemurs of the Lost World

**Exploring the forests and
Crocodile Caves of Madagascar**

2nd Edition

## Jane Wilson

'Excellent and exciting'
*The Good Book Guide*

'Fascinating'
*Geographical Magazine*

'Wilson's nicely written and highly
entertaining account is full of lively
and colourful anecdotes.'
*New Scientist*

# i

## impact books

First published in Great Britain 1990
by Impact Books, 70 Newcomen Street, London SE1 1YT
Second Edition, 1995

ISBN 1 874687 43 9

Photo acknowledgements: *front cover*, Jane Wilson; *back cover*, Simon
Howarth; *colour insert p. 1*, Dave Clarke; *p. 2 top left*, Paul Stewart; *pp. 2 & 3*,
Jane Wilson; *p. 4 bottom*, Mary Styles; *p. 4*, Jane Wilson; *p. 5 bottom*, Dave
Clarke; *p. 5*, Jane Wilson; *p. 6 bottom*, Paul Stewart; *p. 6*, Jane Wilson; *p. 7*,
Paul Stewart; *p. 8*, Paul Stewart.

Drawing on title page is by Paul Stewart

Made and printed in Great Britain by
The Guernsey Press Co. Ltd., Guernsey, Channel Islands.

*Mahaontsa ny fijeriko ny toeran-tsasany eto Imerina*
*Amin'izato tany menany. Moa tsy izany raha heverina*
*No nahatongo tsotra izao an'i Madagasikara*
*Ho nomena ny anarana: 'Nosy Mena' . . . Fanambara.*

*Fanambara ny havoana efa lanaka nodorana*
*Ary dia nokaohin-driaka avy tamin'ny ranonorana . . .*
*Eny no ahitanao, miaraka amin'ny lalan-driaka*
*Ireo tanàna fahagola'zay naorin-drazantsika*

*Tanàna toa mitovy endrika amin'ny tapenaka aminy*
*Sy ny fisoko amam-bala tazana eo an-toktaniny!*
*Ny fantsakana dia tsy misy fa any an-dohasaha any . . .*

*Ny taranaka ho avy dia hihevitra an'ireny*
*Ary hanangan-drindrina hafa ka hisolo tsy an-kiteny*
*'Reo tanànan-drindri-mena mahonena aoka izany!'*

I am moved at the sight of certain places in Imerina with their red soil.
Is this not why people give Madagascar
the simple name of 'Red Island' . . . evocative.

Evoking hills worn by fire and eroded into ravines by torrential rain . . .
It is there you will see, with their road-ravines,
the ancient villages constructed by our Ancestors.

Villages whose face is the gable roof, chicken hut and cattle corral
in the courtyard. But the well is down there in the valley. . . .

Descendants will think of them, and raise up ramparts which silently shall
replace these villages, villages of red walls that ask our compassion!

Dox's poem: *Folihana*, 1969

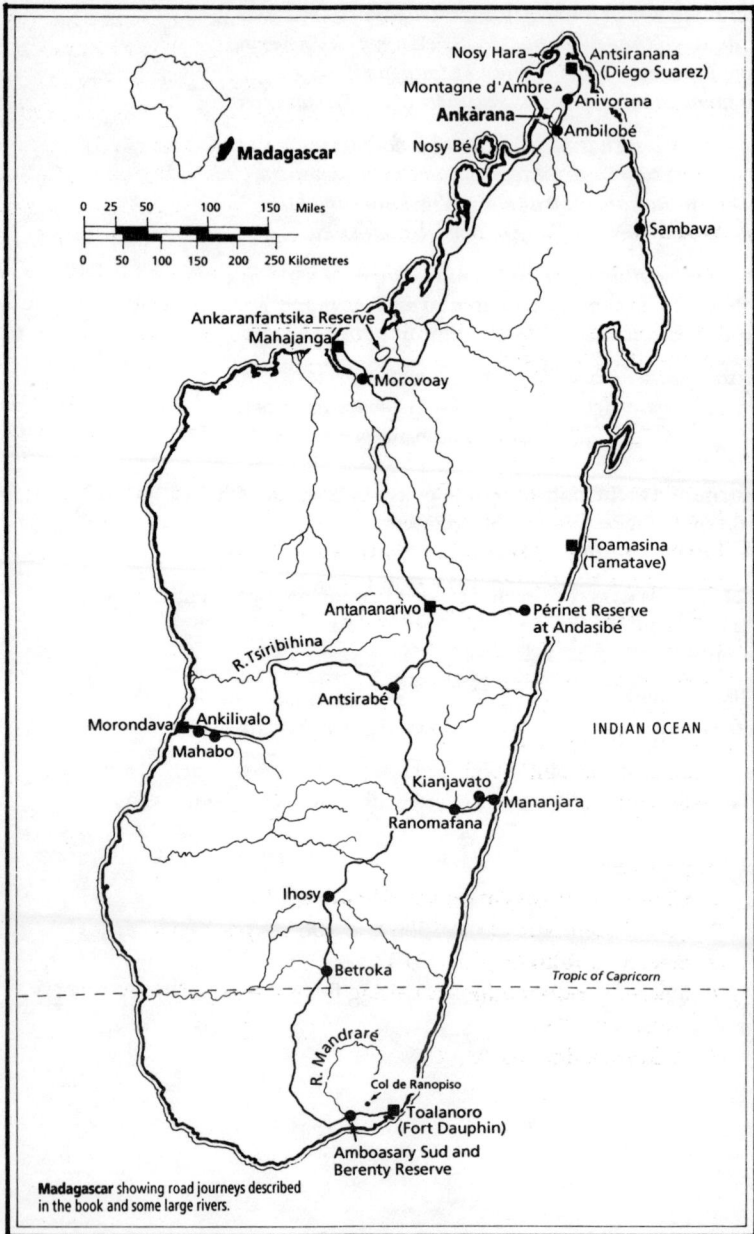

Montagne d'Ambre
**Ankàrana**
Nosy Bé

Nosy Hara
Antsiranana
(Diégo Suarez)
Anivorana
Ambilobé

Sambava

**Madagascar**

0  25  50      100        150   Miles

0   50   100   150   200   250 Kilometres

Ankaranfantsika Reserve
Mahajanga
Morovoay

Toamasina
(Tamatave)

Antananarivo
Périnet Reserve
at Andasibé

R. Tsiribihina

Antsirabé

INDIAN OCEAN

Morondava
Ankilivalo
Mahabo

Kianjavato
Mananjara
Ranomafana

Ihosy

Betroka

Tropic of Capricorn

R. Mandraré

Col de Ranopiso
Toalanoro
(Fort Dauphin)
Amboasary Sud and
Berenty Reserve

**Madagascar** showing road journeys described
in the book and some large rivers.

# Contents

# Preface to the Second Edition

When Jean Radofilao pioneered cave exploration in Ankàrana he found, in the heart of the Massif, footprints of a barefoot man heading into a cave from an isolated sunken forest, but there were no prints to tell that he had ever found his way out again. Jean named the passage *Fitsanantsanganan' ilay olona tokana*, the gallery of the lone barefoot stranger. Intrigued by this macabre story, we too found our way through several kilometres of huge cave passages. It was a relief to reach daylight again in the Isolated Forest, but walled in as it was by 200m cliffs, we felt a long way from home. It took us a couple of hours to scramble the kilometre up and down over the abrasive house-sized blocks which must once have formed the roof of this vast cavern, for growing thick all around was thorny scrub and unyielding lianas. Finally, with lemurs screaming at us in fury and alarm, we had hacked across to the far wall of the sunken forest, and the mud-lined, slippery passages which continued on a smaller scale. This was an eerie, unpleasant cave and I hurried to finish my ecological work. Yet, lurking in sterile-looking muddy ponds, I found several species of blind, cave-adapted shrimps which were new to science. And this was the cave where one of the most remarkable finds in Ankàrana was made since the first edition of this book: a near-complete skeleton belonging, not to the lone man, but to a long-since extinct Sloth Lemur.

As well as the 1987 filming expedition, Ankàrana attracted annual expeditions by Malagasy and American palaeontologists who have discovered that Ankàrana once had an even richer lemur fauna than survives today: including the weird giant Sloth Lemur. It was hitherto unknown to science, weighed about 15 kg and was named in honour of Jean Radofilao. The lemurs which survive at Ankàrana, or are now known to have lived there, total 17. This is a remarkable number of species (they are listed in a new Appendix 1 and our most recent scientific papers on the ecology of Ankàrana are included in an up-dated Appendix 4).

When I first started work on this book, I thought that it would be a record of our exploits in an obscure corner of the globe which would attract few other adventurers. After all, they had been hard expeditions and that scorpion might well have killed me. Yet this is a unique region, which supports amongst the highest concentrations and greatest diversity of primates on earth; it should have come as no surprise then that our descriptions attracted attention to Ankàrana so that now it is on the itinerary of the more hardy ecologists visiting Madagascar.

One researcher, David Lees, wrote of his excitement in seeing huge Sunset Moths (*Chrysidiria*) laying eggs on *Omphalea* succulents (another new species) growing out of the bare *tsingy*. It was a boost to realise that scientists continue to catalogue Ankàrana's abundance, but when I heard of package tourists visiting Ankàrana, I began to wonder whether I had been right in publicising the region. Idylls have been destroyed by writers in the past.

The very fortress-like nature of the Ankàrana Massif, however, should continue to protect it from this new kind of onslaught: no-one has yet reached the largest sunken forest which is guarded by kilometres of *tsingy* sharp enough to bacon-slice anyone who slips. Yet since our exploration work, local guides have discovered gentler routes up onto the *tsingy* in a few places. The film about Ankàrana features the magical, almost crater-like *Lac Vert* which we found so difficult to reach but locals now know an easy route, as well as somewhere to bathe on the way. So access is easier and the steady trickle of more determined visitors attracted to the region and its phenomenal wildlife will help persuade villagers that they live in a very special place. These foreigners will also convince Malagasy bureaucrats in Antananarivo, who may never have seen a lemur in the wild, that outsiders are interested enough in Madagascar's peculiar wildlife to travel many miles and spend thousands of pounds to come and see it all. And Malagasy people will stop telling us that they have no exciting wildlife like lions, elephants and giraffes. They will develop a pride in living with their lemurs, the most enchanting of animals.

Finally I have one plea. If you are visiting Ankàrana, please don't feed the lemurs. They will become an inordinate nuisance and it is bad for their natural ecology.

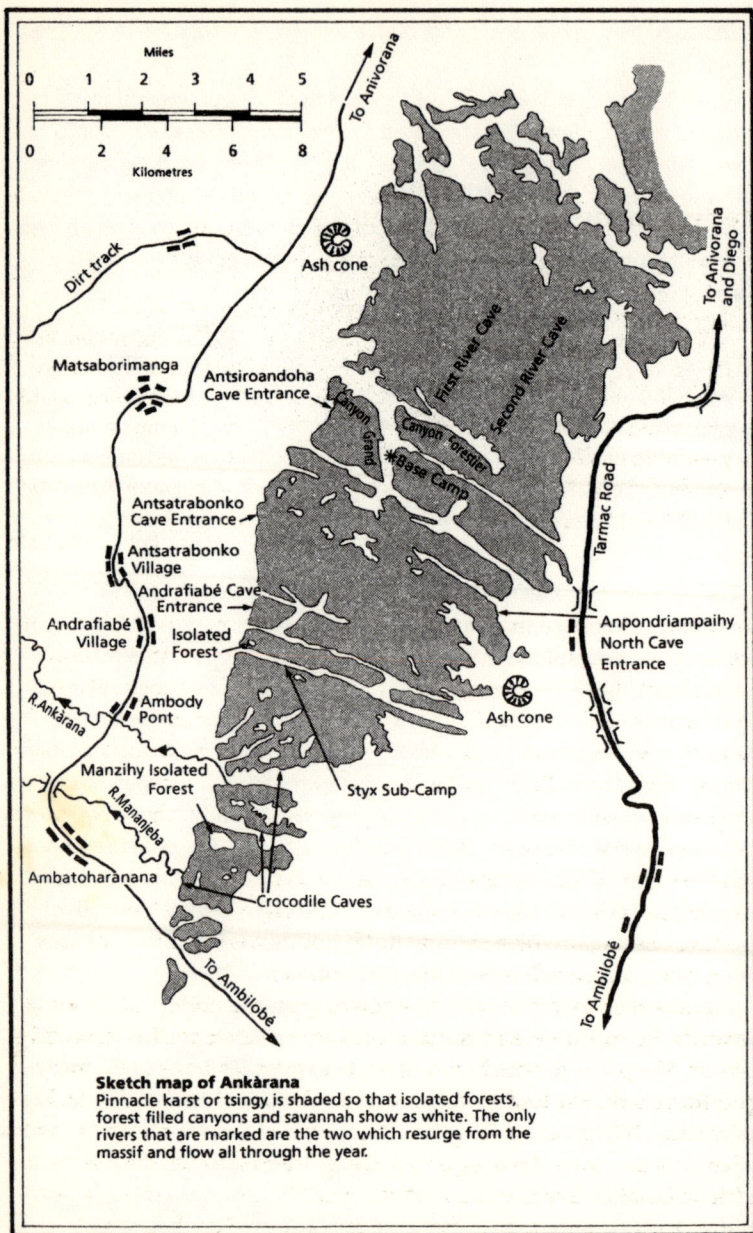

**Sketch map of Ankàrana**
Pinnacle karst or tsingy is shaded so that isolated forests,
forest filled canyons and savannah show as white. The only
rivers that are marked are the two which resurge from the
massif and flow all through the year.

# 1. Return to the Great Red Island

Madagascar is an island lying about 1,000 miles south of Socotra. . . .
You must know that this island is one of the biggest and best in the whole
world. It is said to measure about 4,000 miles in circumference. . . . More
elephants are bred here than in any province. . . . They have leopards and
lynxes and lions also in great numbers. . . . The great diversity of birds,
quite different from ours, is truly marvellous . . . and it is said that . . .
gryphon birds [rukhs] [there] are so huge and bulky that one of them can
pounce on an elephant and carry it up to a great height in the air.

Marco Polo, *circa* 1298

Something disturbed the water deep inside the cave – it was the sort of
noise a large animal would make sliding into the river. After so many
days alone my mind ran riot. I tried to counter fear with logic. If there
were crocodiles in my 'bathroom' I would surely have encountered
them by now, for I had swum the entire length of the little subterranean
river several times. Perhaps it was mud sliding into the water. There
had been only one splash and the ripples died away, as they always did.
I strained to hear more but there was nothing in there. Still I could not
convince myself that I was safe. My bath was hurried and I was soon
out, dripping dry on a boulder, relaxed and enjoying the view out of
the cave once again. Blue sky and fluffy clouds were framed by black
limestone and green leaves of the trees outside.

As I stood up to leave I noticed a gentle grunting noise and, looking
towards the entrance, saw the unmistakable silhouette of a Crowned
Lemur. She paused, with her long tail held over her body like a furry
question mark. She had spotted me. I stood motionless, hardly daring
to breathe. If frightened away from her waterhole now, she might warn
others not to return. Looking away, she grunted softly as if speaking to
a friend outside. Then, reassured, the rest of her troop arrived, looked
in my direction and, to my amazement, continued on their way

down, descending the same familiar climb I had used. They were quite unruffled by my presence.

I fidgeted, tiring of standing so still, but the lemurs ignored me even when I moved. I began to sit down slowly and make myself comfortable, hoping not to scare them. The troop cascaded over the limestone scarcely glancing in my direction. Then the leading female spotted my water container – lurking like a predator – in a crack where I had wedged it. She started making anxious grunting noises, twitching her upright tail to warn the others. The troop took up the urgent grunt-chorus as she scampered back outside. After a few minutes they regained their courage and surrounded the container, tails quivering as they challenged it. It did not react to their provocation and a reckless young male rushed in close and poked it. Still it remained inert. When they were convinced that it was not going to attack them, they continued down into the cave again. Their naïve behaviour – fearing a container but not Man, the deadliest of creatures – so amused and delighted me that I was unable to stifle a chuckle. They took no notice of me, even when I started taking flash photographs.

For generations, lemurs must have been coming here: tiny feet and hands had polished the rocks smooth down to the water. The troop disappeared through a gap in the boulders to a place where it was easy to drink. Five minutes later, they shot out of the cave with muzzles wet and stomachs bulging. This was a dangerous place for them with innumerable dark corners which could hide a Fosa – the lemurs' most dangerous predator. Yet they had to come here. Water was scarce and this one waterhole had to be shared by all the troops living in this isolated section of the forest.

Not wishing to be caught unprepared again, I refilled the water container and left the cave to collect binoculars and notebooks from my solitary campsite at the edge of the forest, then settled down among the boulders outside to await the next troop. It was not long before I was looking into the big round eyes of another Crowned Lemur. She stood on all fours, long bushy tail erect. The light was better out here and we studied each other carefully, just ten feet apart. She was a handsome, grey, cat-sized animal with a face and muzzle more like a fox than her monkey relatives. Her eyes looked wide and startled, but that is the normal expression of lemurs, reflecting their nocturnal ancestry. She too was quite undisturbed by my presence.

She turned her head to look over her shoulder and grunted softly. There was a response from the bushes to my left and she leapt effortlessly across the boulders and down to the cave, checking all around once more before descending into the darkness to drink. The leaves close to me rustled again and in two long easy leaps a male stood in the female's place. He was a little smaller than her and his charming brown teddy-bear face and black button nose made me smile. Between his furry round ears was the triangular patch of black which gives Crowned Lemurs their name. He grunted contentedly and followed the troop leader into the cave. More grunts came from the vegetation. Slowly I turned to look, trying not to startle whoever was there with any sudden movements. I had not seen them arrive, but two grey females were sitting quite close to me. They were cuddled up on a low horizontal branch, their tails wrapped around each other like feather boas. Sleepily they blinked at me, but some crashing beyond made them turn, take notice and start grunting more urgently, perhaps questioningly. The cause of the commotion apeared: a lanky, half-sized, one-year-old male. He bounced rather clumsily through the lower branches, leapt, missed the branch he was aiming for and fell two feet into the leaf-litter. He emerged a little ruffled and sped up the nearest tree. He stopped abruptly when he noticed me and stared boggle-eyed, tipping his head this way and that to regard me from different angles. His enquiring grunts earned him a reassuring response from his elders and he found the courage to bounce past me into the cave. The two females slowly roused themselves and followed.

Several minutes later the five reappeared and scampered two hundred feet up the sheer cliff above the cave. They started feeding on the thorny vegetation above, letting half-eaten *Pandanus* fruits and little stones fall around me.

I was privileged indeed to be in this tranquil glade with such delightful animals. These lemurs survive only in one tiny corner of the extreme north of Madagascar and are fast disappearing as their forest habitat is cleared. Having never learned that Man is a dangerous animal, they are easy to study and yet they are still almost totally unknown. It seemed incredible that I was the first to begin work on their ecology. A study of the Crowned Lemur in its natural habitat was already long overdue; they could even have become extinct without anyone realising. The task was reward in itself and more than ample repayment for the years of preparation needed to get back here to Ankàrana – the 'Place-of-the-Rock' – five years after my first brief visit.

☆

The third largest island in the world, Madagascar is the size of France and Switzerland combined. It is remarkable for its array of ecological relics, and for long it has fascinated European travellers. Few ever visited the island and accounts – including Marco Polo's – were more myth than fact. The most attractive animals are the lemurs, which are primitive primates. Madagascar alone has nearly as many primate species as the whole of the rest of Africa; it has seven of the world's nine baobabs, a thousand endemic orchids and more chamaeleon species than the rest of the world put together. Whole groups of animals are missing. There are no cats or hunting dogs, no antelope, giraffes, elephants or other large wild ungulates, no squirrels and no monkeys. Instead, isolation encouraged the few groups which reached Madagascar to flourish in unlikely ways. Who might have predicted, for example, that lemurs would stand in for absent woodpeckers, squirrels and monkeys and, before they were wiped out, for deer too. The Tenrecs, the oldest of the insectivore mammals and a remote relative of ourselves, have become pseudo-hedgehogs, pseudo-moles, pseudo-shrews and pseudo-watershrews. And Madagascar's Giant Rat hops around like a foot-long kangaroo; it looks like a rabbit, but roars like a lion.

Even Borneo and New Guinea, larger islands renowned for their luxuriant and exotic wildlife, have nowhere near the variety found on Madagascar. It is the island's climate and topography that are responsible for its enormous variety of habitats. A backbone of mountains along the east coast shelters most of the country from the Trade Winds which would otherwise bring rain from the Indian Ocean. East of the mountains, where the year is divided into the Rainy Season and the Season When It Rains, there is rich tropical forest; in the south-west there are scorched semi-arid spiny deserts. There are deciduous forests in the north-west and temperate moorlands in the central highlands. Borneo, lashed by monsoon winds from every direction, has little of these contrasts.

Madagascar – the Great Red Island – is shaped like a left foot. The Tropic of Capricorn runs through its heel in the south and its toes point north towards the Equator. I first went to Madagascar in 1981 with a small team of biologists from Southampton University to study lemurs at Berenty in the far south. After this academic study was completed, we travelled a thousand miles to Ankàrana at the opposite end of the island – in the big toe of the foot. We were cavers as well as biologists, and had gone to investigate intriguing reports of the longest cave systems in Madagascar and probably in the whole of Africa. We knew nothing then of its lemurs and it was not until we reached Ankàrana that we realised what a remarkable place it was. The caverns were of spectacular proportions, but more impressive still was the wildlife which lived in the forests nestling in and around the massif. The area was difficult to explore, but in the ten days we spent there we glimpsed incredible ecological riches. We left full of enthusiasm for a return trip.

Back in Britain, I tried to find out more about the area. At first I assumed that in a biologists' Mecca like Madagascar all the large attractive species would have been well researched by professional ecologists. Yet searching through the scientific literature, I was amazed to find that Ankàrana's furry forest animals were unstudied. Little had been published on Ankàrana except for a few cave maps and some superficial geological studies. There was almost nothing recorded about the fauna of the region, and our rather inconsequential reconnaissance turned out to be the most extensive zoological study ever done there. The Crowned Lemurs, which had visited our campsite every day, had never been studied in the wild before, and (as we discovered much later) Ankàrana was the key refuge for their dwindling populations. I was also rather alarmed to discover that the subterranean rivers in which we had been bathing were inhabited by the world's only cave-dwelling crocodiles. The massif boasted miles of vast cave passages and, where large caves had collapsed, isolated sunken forests grew, walled in by unscalable limestone cliffs. These Lost Worlds, flourishing in the heart of the massif, seemed perfect natural nature reserves, protecting lemurs and a wealth of other rare species, some endangered, others as yet undescribed by scientists. Why was Ankàrana so neglected? Could difficulty of access really have discouraged scientific study? Were the professional ecologists really so unadventurous? Or was Arkàrana not as exceptional as it seemed to me at first sight?

I was determined to return to find out, but it took five years to get back with the right team. I linked up with Phil Chapman, probably

the most active cave biologist in Britain. It did not take long to infect
Phil with my enthusiasm for Ankàrana. The invertebrate fauna of
Madagascar was not well documented and Phil was keen to study
all the undescribed new species that were sure to be hidden deep in
Ankàrana's caves. Knowing how little ecological research had been
done in the remote forests, I was anxious that the project should be a
comprehensive study of lemurs, birds, cave crocodiles and butterflies,
as well as some of the less attractive animals.

The expedition would have to be much bigger than the 1981
reconnaissance. We needed to get a strong team with boats into
the area, so that we could explore the underground rivers and
study their crocodiles. It would have to be big enough to effect
a rescue, too. Ankàrana's wild inhospitable terrain meant that the
expedition members would have to be fit and resourceful. There
are plenty of enthusiastic ecologists but it would not be easy to
find scientists capable of working in Ankàrana's difficult habitats. We
needed ecologists who were also competent cavers, able to penetrate
the isolated forests and abseil into collapsed caves as well as to carry
out scientific studies, regardless of the discomforts of expedition life.
Phil was certainly well qualified for this work. There were others who
had been on big expeditions to Borneo and the Amazon, but would
such people be comfortable with a woman leader? Would I be able
to win their respect and confidence? Would I be able to keep up with
the exploring parties?

I was more confident about my scientific abilities, for I was
trained in ecology and had studied lemurs before, albeit briefly.
I was also now a doctor and was keen that we should run some
clinics where we could start some health and conservation education.
I was embroiled in a 105-hours-a-week job as a junior hospital
doctor, and knew I could not cope with all the work expected of
an expedition leader as well, so when Phil suggested that we jointly
lead the expedition, I agreed, deviously planning to delegate to him
all the tedious bureacratic negotiations once we got to Madagascar.
Phil's fluency in French meant he would easily cope and he already
had a great deal of knowledge and expertise gleaned on numerous
large-scale tropical caving expeditions. My experience was only of a
few small, light-weight expeditions, where all the scientific projects
were limited by what we could carry in our rucksacks or what we
could improvise in the forest. We used to travel so light that Mary, my

sister, further reduced the weight of her luggage by cutting the labels out of her clothes.

There were very few people in Britain with expertise in both caving and natural history, but we knew two likely candidates for our team. Like Phil, Mick McHale had studied zoology at Bristol; Mick had recently accompanied Phil on an expedition to the Hawaiian lava caves and they knew they could work well together. On the few occasions that I had met him, Mick seemed amiable and easy-going. Compatibility and flexibility are as important to the success of an expedition as expertise, so in choosing our team I was interested in character as well as *curriculum vitae*. Mick not only seemed to have the ideal temperament for expedition life, but he was also an experienced caver, very fit and a good field biologist. Neither of us knew Simon Fowler so well. He was bearded, thick-set and tough-looking; people he had been on expeditions with spoke well of him. He was exceptionally well qualified, following a research career in entomology, and had worked on cave invertebrates during a series of demanding and dangerous expeditions to plumb some of the world's deepest potholes in the Picos de Europa in northern Spain. The four of us already made a strong team.

Word soon got round about our Crocodile Caves Expedition. Later I met Kev, a friend of Simon, who told me all about the expedition – not knowing who was organising it. The tales of Ankàrana had grown in the telling and Kev marvelled at the thought of zebras in the isolated forests. Baffled, I then realised he had confused zebras with zebu, African hump-backed cattle. The Lost World images in our publicity literature had caused Kev's imagination to work overtime – perhaps we should have employed him as expedition publicity officer, for he certainly had the power to fire enthusiasm in his listeners.

During the months that the 1986 expedition took to come to fruition, twenty people put their names forward for the team. They all worked hard on planning and fund-raising, but other commitments prevented some from coming with us: a frustrating consequence of the time it took to organise the project. Plans were discussed and changed and discussed again. Names were suggested and dismissed, people showed interest and then made excuses. More names were proposed and the team evolved. Dave Checkley and Sheila Hurd had read my account of the 1981 expedition to Ankàrana and this had stimulated them to mount their own independent spelaeological reconnaissance of Ankàrana.

They were interested in cave exploration and not biological research, but we decided it would be to both groups' advantage to join forces. At that stage Sheila and I were the only women in the team, but since I needed more help with the medical work, I suggested recruiting two more doctors – Maggie and Anne. Lively discussions followed about how much feminine infiltration should be allowed. The thought of taking additional women seemed to conjure up images of a picnic rather than a tough expedition to a remote place. Dave Checkley never quite came to terms with being a member of an expedition led by a woman, particularly one who did not even approach his level of caving experience and skills.

Phil and I started the long business of getting official permission in Madagascar for our research. The country had virtually closed its borders to foreign scientists after Independence, in 1981 we were lucky to get permission to work there at all. By 1985 the process was much easier, since more and more scientists were applying to work there. But it still took over a year to be sure we would be allowed to stay long enough to complete our researches. We applied very early for the support of the Royal Geographical Society. Their approval, which is given only to serious scientific projects, helps earn other sponsorship and we hoped it would impress the Malagasy authorities. We travelled to London for the interview expecting intimidatingly astute scrutiny. While waiting nervously to be called, we looked at portraits of great explorers lining the labyrinths of oak panelled corridors: Livingstone, Younghusband, Scott. Towering above me, Phil clutched an enormous heap of files, maps and papers: he looked confident, organised and impressive. He would be sure to charm them. We were called in. Eight serious mature explorers regarded us from behind a vast oak table. I recognised Lord Hunt. This was surely much more frightening than any expedition hazard.

John Hemming, RGS Director and author of several erudite books on South America, started with some easy questions. How would we get to Ankàrana? What about supplies? How would we evacuate any sick or injured expedition members? To my great relief, the questions did not become much more difficult. Half-way through the interview I began to relax and the one person on the panel that I recognised as friendly, Nigel Winser, was winking at me encouragingly. I was the only person in the room who knew Madagascar and, having been to Ankàrana before, I was bound to sound passably knowledgeable. I should not have been so unsure of myself. Then someone commented on the maturity and experience of our team and asked what we were doing about training the next generation of explorers. This took me aback, for the World Wildlife Fund had just criticised us for being too inexperienced. Fortunately I could explain that we had recruited a couple of 'youngsters' to the team since submitting the draft expedition prospectus to the Society, and we were on the look-out for more.

Then came the bombshell: 'We don't like expeditions being jointly led.' Justifications for our decision to have two leaders were brushed aside by the panel with a brief 'But where does the buck stop?' Phil turned to smirk at me and said, 'With Jane!'

Questions followed about the medical projects and clinics that we planned to run. Did anyone in the team know about parasites? This was one of my strongest points, for I had been a research protozoologist for two years at Oxford and had also screened hundreds of Himalayan children for worms for a Save the Children project. And what about a microscope? We would take an elderly brass monocular as well as using the marvellous little MacArthur microscope; this was the size of a pocket dictionary yet had sufficient magnification to distinguish malaria parasites.

'The MacArthur is useless!' I was startled by my interviewer's aggressive tone, so out of keeping with the distinguished calm of the Society, and I mumbled somewhat defensively. It was not until work had started in Madagascar that I was to learn how tiring the miniature microscope was to use: it was quite unsuitable for screening vast numbers of children, although good enough for examining the occasional lemur sample in the forest.

I hardly let Phil get a word in and he had no chance to impress the board with all the maps and documents he had brought. But the Royal Geographical Society gave us one of their biggest awards and – an even greater compliment – after the expedition was over, I was invited to talk to the Society in the same lecture theatre where Livingstone and so many other great explorers had presented the results of their travels.

After this initial success in fund-raising, we were disheartened by failing to raise much money from the conservation bodies for our ecological research. Reluctantly we slanted the aims of the expedition more towards cave exploration, in line with our major sponsors' interests in the adventurous aspects of the expedition. Ironically, the cavers, who earned the most sponsorship, were to be disappointed by their limited discoveries, and the biological value of our expedition was only recognised in retrospect: there is now talk of designating Ankàrana a World Heritage Site because of our work.

We recruited Roo (Richard) Walters to boost the caving team. Dave and Sheila had been with him on an Indonesian expedition and were impressed with his performance and stamina during strenuous exploration. He was tough, but more relaxed than Dave about losing his macho image by associating with women. Roo commented to me later that the women on the team had a civilising influence and made the expedition atmosphere more relaxed and enjoyable!

Finally, nearly two years after Phil and I first talked of the expedition, we settled on a core of nine British caver-zoologists, expecting to recruit a botanist and other scientific specialists in Madagascar. We ran the expedition democratically so that Phil and I, as leaders, could be out-voted by our team. We had long meetings to thrash out what projects we should undertake. By May 1986 we had obtained preliminary permission to work in Madagascar, had assembled equipment and supplies and had a final meeting to decide how we should transport the caving and scientific equipment. Having experienced the vagaries of Malagasy transport systems and the difficulties that customs officials create, I wanted to keep all our equipment with us or at least send it by air freight. The others argued that we needed to take so much equipment that air freight would be too expensive; we must send a container by sea. I yielded, bowing to the judgement of those who had experience of large expeditions to several continents, but managed to persuade the strong-willed Dave Checkley that we should not take the £7000 worth of powerful radios that he had borrowed. They would cause no end of problems with customs, since the officials feel that only people of dubious political tendencies would wish to communicate by radio. The day before my departure I agonised over what to take as contingency, in case there were problems with the freight, and even followed my sister's example of snipping the labels out of my knickers – to save weight.

# 2. Indri – the Man-dog?

*C'est à Madagascar que je puis annoncer aux naturalistes qu'est la véritable terre promise pour eux. C'est là que la nature semble s'être retirée dans un sanctuaire particulier pour y travailler sur d'autres modèles que ceux auxquels elle s'est asservie ailleurs. Les formes les plus insolites et les plus merveilleuses s'y rencontrent à chaque pas.*

Joseph-Philibert Commerson, 1771

I arrived in Tana, the capital, on Air Mad's only jumbo jet amidst hordes of tourists, trying to pretend that I was superior to them. It was the end of July and I had come ahead of the team to arrange the final permission for our research. Despite seemingly endless preparations in Britain there was still much more to do now that I had arrived in Madagascar, but I was uncertain of what kind of reception I would get. I had received no replies to my letters and was not sure whether this was because letters had gone astray or simply meant that we were not welcome. The Malagasy have a habit of losing papers that are difficult to deal with. It is more polite than saying 'No'. The bureaucrats in Tana, though, were far more accommodating than I had imagined even in my most optimistic moments. They had remembered and appreciated my reports from the 1981 expedition and as soon as they recognised my name they dashed off to find the file on my new project.

I needed all sorts of letters of recommendation in order to get visas to stay more than two months in Madagascar. I visited academics at Parc Tsimbazaza Zoo and Research Station, the University, the Ministry of Scientific Research, the Ministry of Higher Education, the Ministry of Waters and Forests and I even called on the President of the *Académie Malgache*. Unbeknown to us, these people had already discussed our project at length and had agreed to it on certain conditions. We must fund six Malagasy collaborators and also pay them a wage, collect pairs of lemurs for the zoo, supply a large selection of colour slides and educational materials, donate to the Museum half of all the specimens we collected and provide the funds and expertise to set up a butterfly farm!

The list took me aback. We seemed to have been mistaken for a high-powered, internationally-funded academic team, whereas in reality we were just a group of amateurs, with very little money. We were planning to cover the expenses of Malagasy colleagues, but our small budget certainly did not allow for wages nor for building a butterfly farm. And the idea of trapping lemurs was madness. None of us had experience of capturing anything larger than mice; we had never used dart guns and had no idea how to tranquillise wild animals. I was the best qualified in using such drugs, but my experience was of administering them to patients who were more co-operative and considerably less agile than lemurs. Lemurs would surely die if we tried. I clearly needed to negotiate.

Meetings seemed to go on for ever, straining both my patience and my knowledge of the French language. I was grateful when Maggie and Paul arrived, ahead of the rest of the main team, to help with this thankless task and boost my morale. I had long discussions with the Director of Tsimbazaza Zoo, Voara Randrianasolo. He was an astute man and a hard bargainer. I managed to convince him that we were quite incompetent when it came to trapping lemurs alive, eventually persuading him to settle for some reptiles, a new insect exhibit and a small 'butterfly farm' in a large half-derelict cage next to the vivarium. In return he introduced Jean-Elie – just the sort of person we needed. He was an expert in local invertebrates and birds. While he showed me around Tsimbazaza's impressive insect museum, he spouted Latin names. Slowly he eased the conversation around to what money he might expect from us. I stalled, saying that I would have to discuss this with my co-leader and the team. 'But you can decide Docteur Jane; I know that you are *chef superieur!*'

Dr Randrianasolo must have been instrumental in the remarkable improvements in the Zoo in the five years I had been away. Money and expertise provided by the Jersey Wildlife Preservation Trust and the New York Zoological Society, combined with his hard work, had transformed it from an unkempt, scruffy park, scattered with rusting empty cages, into one of the most impressive small zoos I have visited.

Set, as it is, in an idyllic botanic garden surrounding an artificial lake populated with hundreds of elegant white egrets, it presents the beauties of Malagasy wildlife to the people of Tana who so seldom travel into 'the bush'. Plant specimens from other continents were mixed in with, but outshone by, Malagasy endemics. Amongst these was the marvellous trièdre, *Neodypsiis decaryi*, a three-cornered, triangular-stemmed version of the Traveller's Palm, which is endemic to ten square miles in the Col de Ranopiso, south-east Madagascar.

Tsimbazaza means 'place forbidden to children' – an odd choice of name for a zoo, but the title originates from the time when the area was used as an Ancestral burial ground. Children are no longer forbidden, indeed the Zoo and Botanic Gardens are open to everyone. True to the spirit of the Socialist Republic, there is no admission charge. I frequently visited Tsimbazaza to meet Dr Randrianasolo and to revive myself during the interminable negotiations. Paul Stewart accompanied me on one such trip. We had recruited him to study the cave crocodiles. He was someone that the RGS might have described as a 'youngster', an undergraduate biologist, but a cool mature character with a dry sense of humour. I knew him through the Southampton University Exploration Society, and he had just returned from a year-long study of the Black Cayman in the Peruvian Amazon.

After saying hello to various captive lemurs, we approached the crocodile pen. The reptiles inside were huge, inert, smiling maliciously. The idea of studying such ferocious reptiles in pitch dark caves terrified me and reminded me of a patient in Southampton, long returned from Africa, but left terribly scarred after being chased up a tree by a crocodile! Yet basking in the sun, with glazed eyes, they looked as dynamic as the stuffed specimens in the Museum. Paul suddenly started making strangled gulping sounds and responded to my quizzical expression by explaining that this was the call of panicking baby caymans. In Peru it brought mother caymans from miles around. But this Nile Crocodile was clearly not familiar with cayman-speak and remained a seemingly lifeless killing machine. Later, one of them ate a keeper.

The Museum in the park grounds was a delight. Inside was intricately carved woodwork, weaving and the work of artisans from all over Madagascar. There were no ancient archaeological artifacts on display, since Man was a very late arrival on Madagascar – probably within the last two thousand years. But he soon wreaked havoc on the Great Isle. All the large lemurs became extinct, as well as other spectacular giant forms: tortoises larger than those which survive on Aldabra and Galapagos, huge crocodiles and the Elephant Birds which laid two-gallon eggs. Skeletons of some of these bizarre animals were on display.

Even now the fauna is odd. None of Madagascar's mammals is found elsewhere, apart from a few bats, Man and the species he brought with him. More than eighty per cent of the other animals and the plants are endemic to the island. It is still a biologists' delight, a strange evolutionary museum and 'the chiefest paradise this day upon earth', as Richard Boothby wrote in 1630. Although much impoverished since then, the Great Red Island is still an ecological wonderland.

☆

At the weekends, when all the offices were closed, I fled from Tana. Early one Saturday morning Maggie, Paul and I set out for the railway station. It is the most impressive modern building in Tana, with its imposing facade decorated with the only neon advertising signs on Madagascar. Modelled on the stations of Paris, it is over-ornate – considering that only two passenger trains leave it each day. Our train was bound for the east coast port of Toamasina (Tamatave that was) – a two-hundred-and-fifty-mile, twelve-hour journey from Tana. The railway line was completed in 1913, built by droves of unfortunate coolies brought from Canton and Shanghai for the project; many lost their lives before it was finished. The route passes through some spectacular scenery and the single track edges along the walls of steep valleys and snakes around on itself innumerable times as it leaves Imerina, home of the Mérina tribe, and descends from the *Hauts Plateaux*.

Maps show the route passing through a fifty-mile-wide band of rainforest running the length of the island east of the central mountain spine. But we saw no forest. After five hours we reached Andasibé and the half-way station, where for a few hundred yards the track is double and the train from Toamasina can pass the train from Tana. This small village is dominated by the vast Swiss chalet-style *Hotel de la Gare*, and our destination – the famous Périnet rainforest reserve – was close by. We checked in and deposited our luggage in the corner of the huge echoey dining hall. It was barely 11am but all the tables were set for the full French dinner that would sustain passengers for the remaining six hours of the train journey. *Hotelys* close to the station offered an array of good freshly cooked food, but we decided that bananas and French bread would suffice. As soon as we sat down with our lunch, Maurice introduced himself. He had been hovering around since the train arrived and explained that he was the official guide for the Périnet Reserve. *'Oui, oui; c'est vrai.'* And he had seen the Indri this morning. He could take us to see them now. *'Oui, oui.'*

Once our stomachs were full, we grew more interested. Attenborough's early film of the Indri, the world's largest surviving lemur, had really captured my imagination and I had long wished to see one. On my first visit to Madagascar in 1981, there had been no sign of them; only their haunting plaintive 'singing battles' over a mile away had betrayed their presence. At that distance their howling sounds reminiscent of gibbons calling, and it has a similar territorial function. The Indri's song, though, is eerie, and up close it is so loud as to be almost painful.

I am never keen to employ guides, but Maurice's offer was too good an opportunity to miss. We walked together to the reserve entrance where we were greeted by the warden (who happened to be Maurice's father), who asked if we had permits to enter. Of course we had. There was a long silence while we all grinned at each other.

'May I see them?'

'Ah, so sorry; we've left them in Tana.'

The warden's amused response to this obvious lie was charming: 'You are here and your permits are in Tana. Mmm. Permits in Tana, you in Périnet. What a pity – never mind!'

Maurice led us past a small fish farm and into the forest. We were still three thousand feet above sea level, but the vegetation was rich tropical rainforest with luxuriant ferns, orchids and lianas dangling from the trees. He pointed out chamaeleons, Camellias, *Palisandre* (Madagascar 'rosewood' or *Dalbergia* trees) and so many other species whose common names in French I did not recognise. There were superb iridescent Sun-birds, resembling their namesakes on the mainland, but totally unrelated to them. When we came to a spider's web strung fifteen feet across the river, Maurice gave it a good hard tug to demonstrate its strength. It was constructed by *Nephila madagascariensis*, one of the strongest and most celebrated web-spinners. Last century, Reverend Père Camboué thought it would make an even more attractive fibre than silk. He supervised the making of a beautiful royal *lamba*, but it never became a commercial success.

There was not a breath of wind. The rich canopy forest was mirrored in the river. Huge swallow-tailed butterflies and scarlet dragonflies flitted by. There was an explosion of turquoise and a kingfisher sped past, flying low, before disappearing around a bend in the river. Leaving the main path, we plunged into the darkness of the forest, up over a slippery mud bank. Weaving between the samplings and lianas, we disturbed a small troop of Brown Lemurs who grunted with disquiet as they fled; we glimpsed little but their long bushy tails. Then Maurice stopped and pointed up. 'Indri! *Babakoto! Voilà! Oui, oui.*'

I could not believe it! Despite our clumsy approach, there, forty feet above us, looking calmly down, were two great Indris. No – four. We were almost directly underneath them but they were quite unconcerned. Their dog-like faces with their huge surprised yellow eyes peered down at us for a short time. They soon returned to browsing on the leaves around them – a much more interesting pursuit. They were magnificent creatures as large as three-year-old children but with furry teddy-bear ears and rich, thick coats. Unlike all other surviving lemurs, their tails are tiny, just two inches long. The black and white patterns of their fur made them look as if they were each wearing a black short-sleeved jacket with a shawl collar and matching gloves and socks. Their hands were huge, yet remarkably similar to a human's. Indris are monogamous, with a pair-bond which is maintained on the basis of sex for a week every three years. One couple crouched erect on vertical tree trunks, their disproportionately long hind legs flexed to support their weight. The other pair lounged, sitting astride horizontal branches as they nibbled leaves. Sometimes they sat on precariously thin branches, knees drawn up but large feet firmly holding on so that they sat firm. The Malagasy regard Indris as people who never came down from the trees, and these did indeed have intelligent, pensive eyes and charmingly human mannerisms.

Was the Indri actually the Man-dog so fancifully described by early travellers? That *Cynocephalus* featured in accounts both by seventeenth-century European naturalists and by the early Arab traders? The Man-dog they portrayed was a fantastic but intelligent creature which could not possibly have existed. Or did it? Could it have been one of the giant koala-like extinct lemurs or even the Indri? An upright all-but-tailless primate, weighing about sixteen pounds, the Indri has short arms, hands and feet like a man's and the face of a dog. The early tales were so embellished that illustrations featured the Man-dog wearing a fur jacket with a nicely tailored shawl collar!

Lemurs, during their heyday in the Eocene, were a successful group, but they did not adapt to cope with competition from other more aggressive mammals which emerged throughout most of the world. Only on Madagascar were they safe from competition, and slowly they evolved to make use of the enormous range of habitats on the island. Some grazed the savannahs, while others developed into mouse, squirrel, bush-baby, gibbon or monkey-like forms. The Indri adopted the rôle of a great ape. Fourteen lemurs have already become extinct, and some of these must have disappeared quite recently. In 1661, Etienne de Flacourt recorded the existence of the *Tratratratra* as 'large as a two-year-old calf, with a round head and a man's face, front and hind feet like a monkey, frizzy fur, a short tail, and ears like those of a man'. Although this description may be distorted, it is the last accepted sighting of the now extinct giant lemurs. A few may have survived until the 1930s, however, when a French forester came face to face with an animal sitting four feet high and described it as being unlike other lemurs he had seen. It did not have a muzzle but was like a gorilla with 'the face of one of my ancestors'.

Even with a fauna now impoverished by extinctions, Madagascar still boasts more than its fair share of the world's 183 non-human primate species. Twenty-nine lemur species and about fifty sub-species survive – the experts are arguing over the exact numbers. Lemurs are now restricted to scarce patches of forest widely scattered over Madagascar's 227,000 square miles. Distances are large and travel is slow and difficult, so it is not easy to see many of them.

We asked Maurice to leave us to admire the *Babakoto*, saying we would find our own way out of the forest. '*Oui, oui. Voir le Babakoto. Pas de problème. Oui, oui.*' They were large and ape-like, no doubt capable only of ponderously clambering around in the canopy. But then one pair, replete with leaves from that particular tree, effortlessly extended long hind legs so that their huge furry forms sailed easily into the air. There was a thud as each landed, hind legs flexing to absorb the impact. Short arms – like those of a man – were used only to steady and balance. The Indris continued away in a series of prodigious leaps, ricocheting between trunks more than thirty feet apart; as they disappeared into the forest, the thuds and swishing of the leaves in the canopy faded away. We continued to watch the other pair contentedly browsing.

When we first arrived at the reserve we had felt as if we were in the heart of dense Malagasy rainforest. Now, though, as we sat silently during those hours gazing at the Indris, we realised how abnormally quiet the forest was. Where was the background buzz of insects and bird song? Other sounds intruded in on us. The noise of traffic on the road which passed to our right, grating sounds of machinery ahead of us and then behind, the sound of a chainsaw. The home of the Indris here was actually just a pocket of forest only a mile across. On one side a sterile *Eucalyptus* plantation had been planted. Lemurs do not eat *Eucalyptus* and nor do many other animals. Why were foreign nutrient-sapping *Eucalyptus* being grown when there must be so many more suitable native trees which would benefit the soil as well as the wildlife? The road bordered the reserve on another side and on the third the hillside had been quarried away (extracting stone here and graphite and bauxite close by). As if that was not threat enough to the forest, a saw-mill was hard at work at the foot of the quarry. Our necks grew steadily stiffer until Maurice returned to guide us back to the hotel. Not convinced that we were great expeditionaries, he did not believe that we would be able to find our way out of the forest now that darkness was gathering.

I caught the midday Sunday train back to Tana to be ready to continue negotiations on Monday morning. Meanwhile, Maggie and Paul continued on towards Toamasina to clear through customs the fourteen hundredweight of equipment as soon as it arrived at the docks. A week later they returned with tales of the damage wrought by the terrific cyclone which had struck the east of Madagascar five months earlier. Coconut palms were still littered about, on flattened homes or between roofless huts. The ancient clove orchards – so important to the local economy – had been devastated. The warehouses of our shipping agents were no longer secure, but that hardly mattered since there was no sign of the freight and no news of the *Emilia* which was carrying it. My fears were realised. We phoned home to let the others know and they arrived burdened with extra scientific gear and a small elderly inflatable boat.

# 3. City of the Thousand

Ry Tanindrazanay malala ô
Ry Madagasikara soa
Ny fitiavanay anao tsy miala
Fa ho anao, dia ho anao doria.

O, beloved land of our Ancestors
Excellent Madagascar,
Our love for you will never depart
For it is yours, yours forever.

Malagasy National Anthem

That Monday morning was a bad one. I thought I had an
appointment at 8am with Madame Berthe, head of the Ministry of
Higher Education, but by nine she had still not arrived. Was she
already in her office? No, she was at the *Université* but would be back
soon. At 11.30, when everyone was leaving for lunch, I asked again.
She will come this afternoon. I wilted as I realised that I had wasted
the whole morning in that dingy office when I could have stayed with
the Indris. I could now do nothing until the long lunch-break was
over at two-thirty. Even the libraries at Tsimbazaza would be closed.
I walked back to avenue de l'Indépendence and tried to make my
solitary lunch last an hour. Slowly I chewed my substantial *canard
aux poivres vertes*, impatient to be done with all these interviews
but unable to speed up the process. As I left the *Hotel de France* feeling
overfed, a ten-year-old boy approached me and asked for money.
Most of the skin of one cheek was an oozing sore which would
blind him if it spread to his eye. I asked where he lived but he did
not understand my French. His eyes sparkled with delight as I gave
him some small coins and he was gone before I could think what to
do about his impetigo.

I walked back to the Ministry of Higher Education by way of the bank, where I gave money to a pathetically thin leper with no nose. Then on I walked into one of the foul, polluted, road tunnels which burrow through the Y-shaped arms of the volcanic ridge at Tana's centre. The Renault factory ceased production soon after Independence and very few cars have been imported over the last twenty years; spare parts are impossible to acquire. Cars are often held together with elastic and string, and holes in the bodywork give good views of the engine, chassis and road surface. The streets are crowded with ill-maintained, ancient French cars which belch black fumes, and the road tunnels are foul to walk through.

Madame Berthe was not in her office when I arrived back at the Ministry. I waited until five and then walked back into central Tana, resolving thenceforth always to carry a novel so that I would not notice the hours slipping by waiting for the interviews. I walked along dusty streets, past crumbling buildings. The big concrete slabs which should have covered the town drains were cracked, and noxious gases emanated from the foaming black filth inside. Emaciated people in rags picked over the rubbish in the concrete bunkers at street corners. Each sustains a family: human scavengers so efficient that they do not leave enough food to support a sparrow. Tana is ugly; the population swollen to a million by vast numbers of impoverished farmers who have come seeking in vain for employment in the city.

I was meeting Hilary. As I walked up the cracked steps to the Hotel Colbert's *pâtisserie*, my stomach still full of duck, a little girl came up to me and said, 'I'm hungry.' She might have been twelve but was no bigger than a five-year-old. She had no muscles, her hair was brittle, dull and sparse, and her belly stuck out from between her rags as pathetic as on any Oxfam poster. Her eyes showed utter despair: I have never seen such a hopeless look, not even amongst the dying. She accepted my money blank-faced and walked slowly away. The Government, trying to remove such uncomfortable reminders of urban destitution, round up these street children and accommodate them in what was once an abattoir. I did not enjoy the pastries that Hilary bought me.

During my time in the capital, I stayed at the Friends' Centre in Faravòhitra overlooking central Tana. I never quite caught up with all the functions of this institution. It was a hostel for poor young girls who came into Tana to complete their education, it was a centre for training destitute women in handicrafts so that they might make a living, it was a meeting place for Quakers, and the garage even functioned as a distribution point for the government rice ration. It was run by David Andriamparison, a tiny little man, but powerful and dynamic almost to the point of mania. He explained that he wore a beard – rare things amongst the Malagasy – to show that he was a revolutionary, and he had certainly been in prison for the provocative way he challenged the authorities by championing the poor. David was courageous and inspiring, though bewilderingly unpredictable; he worked inordinately hard for his friends, the poor and the Quaker movement, while his very sweet wife stood by him, always smiling, but with tired sad eyes and a constant look of bemusement on her face. There was always a welcome for me there whenever I was in Tana.

Over the following days and weeks, as through David I met people trying to ease the plight of the poor, I began to see a little hope for a few of Tana's destitute. I attended meetings in so many different offices during August that I covered miles on foot and in numerous communal *taxi-bés*. I grew to know the capital, taking more interest in it and noticing more beauty than ugliness. The novel helped me to wait patiently.

☆

In 1610 the Mérina King Andriandraka made Antananarivo, 'Place-of-the-Thousand', his capital and put it under the guard of a thousand soldiers. The city's name is pronounced and sometimes spelt Tananarive, but is usually referred to simply as Tana. The steeply pitched, red-tiled, two- or three-storey brick houses, with their decorated wooden balconies, surrounded by green rice-fields, reminded me of Kathmandu. Both capitals are at four thousand feet above sea level and, like Kathmandu, Tana is in a broad valley, once a vast lake, fringed by hills. Perhaps the eruptions which were responsible for Tana's steep contours also allowed the lake to empty and leave so much fertile land – or did Manjushri's sword drain this valley too? The people – especially the Mérina of the central highlands – are similar to Asians, too, since they came from what is now Indonesia. Malagasy resembles the tribal languages spoken in Borneo and many of the people have south-east Asian features.

The city rises out of the dry lake bed like an island set in a green sea of paddy. Even around the city centre there are pretty little gardens growing gorgeous flowers, Traveller's Palms, bananas and a range of beautiful flowering trees. Crown-of-Thorns shrubs, *Euphorbia milii*, decked with waxy crimson blossoms, have been planted in many traffic islands, borders and gardens. A relative of our garden spurges, this is grown in gardens all over the world, but it originates from Madagascar. Frangipani and other plants that I could not name fill the evening air with heavy tropical perfumes. Small corners are turned over to rice. How strange to be so close to Africa but to feel so much in Asia.

Before the rice-fields can be planted, they have to be puddled – churned over to waterproof them. This is great sport. Pairs of water buffalo are chased around in circles by shouting and singing adults and children thigh-deep in the muddy soup they are creating. By the end of the day, people and buffaloes are plastered head to foot in mud, the fields compacted, waterproofed and ready for sowing. In a few weeks the paddy-fields will be brimming again with bright green rice plants. Towards the end of my stay in Madagascar, the rice crop was harvested laboriously by hand. Threshing, too, looked hard work; it is done by holding the cut ends of the rice stalks and beating the grain-bearing end against a large stone. Not all the boys joined in this work – some ten-year-olds walked around unusually clad in a shirt and knee-length piece of cloth. They walked uncomfortably with a stick propping their skirts out ahead of them. They had just been circumcised.

Contours add to Tana's appeal, but the shortest routes through the city often involve labouring up and down hundreds of cracked, uneven, stone steps winding between the houses and perched gardens. One of our regular walks led us past a stall selling what we christened Kennomeat Cake. It looks as unappealing as dog food, but tastes marginally better. It is made principally of cassava (which in Europe is used to make glue) mixed with peanuts and a little sugar. The entire brown gelatinous mush is then rolled into a banana leaf, so that gluey swiss-roll-like slices can be sold to passers-by. The vendor looked ever hopeful when we passed, but one sample of what was euphemistically called *gâteau* was enough for us. In 1981 a biology teacher friend, Suzanne, often invited us around for *gâteau* whenever she had managed to find flour, sugar and butter.

Then, as the shortages bit deeper, she served Kennomeat Cake and even cassava boiled in sugar water which she also described as *gâteau*. We had difficulty eating this with the relish we had for her sponge cakes.

The Royal Palace is on the highest point in Tana. The flamboyant Queen Ranavàlona II (1868–83) commissioned the versatile missionary James Cameron to embellish the first simple wooden building with a wild combination of French, Italian and Victorian English architectural styles. This dramatic creation, with a vast columned two-storey veranda, gives an impression of a hybrid between the Palace of Versailles and the Natural History Museum in Kensington. It dominates the city, perched on a volcanic dyke above a six-hundred-foot sheer cliff. From this vantage point, called 'the place of hurling' (where Queen Ranavàlona I (1828–61) hurled Christian martyrs to their deaths), it is possible to see how small is the urban centre of Tana. Beneath is the beautiful Lac Anosy: at its best in November when the constantly-dripping Jacaranda trees around the lake burst into a gorgeous rich lilac-blue. Lac Anosy was originally built for a water supply, but it is now fetid and stagnant with urinals draining into it; the only individuals to enjoy being close to it now are egrets, which remain remarkably white despite the filth, and muddy domestic ducks.

Nestling in a rare flat expanse at the foot of the hills is the market. It is busiest on Fridays when it grows to fill the whole of the centre of town. It takes its name, *zoma*, from the Malagasy word for Friday; markets in other towns have assumed different weekday names. The *zoma* is fascinating, but it clogs up the city centre: on Fridays all the bus services and other forms of transport degenerate into chaos. Often there are so many people that it can take an hour to walk the half-mile length of avenue de l'Indépendence. Weaving between stalls protected from the sun by white canvas umbrellas, we had to take care not to trip over children or some huddle of people brewing up rice and meat for lunch. Some played *fanorona*, a game like draughts using counters made from carrot and cucumber on a grid scratched in the sand. In the evening, numerous shivering bundles, enshrouded in little but thin cotton sheets, turned out to be sleeping stall-holders and their families. With darkness came a new hazard; it would be all too easy to tumble into the unimaginable filth of the drains through one of the many missing covers.

The *zoma* was a delight. One colourful corner sold cut flowers, pot plants and rare orchids, elsewhere there were expanses of stalls selling both the temperate crops of the *Hauts Plateaux* and lowland tropical fruit and vegetables. Pineapples are grown all over the lowlands, first brought from Brazil by the Portuguese who were already growing them in Madagascar as early as 1548. Another part of the market sold semi-precious stones, polished fossil fish and ammonites, crocodile handbags and wooden replicas of the *alo-alo* which decorate Mahafaly tombs. Touts played lively tunes on the *valiha*: an instrument made from yard-long pieces of bamboo with about fifteen fibre strings or wires running the length of the bamboo between two leather collars encircling each end. These are not found in Africa, but I have seen similar musical instruments in the Indonesian islands of Sulawesi and Timor. The market also provided almost everything that a person might want: second-hand clothes imported from Europe, recycled (and often rusting) pieces of engine, raffia hats, sisal rope, superb hand-embroidered tablecloths, herbal cures, ampoules filled with honey, wooden furniture and even stripy sisal giraffes. Puzzled to find a representation of an animal which (like zebras!) never existed on Madagascar, I asked one stall-holder why she made African and not Malagasy animals. Her reply saddened me: 'There is no big game in Madagascar; African animals are much better!'

The boy with the sore cheek tugged at my skirt, eyes sparkling as he saw my smile of recognition. I asked the stall-holder if his house was far, but was told that he slept on the streets: his mother was probably a prostitute forced by poverty to sell herself.

'If I gave medicine for that sore, would anyone see that he took it?'

'No,' said the stall-holder. 'He would just sell it!'

I felt impotent and angry, yet he was happy and making a good living. His eyes, the eyes of a survivor, had a wonderful sparkle.

☆

We needed five more local collaborators. So, to the task of negotiations for visas, was added the search for academic volunteers. I visited the University several times to recruit Malagasy researchers. The campus, which is several miles from the centre of Tana, is modern, spacious and attractively set out: small classrooms, offices and teaching and research laboratories surround large rectangular fishponds. Students relaxed on the grass, while nearby soldiers, stationed to control their strikes and demonstrations, slept in the sun, having carelessly left their ancient Russian rifles stacked in pyramids for anyone to take. Most lectures went on in what looked like a wartime, corrugated iron, aircraft hanger – the only building large enough for lecturing to nearly a thousand biological science undergraduates. Most of them never graduated, though I don't think this was entirely due to the fact that the lecturer was totally inaudible whenever it rained.

My descriptions of Ankàrana captivated the imagination of Madame le docteur Voahangy Rakouth. She was a botanist and enthused about the specialised leguminous shrubs which would surely grow amongst the limestone crevices. She would definitely accompany us. I was hesitant, for she was a very plump lady who teetered precariously about her lab in ridiculous stiletto heels, and she did not have any walking boots! A few days later I was relieved when she offered a variety of excuses as to why she could not come after all. She introduced us instead to Guy-Suzon, a colleague who looked much fitter and who told us how much he loved fieldwork. Although many Malagasy academics expressed interest in our project, most were put off by the conditions I described at Ankàrana, and made excuses about not being free. Of those who had more of a taste for adventure, five finally committed themselves to joining us. As well as Jean-Elie and Guy-Suzon, two palaeontologists, Martine and Raobivelonoro, also agreed to come. Like Guy-Suzon, they lectured at the University. The Malagasy part of our team was completed with Jean Radofilao, a mathematics lecturer at the University in Diégo-Suarez and also an obsessional spelaeologist.

Finding academic collaborators was relatively easy. Obtaining visas and permits was quite another story. Despite the interested and welcoming reception at each interview, I found it a strain trying to communicate in French and my diplomatic smile was soon wilting. My first interview with a representative of the *Direction des Eaux et Forêts* was an important one, since this is the government department which controls access to nature reserves. Fortunately Maggie was with me – if I had been alone I would have been rendered totally speechless. Whereas my French is a tenseless, grammarless pidgin, Maggie was not flummoxed by the tone of the interview. There was no introduction and no initial pleasantries. A thin, weasely man addressed us.

'Where is the car?'

'Oh, excuse me. What car? We do not have a car.'

'But you promised you would give us a vehicle when you arrived here!'

He had chosen to interpret our early telexes very differently from our intended message. At one stage, during the preparations for the expedition, we had thought that we might be given a vehicle. We had put out feelers in Madagascar to see if we could avoid the 100 per cent import tax by offering to donate the vehicle to a Malagasy conservation agency when the work of the expedition was over. But the sponsor's offer fell through when plans to make a television film about Ankàrana were delayed until the following year. We had no car.

'We have a problem then, don't we?' He grinned unpleasantly, displaying gappy tobacco-stained teeth.

'Yes, it is a problem of not having enough money, which I am sure you must understand.'

Clearly he did not understand, for he knew that all foreigners were rolling in money and could afford to give away several Land-Rovers. I offered him a calculator, which he slipped into his pocket without comment. While we waited outside the next office to see a more senior person, the Weasel detailed the various zoological topics in which he was expert. Inside we discussed the 'car problem' further. I pointed out cheerily that this would not prevent us from doing good research which we hoped would be of value and interest to the Ministry. The senior person was unimpressed. I offered a reprint describing the work I had done at Ankàrana in 1981. He regarded this with utter disdain.

'It is in English!'

'Yes, but it has a French abstract and surely the Latin species list will be useful?'

He and the Weasel were still unimpressed, so we went to see the *chef du service*. Wearing tinted glasses, he looked an even tougher proposition, but to my relief he listened sympathetically to our apologies and excuses, and then explained to his crest-fallen colleagues that if there was no vehicle, nothing could be done to conjure one up. It was a pity, but there it was. I was thankful to have found someone with normal Malagasy manners. A week later the Ministry of External Affairs received a letter from *Eaux et Forêts* recommending that we have our visa extensions.

It was at *Eaux et Forêts* that we first met Bernhard Meier, a likeable, smiling, German biologist. I asked him where he was working. He had built his own house in the forest and he invited us to visit. Bernhard had arrived in Madagascar at about the same time as me and was also staying for six months. He was in Madagascar to study ways of breeding rare lemurs in captivity so as to ensure their survival. The Broad-nosed Gentle-lemur, which is on the very brink of extinction, was one of the species he was hoping to conserve. This was an animal which interested me, too, for we had found their skeletons at Ankàrana in 1981 and I was keen to meet a living individual. Like us, Bernhard was conducting his research on a shoe-string budget and was perpetually fighting to convince the Malagasy that he had no money and no equipment to give away. But he was a cleverer diplomat than I and had even talked the Weasel into 'lending' him two thousand Malagasy francs (in 1986, worth about £2). Bernhard said he was destitute and so I was pleased to give him a lift back to central Tana in the taxi we had kept waiting. On the drive home, he explained that honesty was not the best way to deal with *Eaux et Forêts*: we should have told them that their vehicle would be arriving soon and furthermore that the British government were considering shipping out several more for their use. At the end of the expedition, just before Christmas, I visited *Eaux et Forêts* again in order to tell them about the wonders we had found at Ankàrana. They were predictably unimpressed when I offered them our preliminary report, laboriously translated into French, and were still asking when the vehicle would arrive.

☆

It was never possible to force the pace of negotiations and often I was left waiting with time to spare. So one day I sought out Madame le docteur Aimée Randriambololona, an old friend of my sister. I first needed to learn how to pronounce her name (something like Randrambool) intelligibly enough to ask her secretary for an appointment. The Malagasy language and Malagasy names are ridiculously polysyllabic: most words look unpronounceable until you discover which selection of syllables can be merged or ignored.

King Andrianampoinimerinandriantsimitoviaminandriampanjaka, for example, or Andrianampòinimérina for short, emerges as something like Amp'nimern.

Dr Randriambololona was a kind, motherly lady. She was Professor of Paediatrics, an academic burdened by her hopeless struggle to keep her country's children healthy. She showed us around the *Hôpital des Enfants* and described the background of some of her patients. The first little girl had been admitted after she had suddenly become unable to talk. Miraculously, she had improved after treatment with quinine. The girl had suffered an attack of the deadly cerebral malaria, despite taking chloroquine. So drug-resistant malaria had reached Tana – depressing news indeed. The Bubonic Plague epidemic, which afflicted the poor each winter, was thankfully over for another year. Now most children were being admitted with acute malnutrition. One seven-year-old weighed less than twenty pounds: 40 per cent of the ideal weight for his age. 'Look how meagre he is,' Professeur Aimée said as she pinched his skin until he squirmed, and tugged at his scanty brittle hair to show how easily it came out. Diarrhoea had tipped him off the nutritional tightrope between just managing to eat enough and tumbling through the downward spiral towards death from some otherwise relatively trivial illness: 2.8 million children like him die of diarrhoeal disease each year. Professeur Aimée introduced us to a boy who had been brought to the hospital all skin and bones but with a pot-belly bursting with roundworms. Having been rid of his worm burden, he soon began to put on weight on a special high energy diet, but once rehabilitated he had no home to go to – he was another of the abandoned children of prostitutes. Like many of these children, he lived in one of the polluted road tunnels, which, at least, was warm. Now he leaves the hospital to spend each day begging and returns to sleep there at night. His medical problems were comparatively easy to treat; his poverty was a disease with no cure.

In 1981 everything had been scarce. Suzanne's husband, a printer, went out of business because he could not get paper. When paper became available he could not buy ink. The very rich avoided the shortages by shopping in Réunion, where they could buy medicines and other luxuries. Men approached us in Tana like touts selling dirty postcards. They would beckon us to see what they had concealed in their coats and offer us balls of black home-made soap.

The only things that seemed to be in abundant supply were President Ratsiraka's *Boky Mena*, his own Little Red Book, and the writings of Kim Il Sung. (Admiring the régime in North Korea, the President has modelled Madagascar's government on Kim Il Sung's.)

The Madagascar of 1986 was superficially richer. The shops were full of expensive imported goods, there were postcards for sale and it was even possible to buy milk, butter, cheese and wine. But the beggars and ragged street children had increased twentyfold. There were some improvements. No longer did Professor Aimée have her annual influx of moribund measles cases. Each previous winter the hospital had overflowed with so many children with measles that they were nursed on the verandas, in the corridors or in any available nook. One in ten of them had died. But in 1986, a few months before our visit, UNICEF funded a comprehensive vaccination campaign within the city which kept the wards empty that winter and saved many, many lives.

☆

The meetings continued: I had to visit the Ministry of External Affairs, the Ministry of the Interior, the Finance Ministry, Customs and Excise. We also needed a certificate from the Ministry of Health saying that the medicines we had imported were efficacious: a device to protect Malagasy people from wasting money on out-of-date, useless or even dangerous drugs. I also browsed around various laboratories offering to collect specimens or information for any local ongoing research. One biologist I met was working on the control of cattle liver fluke and I promised to collect for him the snails which harbour the worms. Leaving his office after a long involved discussion about my genealogy and the advantages of belonging to an island race, I discovered a WC and decided to make use of this rare resource. I shut the door – and found that there was no handle on the inside. The room was on the fourth floor and there was no way I could leave via the window, dressed as I was in my interview skirt. Having failed to pick the lock with a pen and a credit card, I resorted, embarrassed, to shouting. Ten minutes later I was let out.

The weeks went by and I began to worry. The weather at Ankàrana would not let us work beyond mid-October and the more time we spent in Tana now, the less we would have at Ankàrana. After nearly a month of intensive negotiations, I was relieved when our visa extensions and permits were finally granted and we could, at last, start our first period of fieldwork. Then came the battle to secure tickets for the entire team to fly up to Diégo; many flights were booked, for this was the tourist season for Malagasy and foreigner alike. The final little chore, which took several days to organise, was to hire a light aircraft for a day so that Dave and Sheila could do an aerial reconnaissance for caves in another limestone area: the Kelifely Massif, in the north-west of the island.

By the end of August, the main team had arrived from England. Amongst them was entomologist Simon Fowler, but Aeroflot had lost his luggage and he wondered if he could improvise a butterfly net and collecting equipment from the materials available in Tana. Three more ecologists were expected in September and then finally, in October, Simon Howarth would join us to help with the medical work.

# 4. How many Coconuts?

As there are no roads or railways, the traveller must content himself
with the only kind of native conveyance found in the country – the
palanquin . . . not the luxurious arrangement used in India [but] a
much rougher apparatus, and one better suited to the exigencies of the
uneven and broken country . . . must suffice the most fastidious traveller
in Madagascar.

The Malagasy bearer is a curious creature, of whom you can never be
certain until you have him away with you. Probably when all is tied on
the poles ready for starting, and sometimes after the baggage has started,
the palanquin bearers will ask, with the almost perfect show of innocence,
what wages they are to receive, as though they had not been bargaining an
hour or two the previous day, and professedly come to an arrangement.
This generally means trouble, and the traveller may think himself favoured
if he is able to leave at all that day.

George A. Shaw, 1885

Having at last obtained our six-month visa extensions and most of
the permits allowing us to start work, there was still no news of the
freight shipment and our equipment and nothing could be done to
speed its arrival. By now I was desperate to leave red tape and city
life behind me and get out into the field. Fortunately, I had most of
the equipment I needed.

Entrusting ourselves to Air Mad, I flew north with Maggie, Paul,
Simon and Nick. This left Phil and Anne to spend two days tidying up
the final bureaucratic details and to try and sweeten the officials at
the *Direction des Eaux et Forêts*. Phil got on better with the Weasel.
When he asked him for a special permit to work at Ankàrana, he said
that since Ankàrana was not a reserve, we would not need permits.
Phil suggested that the Weasel consult his records, and only then did
he realise that *Eaux et Forêts* should in fact be controlling the area.
Permits were laboriously typed in pentuplicate and Phil was given

one. We need hardly have bothered, though, for there was no warden to check our authority to enter.

The 4am start from Tana left my companions unable to keep awake for the one-hour flight north to Diégo-Suarez. I was too excited to sleep and full of anticipation for my first glimpse of the Ankàrana Massif for five years. I craned to see. Compared with my first visit, I was really travelling in style like a proper *vazaha* (European). Five years before we had negotiated, over the space of a whole week, for six places in a new Peugeot 505 driving all the way to Diégo. After we had finally settled on a price and departure day, there were further excuses and delays. The driver said he would have to charge more if only eleven passengers were travelling since usually he would fit in twenty! Eventually we agreed to a surcharge. The 'discussions' echoed the experiences of George Shaw when he tried to arrange to travel by palanquin a hundred years before. Malagasy friends commented that if we had been French, we would have torn the Peugeot-owner's car apart early on in the increasingly heated negotiations. They were impressed with the calm way we had coped with the taxi-driver's blackmailing methods, although it had been a superficial calm. Once we began the journey, though, our driver's character changed from hard businessman to thoughtful host. He watched over us carefully to make sure that we found enough to eat at each food stop and constantly enquired whether we needed the WC. The trip took two days. We often helped push the car out of deep ruts and pot-holes or across small rivers, wondering as we paddled whether we would catch Bilharzia. In reality it takes the parasite ten or fifteen minutes to penetrate skin and after our short immersions the parasite would have dried and died before it could infect us.

Now in 1986, the view from the Boeing 737 window was of Imerina, the rolling *Hauts Plateaux* which surround Tana. The scene looked desolate: a denuded dry zone left desiccated and singed by six rainless months. Soon the first showers would revive the shrivelled yellow grass and water the rice terraces. At the beginning of this century the French geographer, E-F Gautier, uncharitably described Madagascar as having the colour, consistency and fertility of a brick. I could now appreciate where he found his inspiration. From the air it was also clear why conservationists are so worried about the fate of Madagascar's unique wildlife. Landslips, great red fan-shaped gashes in the hills, bore witness to the disastrous effects of forest clearance and overgrazing.

The gently undulating central plateau gradually gave way to lowland savannah. Patches of scrub and forest punctuated the landscape and the great red rivers loaded with irreplaceable topsoil snaked out to the coral fringed coast where they muddied the deep clear blue sea. As we continued along the coast the ground was obscured by embryo rainclouds building up for the approaching wet season. I dozed a little and then, through a break in the clouds, saw black limestone far below. Another break and a glimpse of a thin green line: forest that shelters beneath the six-hundred-foot cliffs along Ankàrana's north-western edge. I wanted to share my excitement with the others, but they were still asleep.

A little later I saw the round outline of an ash-cone made by a small, long dormant, volcano. A vivid patch of bright green vegetation grew in the centre. Further on still we skirted the extinct volcano of Montagne d'Ambre. An angry black anvil of cloud hung above the peak, spitting out lightning and warning us not to come too close. This is one of the wettest places in Madagascar, receiving even more rain than the eastern rainforest belt. Its permanent halo of storm clouds, where each evening there was a spectacular lightning display, gives the place a climate of its own: like a patch of rainforest transplanted into the dry western savannah. Many of the trees within this National Park have gone, so that all that remains now is a few square miles of degraded forest at the summit, looking like a green snowcap surrounded by the bare red laterite, savagely cut by ravines.

The huge natural harbour of Diégo-Suarez came into view. Its rather unMalagasy name commemorates two Portuguese admirals: Diégo Diaz, who in 1500 was the first European to see the island, and Fernan Soares, who directed the first wave of white settlers in 1506. When Diégo Diaz returned with news of his discovery, it was assumed that the island was the Madagascar that Marco Polo had written of but not visited and as early as 1502 it appears on Portuguese maps as Madagascar. All the old colonial names are being replaced by polysyllabic Malagasy ones, so that Diégo-Suarez is now officially called Antsiranana, meaning The Port. But the new name is yet to catch on – everyone continues to call the town Diégo. We circled over the square pans for concentrating sea-salt and touched down.

'Did you see it?'

'See what?'

'Ankàrana, and the forests – fantastic!'

My enthusiasm was received with bleary disinterest.

Mick and Roo were grinning amongst the welcoming throngs; I had sent them up ahead to start organising the next leg of our journey and also to try and find out what had happened to the freight consignment. After it had failed to appear at Toamasina, we learned that the *Emilia* was due to come to Diégo. Perhaps our equipment would turn up here.

We were whisked off in three dilapidated 2CV taxis, so crammed in that we linked arms so as not to fall out through the unlockable doors. Fortunately it was not far to the *Hotel Fiadànana* – not at all the peaceful haven its name implies. It looked cheap and disreputable from the outside and the iron doors on each room made the place feel more like prison than hotel. Later I discovered that the hotel had rooms designated as *chambres de passage*, which were distinct from rooms to sleep in! We rented some rooms and divided ourselves so that girls were with girls and men with men. This encouraged the gay *patron* to leap to the wrong conclusions. He soon took a fancy to the macho members of our team and took every opportunity to express his disgust that they had chosen to travel in the company of women. Often, as we returned from some shopping trip, his voice would echo down the corridor: 'Oh, you naughty boy Phil!' or 'Where is beautiful Roo?'

Diégo's two special attractions are the British war cemetery, for those killed in the landing to take Madagascar from Vichy France in 1942, and the beach. What we first took for the beach turned out to be the town's open-air abattoir; the best place for bathing was fifteen miles further round the bay, at Ramena. The taxi-ride out there took us past numerous contorted baobab trees, stunted-looking at less than twenty feet high. The beach was a vision of tropical paradise. Soft clean white sand, fringed with coconut palms, swept down into inviting azure sea, so clear we hardly needed masks to see the colourful creatures beneath the surface. Large, highly venomous and rapidly lethal sea-snakes, marked like leopards, lolled around lethargically. Little Boxfish, bright yellow, orange-spotted cubes with a mouth stuck on one face, swam hyperactively despite their unstreamlined shape. Littered around the sandy bottom, rolling gently back and forward with the motion of the sea, were warty black Sea Cucumbers. I dived down to pick up a couple. In South-East Asia these are a delicacy but Jean-Elie was as revolted as we were at the thought of eating them. 'Lobster is better!'

he said. I gave the Sea Cucumbers a few firm squeezes, demonstrating their efficacy as water-pistols.

Fishing canoes were beached all along the strand line. Each canoe was a single dugout log with planks built up on it to raise it high out of the water. The fishermen perch on cross-slats, which gives them a good view of their prey for it is about five feet from the bottom of the dugout log to the slats. Although the outrigger-canoe is now found all around the Indian Ocean as far as Africa, it originated in South-East Asia. Some take this as evidence of the early migrations which first brought people to Madagascar. The island's early history is obscure, but it was uninhabited until very recently. The first settlers knew how to cultivate paddy-rice, had outrigger canoes and may have sailed straight across four thousand miles of Indian Ocean. The 1985 Sarimanok Expedition proved that the voyage was possible in that kind of vessel. These 'proto-Malagasy' must have left the Malay–Indonesian archipelago sometime after the introduction of iron (300BC–AD200) and before the introduction of the Hindu religion (2nd–5th century AD).

The South-East Asian colonists were followed by migrants from East Africa, who brought Negro features to the coastal peoples, certain cultural practices and zebu. Then came Arabs, who dominated trade in the Indian Ocean by the tenth century and established communities along the coast, especially in the north. Later still came Europeans: Portuguese, British, then French; and it was Welsh missionaries (the first arrived in 1818) who introduced a script for the language, when they translated the Bible into Malagasy. A few Islamic holy men had written Malagasy using Arabic characters, but this was never widely adopted, and the Roman script became popular with the growth of Christianity. Indians and Chinese also settled on Madagascar. Now about 0.2 per cent of Malagasy residents are Europeans, mainly French, and there are a similar number of Indians, with about 0.1 per cent of Cantonese.

Diégo is a thriving town in a prosperous corner of Madagascar. It is small and pleasantly cosmopolitan, with attractive, but faded and peeling, French colonial architecture. Once an important port and home of Madagascar's only shipyard, it grew up around the world's second largest natural harbour (after Rio). The docks are not used much now, but the whole town still comes alive whenever there is a ship in dock and this is the time to visit the nightclubs. I loved the infectiously rhythmic Malagasy disco songs, but one evening, at the *Nouvelle Hotel*, these were replaced by grating accordion music. The delighted Spanish sailors, frisky and determined to enjoy their shore-leave, responded by bull-fighting across the dancefloor. One of the sailors, a small unattractive dumpling, fancied his chances with Maggie. His proposition, 'You. Me. Bed!' so amused her that she was incapable of a suitably withering look. A stream of sarcastic French, however, had the desired effect and he wobbled back to the bar in search of more inspiration. The men of the expedition were disappointed by the change: they wanted to continue watching the local dancing. The style, adapted to cope with the hectic East African pop beat, involves doing slow stately rhythmic circuits of the dancefloor, and the local girls cruised expertly in circles while rotating their bottoms so that they looked almost prehensile: an enthralling trick.

Roo and Mick had negotiated the hire of a lorry from a Libyan entrepreneur who hung around in the *Hotel de la Poste*, the classiest in town. It was worth visiting just to see the skin of a twelve-foot-long crocodile hanging over the bar, but it had also been Captain Steve's *pied-à-terre*. Friends had suggested we sought out Captain Steve, Diégo's only resident Englishman, since he had all the essential local 'connections' and would be sure to help us. Steve had mysteriously made a lot of money from what he described with a wink as Salvage Work. He had helped us out a great deal in 1981 seemingly only because he enjoyed being able to speak English to us, rather than his usual Cockney-French.

The beautifully made-up barmaid told me that Steve had been forced to leave Madagascar the year before. She winked cheekily at me and confided, 'He's gone to Mauritius, but he'll be back!' Pity. Steve had suggested that when we came back to explore the subterranean rivers and Crocodile Caves he would come with us and provide inflatable boats tough enough to resist puncture on the limestone. But even without Steve's boats, we would need a lorry to transport our equipment and food as far as Matsaborimanga, about eight miles from where we planned to set up base camp. At Matsaborimanga we hoped to hire bullock carts and guides. *Chariots-aux-boeufs* may be a slow, uncomfortable means of transport, like palanquins, but they can get to places inaccessible even to four-wheel-drive vehicles.

Mick and Roo were a great team, although completely unalike in physique and temperament. Mick was clean-shaven, thin and athletic, while Roo was bearded and solid. Roo, an electronics whizz-kid, was efficient and hard-working and could not cope with the speed at which things got done in Madagascar. Mick was much more easy-going. He was a totally incompetent linguist but communicated well simply because he was so friendly and outgoing and did not care if he made a fool of himself. He was a perfect balance for Roo's short fuse. Mick would describe some of their interviews as '*stressant*' and occasionally had to drag Roo from an office before he completely lost his temper. They had been trying for several days to talk a local factory owner into selling sixty-five pounds of carbide to fuel our caving lights, finally succeeding when they managed to convince them with official letters that we were responsible enough to handle such explosive material. The receipt was made out to Monsieur le docteur Michel of the Ministry of Scientific Research, which made Mick feel very important.

Purchasing local spirit to pickle specimens was a simpler task. We approached a disreputable-looking bald Chinese shopkeeper, clad in a grubby white vest and shorts, who demonstrated the strength of the *rhum* by pouring some out and then setting light to it. He sold us sugar, noodles-with-cockroaches and tinned foods, and told us that if stung by a scorpion we should pulverise the creature and apply it as a poultice. I laughed at his advice, for I was not worried about scorpions.

In the poor south of Madagascar people subsist on cassava and *brèdes*. Here in Diégo the market was full of good foods. We needed enough for two months and began days of bargaining for rice, maize, beans, dried fish, dried bananas, oranges, peanuts, white cabbage, pumpkins, garlic, chillies, root ginger (and – mistakenly – root turmeric, which was much too subtle for expedition cookery), chives, coriander, coconut oil, a bundle of unappetising dry leaves and twigs which we were told was Malagasy tea, real tea, home-grown coffee, sugar, wild honey, salt, chocolate, biscuits, some locally tinned jam and meat and even a few baobab fruits. I asked the price of a basket at one stall, but did not hear the price clearly so repeated back, 'A thousand francs?' The stall-holder looked puzzled and said with disarming honesty, 'No, 700!'

Fortunately the traders were honest and patient, for prices could be quoted either in *ariary* or in francs (there are five *ariary* to the Malagasy franc), but since they never specified which units they were using, there was endless scope for confusion! We expected the stall-holders to be delighted by so much new trade, but some looked mildly put out when we bought their entire stock, thus depriving them of amusement for the rest of the day. The concept of bulk buying seemed to baffle them, too.

'How much are the coconuts?'

'150 Malagasy francs.'

'OK, we would like to buy a hundred.'

'No, they are 150.'

'Yes, we would like a hundred.'

'No, they are 150.'

'Yes, we would like a hundred coconuts each costing 150 Malagasy francs.'

'No, they are 150.'

Only by theatrically loading the coconuts on to a rickshaw were we able to convince the bemused stall-holder that we really did want to buy a hundred coconuts.

We also bought some treats and goodies for our first week in the forest: samosas, French bread, banana fritters, sesame and peanut brittle, tomatoes and grean beans. Soon we had about half a ton of food stacked in our cell-like rooms and in the hotel corridors. The shopping was completed when we found a pestle and mortar (to grind the salt, spices and maybe a scorpion or two), some nails, a hammer, saucepans, a spade and some poor quality machetes; called *coupe-coupes* locally, they were too soft and blunt to 'coupe' anything.

While all this shopping was going on, the rest of the team caught up with us. The last four to arrive joined us on the beach the day before we left for Ankàrana. Dave and Sheila had done the aerial reconnaissance with Phil the day they arrived. Phil was bubbling with excitement as he recalled the reconnaissance aeroplane plunging along the limestone cliffs and ravines: 'Probably one of the most impressive areas of tropical karst I have ever seen. It was depressingly barren, though. All the forest had gone, except in a few inaccessible ravines.' Dave, logistics expert, immediately checked to make sure that we had enough supplies and food; we would not starve. Dave and Sheila arrived in Ankàrana the following day (just two days after their arrival in Madagascar), quite oblivious of all the difficulties and frustrations I had experienced in the month I had already been in the country.

☆

I had decided not to travel to Ankàrana in the lorry with the lads but would try to set up a life-line through the town of Ambilobé, our closest link with civilisation. It had electricity sometimes, telephones, a small hospital and, according to the map, even an airfield. As Medical Officer to the expedition, my recurring nightmare was of someone falling onto the ferocious, spiky limestone. Without a few basic facilities even three doctors would not be able to cope with severe trauma and compound fractures, so a quick evacuation would be necessary and Ambilobé seemed the best escape route. The medical trio could then nurse any casualties in the local hospital until they were strong enough to fly home. We also hoped that, through the Ambilobé doctors, we might be able to recruit a local health worker to join our team. We wanted someone to teach us about the local customs and *fady* (taboos) and to assist with translation. So, as the main team prepared to drive to Ankàrana from the north, as I had done in 1981, Anne, Maggie and I (the three doctors) set off to find a bus to take us to Ambilobé at the massif's southern tip. The map showed a track running north from Ambilobé up to very close to where we proposed to set up base camp. On my last visit I had heard that it was not possible to drive to the massif from Ambilobé because a bridge had collapsed. I now hoped that five years later, it might have been repaired.

The Diégo bus terminus on the edge of town was an expanse of sand and oil and a chaos of dilapidated buses and minibuses. Several were being bump-started by their passengers. We were directed to the one new minibus ('a present from the people of Japan'), which was just leaving. Twenty-eight people were already on board. Maggie and Anne claimed the two remaining front seats and I made myself comfortable on the spare wheel at the back, ignoring people beckoning me to join them sardined into the seats in the centre of the bus. Many more people arrived over the next hour and piled into the already full seats while I congratulated myself on my wisdom in choosing the comfort and exclusiveness of the spare wheel.

We sped south along the first thirty miles of newly tarmacked National Highway 6. Just beyond Anivorana, the money for the road repairs had run out – the remaining forty miles to Ambilobé was in such terrible condition that it was difficult to know whether the road had ever been metalled. The journey took nearly five hours as we stopped every half mile to let on more people. Soon I was envying Anne and Maggie their prime positions, crammed into the front seats with ten adults and three vomiting children. My little haven now had fifteen people packed into it and my vista comprised the crutch of some very soiled trousers. I wanted to see Ankàrana as we drove past its eastern flank but, standing up, I could only find space on the floor for one foot and saw nothing but bits of my fellow passengers. The balancing act was punctuated by frequent stops for the men to relieve themselves (there was never enough time or cover for the women) and to let even more people on. The journey was interminable.

What a relief to arrive finally at Ambilobé: the name means the Place-where-the-*Bilo*-is-danced . . . in a special ritual to awaken the Ancestors. It was dusty, sleepy and run-down, and much too hot for us to think about dancing. Unlike Diégo, it was particularly unattractive on first arrival. The bus depot was hemmed in by corrugated-iron shacks. Thirsty, we entered one of these and were offered warm Three Horses beer or *Bon-bon Anglais*. Looking as innocuous as lemonade, *Bon-bon Anglais* is as disgusting as the lurid-green *Inca Cola* of Peru. It is cloyingly sweet with a nauseating taste of perfume, supposedly reminiscent of English sweets. Malagasy friends found the irony of the English disliking *Bon-bon Anglais* hilarious.

As soon as we emerged from the *hotely*, we were surrounded by taxi-touts trying to persuade us to go on to the island resort of Nosy Bé, another sixty miles further south. We grabbed our bags and fled towards town. The centre was pleasantly shaded with numerous mango trees and the many plants growing in half oil-drums gave the town a homely, friendly feel. Some of the streets were tarmacked, some cobbled and all were covered in the ubiquitous red dust. Each house and shop had a little veranda to sit out on or to display brightly coloured materials and plastic bowls. Whitewash on all the buildings was either peeling off or was streaked with black mould, the corrugated-iron roofs were rusting, and so were the stripped shells of ancient French cars which lay decaying at most street corners. The market was stocked with all sorts of vegetables and luscious fruits. I went to look at what I thought were currant buns, but when I approached the 'currants' flew off. Stall-holders selling fresh fish or sweet sticky things were constantly whisking flies away. The whole scene was made more colourful by the women in their traditional northern dress: gaudy printed cotton *lamba oany*, often pulled over the head Arab-style, and with hair neatly plaited into a bun. The more the colours clashed, the better they seemed to like them: red with puce, pink and orange or purple and green. Some wore yellow face packs which I first mistook for some horrendous dermatological affliction. Apparently they restore beauty after childbirth. People returned our incredulous stares, laughing at our white skins and shouting, '*Vazaha!*'

The *Hotel d'Escargot* was the only hotel. Here, at last, we could go to the loo. The *maîtresse* was Madame Assisty, the same kindly middle-aged Indian lady who had made us so welcome five years before when, *en route* for Ankàrana, we had arrived exhausted by road from Tana. She seemed to remember me. Unchanged after five years, her myxoedematous bulk was still bound up in a faded *lamba oany* (the same one?) tightly wrapped around her ample bosom like a bath towel. Her long grey hair was stuffed up in an untidy bun. She had married a Cantonese. Like the Diégo shopkeeper who had sold us the *rhum*, he too was balding and wore a grubby white vest and shorts. He owned the general store adjoining the hotel: a wonderful place with shelves up to the ceiling stuffed with dusty tins and boxes. An overpowering atmosphere of rum emanated from a row of metre-high metal drums. He decanted from these one of three grades of the inflammable brew into whatever container his customers brought. Their son, Zo-Zo, proudly described himself as an Indo-Chinese salad. He also explained the pedigree of each of his friends when introducing them.

The food at *Hotel d'Escargot* was mouth-watering, despite the primitive conditions of the kitchen: lobster, shrimps, fish, tasty buffalo steaks or meat mixtures with rice, all cooked on hefty Chinese-made paraffin stoves. Madame Assisty shuffled around her kitchen, with a huge well at its centre, supervising the cooking or kicking the ducks which wandered between her feet. Her main pleasure in life was to talk. She paused to draw breath only when forced to; she would stop in mid-sentence for a strident inspiration, only to gabble huskily on. Despite all those words and her nice straight-forward French, I can't remember much of what she talked about, apart from constant requests, through a curled upper lip, for a tonic to cure her fatigue. Madame Assisty told us that this was the cool season. It would only get hot, she said, between October and January. Ambilobé is in a heat sink with none of Diégo's cool sea breezes; the heat made us languid and lifeless and my first thought was of cooling under a shower. The door of the concrete bathroom had disintegrated long ago and had been replaced by some flattened oil drums in a wobbly wooden frame.

It would not stay shut. Inside was a rusting oil drum which had been filled from the well. Floating on the water was a plastic mug which gave a clue to the local bathing technique: sploshing the water all over me felt the height of luxury.

Next morning we went in search of the doctor. The hospital out-patients' clinic was in progress and fifty people were waiting.

'Could we see Monsieur le docteur?'

Much to our embarrassment, we were shoved through the throngs and straight in to see him. Briefly we explained our mission and suggested that we arrange to meet him at a more convenient time. He called in his colleague and we talked. The senior doctor had been working here single-handed for years. He looked after the sixty-seven-bedded hospital and, with support from *aides sanitaires*, was GP to the 160,000 people of Ambilobé and environs. By comparison, GPs in Britain look after about 2,500 people and can refer to the district hospital. This man saw 150 out-patients each day, but the numbers did not worry him. He was frustrated by the limited treatments he could offer. Supplies of drugs and dressings were his biggest headache: he was only able to dispense penicillin. If anyone needed anything else they had to buy it in Diégo – even intravenous fluids. The doctors were working under difficult conditions; the electricity supply was at best intermittent and there had been no water in the taps for eighteen months. Both doctors were of the Mérina tribe from the *Hauts Plateaux*. The Mérina are the most numerous and intellectual of the eighteen Malagasy tribes and make up almost a quarter of Madagascar's population. They were first to unite the country and still hold most of the top administrative posts all over the island. The doctors seemed to look down on their unsophisticated patients, although in a paternalistic rather than a critical way. They were sympathetic, and their training at the Medical School in Tana, set up by Protestant missionaries in 1886, left them knowledgeable and inventive when it came to finding ways of surmounting the difficulties of their practice. The junior doctor was recently married to a government servant stationed in Tana and had hardly seen him since their wedding. She said that his transfer to Ambilobé 'might be possible next year'. She was resigned to the separation, explaining that professional women are often expected to sacrifice their private lives for their careers. It will be better, she said, when she is more senior. The doctors were baffled by our desire to go to somewhere 'even more primitive' than Ambilobé.

'We must go and meet the King. He knows the area well and will help you. Is it convenient to go now?'

'Yes, it's convenient for us but we will not disturb you now. We can go after you have finished your work.'

The King was Prince Tsimiharo III, heriditary 'king' of the Antankarana tribe (the 'people-of-the-rock'), and we had been looking forward to meeting him. His ancestors were buried inside certain Ankàrana caves and we did not want to give offence by entering them by mistake. The King no longer had any official power, but he was still greatly respected and his approval of our project would ensure a welcome wherever we went.

The five of us trooped out through the growing queue of patients to find him. He worked as a policeman and was easy to find. It was still early, yet he insisted that we each drink two bottles (*grande modèle*) of Three Horses beer. He seemed a kind and civilised man who was impressed with our wish to deal with some of the medical problems in the villages close to our camp. He was most concerned about our welfare, though, and asked three times whether we ate rice. He knew foreigners could not eat rice and therefore would starve. Clearly he did not see us as the tough, independent women that we thought we were. He said he would visit us.

The more the doctors learned of our intentions, the more their bemusement increased. Why work in such a remote place? Why not work in Ambilobé with them? Once we had convinced them that we were determined to go to Ankàrana, they expressed their worries about us ever linking up with our team again. We tried to impress them with stories proving that we were intrepid and resourceful, but they continued to regard us like little lost sheep. They left us at our hotel while they found out about the bush-taxis. The beer and the heat had sapped our strength and enthusiasm, and we were pleased to be able to relax. Here Anne sat reading with her feet in a bucket of cold water, and after another 'shower', I settled down for a long siesta.

All we could offer in return for the doctors' kindness was our gratitude and some medicines, which are in such short supply in Madagascar. They were pleased with the common antibiotics, though puzzled by Flagyl suppositories. Over dinner, they told us to be ready for a 4am start the following day. We were up and packed at dawn and finally squeezed aboard the *taxi-brousse* at 2pm.

# 5. The One-eyed Abyssinian

*Izay marary andriana*
The ill are noble.
Malagasy proverb

The bush-taxi toured the town a few times touting for more passengers, then finally headed north. At the edge of town we were struck by the poverty and the smells of absent sanitation; the red sand seemed to be waiting to invade the minute huts-on-stilts that each large family inhabited. We soon left the once-metalled main road and turned west onto a dirt track. We bumped and lurched along, swerving to avoid the potholes, past fallow paddy-fields, cassava patches, mango trees and banana plants. Beyond stretched the savannah, deserted except for the occasional grazing zebu. A large cloud of red dust followed, and overtook us when we slowed to negotiate particularly large potholes or river beds. The track passed through a river-cut gash in the Ankàrana outcrop, here eroded into ferocious spikes topping an imposing grey wall of limestone three hundred feet high. We passed through the great barrier of the Ankàrana Massif and, looking north along the line of the Ankàrana Wall, it seemed to go on for ever. How far was Matsaborimanga and base camp now?

Travelling with us in the *taxi-brousse* was Abdulla. He was a health worker, the *aide sanitaire* for the village of Ambatoharanana. A relative of the King (as we might have guessed from his substantial girth), he spoke excellent French, or at least better French than I did. An hour before sunset we reached Ambatoharanana. I was dying for a pee again. Abdulla invited us to see his *'hôpital'* – I looked as enthusiastic as my bursting bladder allowed. I prayed that his hospital would be small. Abdulla led us through the village: a muddle of tiny houses, most thatched and all perched on stilts. The 'hospital' was not much larger than the other houses. It too was on stilts but had a corrugated-iron roof which made it stiflingly hot and airless inside. There were four beds, each with a mosquito net full of holes. Under one, lying on plastic sheeting instead of bed linen, lay a man who groaned and rocked his aching abdomen. Perspiration poured off his emaciated body. Abdulla demonstrated his training and how ill his patient was by prodding him sharply in the stomach. The invalid curled up and his groaning grew louder. I felt sick. *Aides sanitaires*, who are male, educated and leading village figures, are given a whole year's training to provide a basic primary health service. They organise immunisations, treat what they can with penicillin, chloroquine, aspirin and antiseptic, and can refer patients to the doctor. He showed us his meagre dispensary while I tried tactfully to ask about the man with belly-ache. Would the doctors come and see him? Shouldn't he be evacuated to Ambilobé? 'Maybe tomorrow,' came Abdulla's answer.

Abdulla asked us if we wished to use the bathroom. Baffled, but hopeful still of finding somewhere discreet to squat, I said 'Yes', and he led us out between the little huts to the edge of the village and waved vaguely towards some kapok trees. Once I had emptied my bladder, I could take more interest in my surroundings. It then struck me how out of place the kapoks were. All across the northern savannah kapok had been planted for shade, for material to stuff mattresses and as a source of vegetable oil. It is native to Central and South America, but Madagascar is now one of the world's largest exporters of kapok products. A strange-looking tree with buttresses and shiny green bark, its geometrical horizontal branches make it distinctive so that on Pacific islands it is used to mark boundaries. In colonial India it was known as the 'PWD tree': the sort of tree that might be designed by a Public Works engineer. Now its eight-inch fruits were bursting with cottony fluff and small hard round black seeds. Stars appeared as we sauntered back to the village and dozens of bats flapped their three-foot wings silently and eerily above us. They would be going to forage for fruit in the Ankàrana forests now that the kapok was no longer edible. How strange to see these Asian *Pteropus* bats here so close to Africa.

The toothless *président* of the local *fòkon'òlona* (a council of village elders) was our hostess. Members of her family brought rice and a thin soup with some leaves floating in it. We suggested that we could sleep under the stars where it was cool, but they insisted on turning the family out of their communal bed. We did not sleep well.

At 4am Abdulla woke us. It seemed an uncivilised time to rise, but starting before dawn meant that we could walk a good part of the way while it was still cool. Beyond Ambatoharanana, a half-decent dirt road continued across a substantial bridge over the Mananjeba River, where Paul was later to see so many signs of crocodiles. Why did the *taxi-brousse* stop just before the bridge? Less than an hour's walking gave us the answer. The track was cut by steep dry riverbeds and a huge tidal swamp. When we reached Ambody Pont, there was no sign of the bridge that gave the place its name. In 1981 I had approached the massif from the north, and so had not realised there would be such barriers making walking or bullock cart the only practicable means of getting about. Even a four-wheel-drive car might not get much further than the thigh-deep River Ankàrana.

It was only 6am but the temperature was already climbing. Dust was everywhere: it dried our throats and turned us brick-red so that wading across the river felt delicious. We plodded on, blissfully unaware that we still had another twenty miles to go. Looking at my companions, I wondered how Maggie and Anne would fare on this walk and on the expedition? I did not know either particularly well: they had been amongst the 120 students in my year at Southampton Medical School. Neither had been anywhere very remote before, but they seemed prepared to have a go at anything. Anne was a giggly extrovert and was great fun to be with. She was fit, lithe and bouncy, looking as if she could cope with anything the expedition might throw at her. Maggie could not have been more different. She was quiet, and at Medical School I had hardly noticed her. Then she turned up on a parachuting course and I was amazed at how she took the sheer terror of the first jump with a quiet calm smile. Subsequently we found we had a great deal in common and when I suggested she come to Madagascar with us, she said 'OK', and with no fuss and few questions she simply turned up in Tana ready to start work. She was the cool, steady sort of character who would thrive on an expedition.

The countryside became wilder and more interesting. It was more as I remembered: dusty savannah covered with shrivelled yellow straggly grass similar to the Savannah-with-Palms which covers so much of the drier lowlands. The palms and a few thorny bushes retained green leaves and some bore delicious juicy miniature plums or lovely yellow, orange or red flowers. Others produced seed pods the shape of model spaceships, waiting for the rains when they could germinate. My favourite savannah plant was the stupid-looking bulbous-bottomed Elephant's Foot Tree, *Pachypodium*: fifteen feet tall and endemic to Madagascar. Now it was naked and looked dead, except that at the tip of each tentacle-like branch grew a bouquet of large beautiful white flowers. Half-inch coin-shaped leaves appeared later, between the spirals of thorns which covered the plant.

Looking east, to our right, we saw the Ankàrana Wall again. Black limestone cliffs rose over six hundred sheer feet out of the red savannah, and further north were the orange ash-cones of extinct volcanoes that I had seen from the air. Their solidified lava form remains as smooth black basalt boulders littering the plains. Ancient eruptions had cracked the Ankàrana Massif from top to bottom in many places, like a tile under a boot. As we walked parallel to the cliffs we could see the resulting canyons which cut right through, west to east. The jagged segmented cardboard-cut-out horizon of the Ankàrana Wall, surrounded by dry plains dotted with palms and *Pachypodia*, was a world away from the African savannahs and their stunted acacias. We walked in a strip of land barely fifteen miles wide, between the Ankàrana Massif and the coastal mangrove swamps. After several hours, more kapok trees appeared on the horizon as geometric as telegraph poles. We were approaching another of the several villages scattered on this fertile but dry savannah. This village seemed familiar: it was Andrafiabé, where in 1981 our drunk pick-up driver had left us, shouting, '*Alors! On y va! En safari!*'

That time we had travelled in a car belonging to a most disreputable expatriate: a 'business associate' of Captain Steve. We did not at first even know his surname, but Georges was well known in Ambilobé and people seemed frightened of him. By local standards he was expensively dressed – a shifty-looking character with a hawkish nose and a glass eye. He described himself as an Abyssinian. We introduced ourselves as Steve's compatriots and he welcomed us warmly. Steve later explained with a sinister grin that Georges owed him some Big Favours.

Georges Kharma proudly showed us around his timber yard: stacked high with enormously valuable and supposedly protected *Palissandre* rosewood. His only response to our undiplomatic expressions of surprise that he should be trading in *Palissandre* was a smug grin, while his good eye twinkled mischievously. I recalled a conversation with the Attorney General in Tana a few weeks before. He had invited the expedition team to dinner and put on a bewilderingly lavish meal: a whole roasted suckling pig with French wine and cheeses flown in from Réunion. We and the other twenty guests dined on a magnificent fine-grained table made from a single plank of *Palissandre*.

Undiplomatic as ever, I commented that the table must be very old for it would not now be permitted to cut down such a superb tree. 'No, it is not very old,' the Attorney General replied. 'Permits are available to certain people.'

For reasons we never did understand, Georges did everything he could to help us. Had we been forced to walk to Ankàrana with all our equipment, we would not have been able to carry enough food for more than a couple of days. Georges assured us that since he owned a variety of vehicles, transporting ourselves, all our food and luggage to the caves would be no problem. He lent us one of his pick-ups with an ebullient driver who smelt strongly of *rhum*. The driver took us shopping for food and paraffin, but we had not brought enough containers to transport all the paraffin we would need. '*Oh, pas de problème!*' shrugged the driver, as the garage attendant dispensed the *pétrole* into Three Horses beer bottles (*grande modèle*) sealed with twists of brown paper. They looked alarmingly like Molotov cocktails.

We also needed a sack of rice. Our driver's face momentarily clouded as he pondered the difficulties of buying rice in bulk. Then it was back to all-smiles and enthusiasm again: '*Pas de problème!* Georges will fix a *spéciale* permit.' The Government had tried to curb the black market in rice at the beginning of the eighties by introducing fixed prices and a rationing system. Road blocks were set up to prevent rice being moved around the country. So transporting sacks of rice was illegal unless authorised by a permit . . . but Georges somehow had access to supplies of 'official' documents. We grew increasingly uncomfortable about having anything to do with this man's dubious activities – but he did get us to Ankàrana with a fortnight's supply of food.

The following morning the driver arrived early, still apparently drunk and ecstatic about the prospect of this expedition into *la brousse*. We sped off up towards Diégo, around the northern end of the massif and into the dusty savannah where the only tracks were for zebu and their herders. We took it in turns to nurse the leaking Molotov cocktails, cradling them as the pick-up lurched. It was a long hot uncomfortable trip, but the driver's enthusiasm never waned. Even when we reached places littered with twelve-inch basalt boulders, he sped on undaunted, shrieking with delight, until the pick-up was stuck, rocking with two wheels off the ground. He found this hilarious and tears streamed down his face as the six of us manhandled the Toyota back onto four wheels again. An even funnier joke was to speed off again, showering us with more dust as he shouted, *'Nous faisons la safari!'*

We never did find the dirt track that would have taken us all the way to Andrafiabé, but instead meandered across the savannah negotiating numerous steep-sided dry riverbeds and miniature ravines. Dusk was gathering when we finally arrived and we were taken to see Princess Manarovika. She was a scrawny, pleasantly barmy old lady who offered the traditional Malagasy greeting, 'What's the news?'

'No news,' we politely replied.

She spoke a language with a fair amount of French in it and was very welcoming. The driver cheerily took his leave; we wondered if we should let him go – how would he manage to navigate across the trackless savannah at night? *Pas de problème!* He would come back in ten days to collect us. And he did.

The long day's *travails* speeding across the desiccated savannah had turned us brick-red, and smiling sent slicks of dust avalanching off our faces. We stank of stale sweat and paraffin.

'Would you like a wash?'

Princess Manarovika directed us to the village water supply: a large stagnant puddle in an all-but-dry riverbed. In my ignorance and enthusiasm as a first-year medical student, I proclaimed the pool 'the perfect place to catch Bilharzia', so we returned to the Princess's hut still stinking and brick-coloured.

'Had a nice wash?'

'Yes, thank you.'

Smiling in response to her puzzled enquiry, we felt cakes of congealed sand cracking about our eyes. I expect she thought us as barmy as we thought her. Over dinner – rice and chicken again – she asked lots of questions and prattled on about the old days. Her French-with-Malagasy was difficult to understand but I did gather that we need not fear scorpions: 'They never sting white people!' She pointed out a hut-on-stilts where we could sleep. Inside half of the floorboards were missing and I listened to rats – ordinary Brown Rats – scuttling around underneath me. But not for long: I was soon asleep. The following morning the Princess helped us negotiate the hire of a *chariot-aux-boeufs* to take food and equipment to a campsite at Andrafiabé Cave.

☆

Memories of this 1981 visit came flooding back as Anne, Maggie and I approached Andrafiabé village and it seemd odd to have arrived so uneventfully this time. A man came out of his hut grinning broadly, and said: 'Good morning!'

I was amazed to find an English speaker here, and pleased too, for I was itching to ask after Princess Manarovika. She had been rather frail in 1981 and I wondered if she was still alive.

'Good morning. How are you?' I replied.

'Good morning. *Bonne zour.*'

Clearly we were not going to have much of a conversation.

I tried: '*Manao ahoana tompoko.*' (Hello.)

Still he did not respond, so I offered: '*Veloma tompoko.*' (Goodbye.)

We walked on past the stagnant village water supply which I now knew was totally unsuitable for the fastidious Bilharzia snails. By mid-morning we had reached Matsaborimanga, the village nearest to our base camp. Sheila and the men had arrived there in the lorry a couple of days earlier. Following Jean Radofilao's advice, they had met Simagaul and through him hired guides and a *chariot-aux-boeufs* to get the equipment and supplies to the campsite inside the massif. Jean had employed Simagaul on numerous occasions for he knew Ankàrana and, unlike some of his fellow villagers, was not frightened of entering caves.

Abdulla introduced us as Important Doctors and we were shown into the cool of a large new schoolroom which soon filled with spectators. Clean new rush mats were brought and, with amazing speed, lunch. We must have been eating someone else's. I squirmed with embarrassment, feeling parasitic, but these people were relatively rich. The children all looked healthy: none had the protruding ribs of Tana's street children and the poor villagers of southern Madagascar. My travels in local buses and bush-taxis, stopping to eat hurriedly at roadside *hotelys*, had prepared me for the usual fare: a congealed mound of cold rice to accompany a piece of chicken neck or some more unappetising member floating in a thin, lukewarm stock. Solidifying fat globules made it rather unpalatable unless you were really hungry. Village food was much the same. To accompany our lukewarm rice, we were given some watery, fatty soup which contained a few small pieces of chicken skin and some *brèdes*. *Brèdes* looks like camomile. It is often served floating in a lot of hot water, a refreshing drink which produces a pleasant tingling sensation in the mouth and washes the grease off the palate. Even rich Malagasy have a great appetite for fat, and to be at its best, meat should wobble with adiposity.

Our host was a balding man who looked well over sixty; he hobbled with arthritis. He was the grandfather of Arman, one of the two men whom the others had employed as guides. Grandfather did not respond to our greetings; was our pronunciation so bad? With solemn relish, he tucked into what looked like part of a fossilised archaeopteryx. The chicken's feet disappeared with much crunching of bones, demonstrating one of the numerous *fady* (taboo) which control relations within families. The legs of fowl are reserved for the head of the family in Antakarana households. Other tribes have completely different customs: amongst the Mérina tribe, for example, chicken feet are given to children.

Abdulla asked if we were tired; pillows (stuffed with local kapok) were brought and we were left to sleep. It was 11am, but we were exhausted already.

☆

Later we had a look around Matsaborimanga. There was one shop which sold plastic bowls, cigarettes, matches and Three Horses beer, but nothing else. The village was a muddle of houses. All of its seven hundred people lived in small wooden boxes on stilts roofed with thatch or corrugated iron. All over Madagascar, the houses are rectangular and on stilts. In the west their walls are wattle daubed with mud and roofs are thatched with wild grasses. In eastern Madagascar the houses are thatched with Traveller's Palm leaves. Nowhere on Madagascar will you find the circular huts of Africa.

Like all villages to the west of Ankàrana, Matsaborimanga's existence is only possible because the massif acts as a reservoir, discharging water even throughout the annual six-month drought. The water is crucial for growing 'the best rice in all Madagascar', as the people of Matsaborimanga proudly boasted. The Malagasy love rice and like to eat it three times a day; they claim to have the highest per capita rice consumption in the world. The villagers were equally proud of their ingenious machine for milling rice. It comprised a heavy wooden hammer supported on a pivoted log fifteen feet long. The hammer was counterbalanced by a tipping wooden bucket which filled with water from an irrigation canal. The hammer was raised as the bucket filled and fell as water spilt. It was marvellously simple, very slow, but extremely effective.

Happy children chased scrawny long-legged roadrunner chickens or threw zebu dung at each other. Originally zebu were brought from mainland Africa with their Swahili name, *omby*. Now there are said to be at least ten million zebu on Madagascar; they probably outnumber the human population. Although zebu are used as draught animals, they do not feature in the family's menu and any milk they produce goes to the calves. The Malagasy do not have a taste for milk – presumably, like South-East Asians, they cannot digest it. Zebu are a status symbol and herds are kept to be slaughtered at funerals. Especially in southern and western Madagascar, the skulls of hundreds of zebu sacrificed at funerals are used to adorn tombs. Some Malagasy dialects have 140 or more words to describe the various combinations of black or brown splodges and patches on the off-white zebu hides. The colours are important: black and white cattle are especially prized for slaughter at funeral ceremonies - a curious parallel with the Toraja people of Sulawesi in Indonesia.

Abdulla reappeared just after three to say goodbye. We offered to take his photograph, which pleased him greatly. He grabbed the nearest lady and embraced her, adopting a self-important expression until the click of the camera shutter told him he could relax and grin broadly again. Then everyone wanted a picture and we decided that it was time to leave. Two men from Matsaborimanga came to show us the way.

A couple more hours' walking brought us to the forest which flanks Ankàrana. I was flagging and it seemed that we still had a long way to go, so we paused to sit in the welcome shade. Dripping with sweat, I gulped down some warm plastic-flavoured water. The track deeper into the forest had breached the canopy and allowed enough light for pretty shrubs to grow. A plant like a diminutive *Mimosa* caught my eye. It had lilac pompom flowers and red truncated pea-pod seeds. The delicate little pinnate leaves were touch-sensitive so that merely brushing past them induced the leaves to fold up and all but disappear. Once this had happened, any grazing animal would likely move on to more obviously succulent fodder. While playing with the touch-sensitive leaves, I noticed movement in the trees nearby and turned to see three dark forms leaping across the gap in the forest above the track. I struggled excitedly to my feet but was too slow and saw little more than quivering leaves and branches. Even this glimpse of lemurs elated me and I wanted to rush on to camp and start work. But as we walked on, the exhaustion returned. I peered into the forest, looking for the limestone cliffs that would tell us we were at last inside the massif with only two more hours' walk. All I could see was trees. Then suddenly we arrived at the camp, having been unaware that the forest path we were following was inside a canyon. The forest was so thick that we had not been able to see the canyon walls, yet we were now nearly two miles inside the massif and almost completely walled in by limestone.

It was the end of August, a whole month since my touch-down in Madagascar. Tents, mosquito nets and hammocks were scattered between the trees: our base camp looked comfortable and civilised. I handed out some peanut brittle to celebrate the team's arrival at Ankàrana at last. This made the lads yet more pleased to see us; they even offered to brew up some coffee. This time we avoided the problems of transporting paraffin and cooked on wood fires rather than on stoves. As the men rekindled the fire, they began to tell us what they had achieved in their first two days. They had started local exploration and had dug pits for a compost heap and, out of sight, a latrine. The latrine had been sited by an expert: it was possible to squat unseen amongst the bushes, yet be able to spot, and warn off, other would-be users of the facility. It was not necessary to whistle while answering nature's call.

Eleven of us (four women and seven men) had come from Britain and we had been joined by Jean-Elie Randriamasy, the entomologist from Tana, and also Christian and Armand, both in their late teens, who we had employed as guides in Matsaborimanga. Jean Radofilao had also arrived with his son and daughter. It was Jean's writings which had first drawn my attention to Ankàrana. More than twenty years ago, he had come from France to teach at the University for two years. Now he had adopted Malagasy citizenship and had no intention of returning to France. His particular academic interest was in the mathematics of movements of galaxy clusters – not just stars or even galaxies but clusters of galaxies. He had taken on a task of a similarly mind-boggling scale when he decided to map Ankàrana's complicated topography. Lately he had been going to Ankàrana alone at weekends with little more than a rucksack full of French bread to sustain him: his vegetarian diet, he said, kept him healthy and strong. He did not look it, though, for he was a greying, thin, slightly stooping figure, not at all my image of an intrepid explorer, but he had surveyed miles of unknown cave passages, mostly completely alone. In 1981 I had found a tree that he had dragged a mile into a cave to help him scale a loose, rotten, vertical climb 120 feet up into a hole in the roof. He thought nothing of attempting such a dangerous assault by himself, deep inside a cave in a very remote area, and never mentioned the risks he had taken. Yet he had survived two decades of cave exploration. Mick, the fit, effervescent, outdoor sports instructor in his mid-twenties, joined the greying Jean on one of his exploratory trips. Mick had hardly been able to keep up and came back absolutely shattered – another '*stressant*' experience. When I asked Jean whether their trip had been a good one, he responded: 'Eet was 'ard; eet was too 'ard!' We soon grew accustomed to Jean's amazing capacity for work and his over-serious personality. I do not ever recall him laughing or making many jokes, and it later transpired that he described most of the days he went exploring as 'Too 'ard!' This and 'Ze cave she was blocked wiz bolsters' were his two stock phrases. His English was fluent, but learned from books, so he had a very strong and rather charming accent. The Malagasy understood his version of the English language much better than ours.

Jean was a mine of information about Ankàrana and the Antankarana people. Throughout the weeks he spent with us, he continued to provide tantalising facts about the region. He said that there were definitely no blind fish at Ankàrana but there was a large cat-like animal.

'Ah, I would love to see the Fosa!' I said.

'Oh no, this is not the Fosa. I have see *him* many times. There is another cat, *approximately* half as big again and very fierce. The Antankarana men are very frightened of him.'

'But the Fosa is Madagascar's largest carnivore . . . there *was* an animal which was a metre and half long, but that died out hundreds of years ago.'

'Did it?' he said, mysteriously. 'There is a lot still to be discovered at Ankàrana.'

Jean would elaborate no further.

Pleased as I was to see everyone again after the trek from Ambilobé, I was keener on bathing than on swapping stories. We had not washed for two days. I asked Simon where our water came from. 'It is a bit of scramble. You'd better put towels, clean clothes and your womenish things into a day-sack.'

Simon led us deeper into the forest to a steep slippery mud climb down to the gaping cave mouth. I could see it would be difficult to emerge pristine and mudless after our bath. We entered a chamber perhaps thirty feet high and from beneath us came the sound of rushing water; there were rapids inside. It was indeed a bit of a scramble to get down to the river. Simon led us over large angular boulders and down to where hardly a glimmer of light penetrated; the darkness was welcome for it gave the privacy for a proper wash. Then with uncharacteristic discretion, he left us at a good bathing spot where a slab of rock sloped gently into the river. The limestone was sharp, thrown into knife-edges in places, and we had to take care not to lacerate our feet in the gloom. Our hugely magnified deformed shadows danced like deranged giants on the cave wall ahead of us as we set up our headlamps to illuminate our bathing place. Rumours of crocodiles in the river caves were forgotten. Shining the light around, the torch caught flashes of white water. The rapids were not far downstream and the river boiled and swirled between the rocks, disappearing noisily into the next part of the cave. How excellent. How exciting.

We edged down to the sandy river bottom. I plunged in fully dressed and floated out to where the river was waist deep – so cool and refreshing. I covered my clothes in soap, shampooed my hair and lay back in the water, floating gently downstream. Relaxed, I watched slicks of shiny white lather glistening as they floated away towards the rapids. I peeled off a layer of clothes and repeated the process until my washed clothes were all heaped up on the limestone slab and I felt clean and cool lying in the water. Something brushed my leg. Crocodile! I exploded out of the water. I saw nothing as I lunged towards the bank but in groping around, desperate to get out, I found the branch responsible for my scare. Why was I so jumpy? Wasn't this a safe place?

'What happened?' Anne asked. I tried to laugh off my cowardice. 'Do you really think there might be crocodiles in these caves?'

'I don't know,' I said.

# 6. Amongst the Pinnacles

Those lemurs're the daintiest little animals extant.
Neither cat nor monkey, they've been dowered by Nature
with the privileges of both. Beauty with agility . . .
Alfred Aloysius Horn, 1928

Ankàrana is a tiny ecological island within Madagascar's island-continent. It lies almost at the northern tip of the island, only fifty miles south of Diégo. Although just thirty miles from the east coast, it is sheltered by the eastern hills, and since rain falls for only half of the year, the forests are deciduous but lusher than most other dry tropical woodlands. Yet it is close to the Montagne d'Ambre, the highest peak in the vicinity, where it rains most days and is one of the wettest places in the country. Rivers flowing from the mountain pass through the massif, irrigating its forests and going on to water one of the best rice-growing areas of Madagascar. Away from these rivers, the landscape is dry savannah dotted with palms where cattle have a hard time finding anything to eat from March until the rains transform the dusty savannah into lush grazing in October.

Habitats within Ankàrana's small area – just twenty miles by five at its widest points – range from desert-like conditions on bare limestone to rich forest in deep canyons. Rising abruptly out of the flat dry savannah, the jagged and grotesquely eroded massif looks unwelcoming. The terrain does not deter the agile lemurs, however; searching for food, they scamper over the spikes and skim down to browse in the trees. A few metres below the hostile spikes, in canyons cut into the massif, there is rich forest: as rich as any tropical woodland. Even at the denuded forest edges, wildlife abounded and there would be much more living in the largest sunken forests within the massif. Yet I had found no trace of any ecological work on the area. A little had been written on its subterranean crocodiles and on the royal cave cemeteries. The *Guide Bleu* for Madagascar has a couple of paragraphs on Ankàrana, but no one we talked to in Tana had heard of it, and even the Madagascar Airtours agent in Diégo hardly knew that Ankàrana existed. Rich and unique as Ankàrana's wildlife was, it had been neglected, even though the area was designated a Special Reserve in 1956. By 1986 its reserve status was still unknown locally and overlooked nationally. There is no warden and no control of timber felling.

We had come to Ankàrana to compile an ecological inventory, the first such catalogue for any Malagasy reserve. We needed to explore the massif, map the forest types and the caves, listing which species favoured which habitats and which of the larger species might be vulnerable to hunting and forest exploitation. Even compiling a simple list of animals involves a great deal of work, using a variety of ecological techniques and, often, inventiveness. Each of us was responsible for one or more animal groups. Phil and Jean-Elie compiled the bird list, and Phil also had to referee arguments over which species were actually present and which were misidentifications by less knowledgeable members of the expedition (like me). Such arguments became easier to resolve as we all became more familiar with the common birds at Ankàrana.

Simon Fowler had the job of organising the invertebrate surveys. Some of the butterflies were spectacularly beautiful, but he was most interested in the smaller and less appealing insects which might reveal new species evolving in various isolated parts of the massif. Most of his insects could not be identified until he got back to Britain, so he collected specimens from different locations. Then back in Cardiff, the excitement, momentum and cameraderie of the fieldwork long over, he would face the invidious task of identifying and interpreting his collections. He hoped that comparisons of the insect faunae of various forest types (and in particular between different isolated forests) might produce some interesting biogeographical information. It would also help to sort out which cave-dwelling invertebrates were really restricted to the cave environment. He also photographed the most colourful butterflies, the larger bugs and the gross but spectacular leaf-mimicking stick insects and mantises. Portraits of such eye-catching representatives of the unique fauna would surely attract interest in the conservation of Ankàrana.

The reptiles of Ankàrana were of particular interest because they included the world's only cave-dwelling crocodiles. It was Paul's job to find out how they were adapted to cave life, whether their survival was threatened, and to determine which caves had crocodiles in them. He received less enthusiastic co-operation for his project from the other expedition members, for while everyone was happy to look at birds, the reptiles and amphibians were difficult to spot and few wanted to venture near caves which were even *rumoured* to house crocodiles.

The mammal studies were more popular. Mick was responsible for the special study of the ecology of bats, their parasites and the diseases they harboured. Exploring parties recorded where bat colonies were located so that he could later visit them, collect specimens for national museums, blood samples and parasites. My particular interest was in Crowned Lemurs and I planned to spend most of my time studying them. I also had a special ambition to find further traces of the rare Broad-nosed Gentle-lemur, for there was a possibility that it still survived at Ankàrana. Having discovered their subfossilised skeletons in 1981, I was keen to return to the site where we had found the bones and thus discover when and how they had got there. Collecting information on the other mammals would be difficult. Most of the small mammals were aestivating (a summer dry-season equivalent of hibernation) and our small mammal traps were still somewhere at sea. We had also been asked to keep a special look-out for the little know White Breasted Mesite. Not all of our projects were biological. In 1981 we had also found fireplaces inside some caves and we wanted to map such sites to help an American archaeologist who planned to follow us.

Before we could start on detailed studies, we needed to get to know the massif. The day after Sheila and the men arrived at Ankàrana the entire team had set off to find the *Canyon Forestier*, following leads from a previous French expedition. Armand and Christian led at first, but were soon lost, so the explorers decided to rely on their compasses. They spent all day shambling around in the jungly bottom of what became known as the *Canyon des Anglais Perdus*. Even while floundering lost they found evidence of human settlement: pottery and some *Lepilemur* bones. After that first day the explorers split into smaller groups. Cavers Roo, Dave, Sheila and Jean Radofilao formed the backbone of the reconnaissance teams. Dave and Sheila

were the most energetic and hard-working explorers, undistracted
as they were by zoological interests. They could only get a month
off work and seemed determined to do more exploration in their
three-and-a-half weeks at Ankàrana than the rest of us in months.
It was they who first found the Second River Cave, the subterranean
waterhole where I was to do much of my lemur work. They planned
a two-day trip to explore the far reaches of the *Canyon Forestier* but,
though they covered a lot of ground, by the end of their first day they
had failed to find any water or anywhere comfortable to bivouac.
They ended up sleeping fitfully on a gravel hummock dreaming of
cool mountain streams, swimming pools and chilled beer. Dave came
back from that trip saying, 'I fancy a light day tomorrow. . . . Oh, by
the way, we saw a lemur in a hole in a tree.' He went on to describe
a soft, honey-coloured, big-eyed nocturnal lemur. It had a long dark
plumed tail and black stripe up its back which forked to cross its
eyes. This was the little Fork-marked Lemur, so named because of the
markings on the face which make it look cross-eyed. It is unusual in
being especially adapted to feed on gum exuded from certain trees. I
congratulated them on being the first to record this attractive, elusive
lemur at Ankàrana, but they did not seem overly impressed.

Dave had forgotten his exhaustion by the following day and was
blazing trails again with a seemingly endless supply of energy. Again
that evening he announced, 'Yes, I'll have a light day tomorrow. I'll
just stay near camp and do a little local *prospection*' (already we
were adopting Jean's franglais). He never did allow himself to rest,
though, and even a nasty conjunctival abrasion did not slow him
down. Characteristically, he did not complain about his eye which
must have been very painful. No wonder he had the reputation of
being one of Britain's toughest cavers. I admired Sheila even more
for keeping pace with him, and never losing her smile.

Ankàrana's striking limestone pinnacle karst is called *tsingy* locally
because of the odd resonant sound it makes when struck. It is a
hostile environment: the top of the limestone has been eroded into
spectacular razor-sharp spikes, ferocious ridges and unstable blocks.
Delicate, beautifully fluted, wafer-thin knife-edges are arranged so
that a fall would neatly bacon-slice an unwary explorer. The massif's
small size seemed to favour our exploration efforts, but we hardly
foresaw the difficulties we would have in moving about. I had few
illusions about being able to cross the *tsingy*, but I hoped to enter

the isolated forests through the caves that riddle the massif. I could
not foresee that many of these subterranean corridors were blocked
with boulders or water, and even the forested canyons were far more
impenetrable than they first seemed.

Situated beneath the forest canopy, within the *Canyon Grand*,
base camp was a good place to start our ecological work. Although
well over a mile inside the massif, it allowed good access both to
forests deeper into the massif and also the outside, because it was
at the end of an old logging trail. Tracks, some wide enough for a
bullock cart, had been cut further into most of Ankàrana's forested
canyons during the 1940s for selective logging by local villagers.
These provided routes towards the centre of the massif, but they all
stopped abruptly after a short distance. Many of them had breached
the canopy and so allowed sufficient light to penetrate the forest
floor for pretty herbaceous plants to sprout. Amongst the attractive
flowers was the amusing touch-me-not *Mimosa*. The areas that most
interested us were inaccessible from the trails, for we wished to
study the undisturbed forest. According to aerial photographs taken
in the 1940s, vast caves had collapsed in the centre of the massif
allowing pockets of isolated, lush, river-fed forests to grow in closed
depressions, and yet more rich forest grew in the canyons which split
the massif.

We began exploring in pairs on day trips, making notes on the
birds and other animals, compiling species lists and reporting back
to those running the various research projects. The most enthusiastic
biologists delighted in bringing me assorted dried faeces (sometimes
many more than I wanted!). Roo wanted to know why I was so
fascinated by 'a load of old poo'. He did not listen as I explained
that it would reveal what various mammals ate. More welcome than
the faeces were tantalising reports of even richer forests beyond some
difficult obstacle or sheer drop, or of seeing lemurs in forests I had not
visited. Though most of our time and effort at the beginning went into
exploration, at the same time we were collecting valuable ecological
information.

Most exploring groups were back long before dusk, so when
Phil, Anne and Maggie had not returned an hour after dark, my
imagination began to sift through the various accidents that might
have befallen them. They had gone to explore off-shoots from the
*Canyon Forestier*. Just as discussions had started about whether we

should look for them that night or in the morning, Phil, grinning as usual, led the two shattered doctors stumbling into camp. 'We've been exploring probably the most impressive *tsingy* in Ankàrana!' Phil announced. Later, and without enthusiasm, the doctors retold their adventures. They had found another new canyon and a beautifully decorated small cave, but had then become lost, tangled up in dense spiny forest. Phil had led them up onto the *tsingy*, over a high limestone spur and back into another forest pocket. Up and down, over *tsingy*, through forest and over *tsingy* again, so that as the sun set they were stuck up on the *tsingy*, still uncertain which way was home. Just before the light failed completely, Phil had sensed the way back to the First River Cave and the now familiar ground of *Canyon Forestier*, but this was long after the ladies had gone well beyond the point of total exhaustion. They had reached the cave in complete darkness and plunged inside to sit in the stream, blissfully guzzling and splashing water over each other. After that experience they always managed to find better things to do whenever Phil suggested exploring together again, although it did not deter Anne from joining Phil's follow-up expedition to Ankàrana in 1987.

Even on day trips water was a problem. Exertion in the tropical heat soon parched us. We were reluctant to carry more than the minimum of a litre – enough for survival but insufficient to quench our thirsts. When Guy-Suzon joined us later he advised that drinking throughout the day would make us more thirsty. He only replenished his lost fluids in the evening! None of us felt moved to follow his spartan example. Where possible, we moved around the massif through the cave systems where it was cooler and the going was much easier, but only rarely did the underground routes take us where we wanted to go. Most often we had to hack our way through the forest. This was strenuous and we would be lucky to progress more than half a mile a day in the densest forest tracts. There was the additional difficulty of route-finding, too. Aerial photographs of the Ankàrana Massif made navigation within the steep-walled canyons appear extremely easy. The photos were misleading, though. In many canyons the forest was so dense that it hid the canyon walls from view and masked nearly all landmarks. Exploring parties would end up in an unimagined side canyon, unsure how to go on. It was all too easy to walk in circles, too. Tracks would be cut laboriously along a compass bearing, but even this technique was not foolproof since the basalt forming the canyon floors was magnetic. Sometimes it made the compasses inaccurate by only a few degrees, but at other times they spun in circles. One group encountered a freshly cut trail through a particularly remote and inaccessible corner of a forested canyon. Believing their compasses, it took them a long while to realise the origin of the new track. It was the one they had just cut themselves: the explorers had moved in a complete circle!

After several days jungle-bashing, exasperation would drive us up onto the *tsingy*, to be fried in the merciless sun and lacerated on the sharp limestone. Progress up there was even slower, and we would recall the cool of the forest and descend to explore at a lower level again. The contrast between the lush forest canopy and the *tsingy* could not have been greater. At midday the bare grey limestone was uncomfortably hot to touch: there was little shade and no soil. This was a harsh xerophytic zone, an unforgivingly hostile environment. The limestone itself was spiky, eroded into needles and sharp pinnacles. Near base camp, the massif was relatively low and so it was fairly easy to climb onto the *tsingy*. Further south, the *tsingy* rose to over nine hundred feet: the first six hundred feet was almost sheer cliffs, so that access to the top of the plateau was impossible. We envied the lemurs who skipped about high up on the *tsingy* on their way to the isolated forests inside the massif.

Where progress over the *tsingy* was possible at all, it was slow, painful and dangerous. It shredded clothes, ruined boots and lacerated our hands with repeated abrasions. Yet we needed to travel over it to survey the massif properly. I was constantly concerned that people would slip and sustain some really serious injury, but I had not foreseen an additional hazard. Simon returned to camp from one sortie asking for medical attention after an 'attack by sea urchins'. There, still firmly stuck into his hand, was one of his assailants. Another harpoon bur was attached to his shirt. These ferocious seed-pods were almost impossible to remove without sustaining further cuts on the hand to disentangle them. To remove the bur unscathed, I put on leather gloves. The source of the harpoon burs were small trees which later produced incongruously pretty yellow flowers.

Mick was the first real casualty. One day he appeared with blood dripping from a bone-deep laceration on the knuckle, inflicted by the razor-sharp edge of a palm leaf. Dave, who never expected any sympathy himself and was the least sympathetic and most bloodthirsty of us all, cried, 'Ooh! Great! Stitch it up!' Mick was in pain, although trying hard not to show it, and I was reluctant to increase his discomfort with sutures. Even local anaesthetic stings before it numbs. Deciding that stitches were unnecessary, I cleaned and splinted his finger straight with a twig, so that for the next few days he wandered around camp constantly pointing at things. Dave was most disappointed.

Apart from this, we avoided injuries almost completely. Most of the medical problems at Ankàrana were small cuts and grazes which required only cleaning and dressing. There were mouth ulcers (probably a consequence of our poor diet, which was increasingly lacking in fresh vegetables as time went on) and a few sore throats. To everyone's surprise, we did not suffer from the usual skin problems that are a part of life on expeditions to rainforests: disintegrating feet, septic mosquito bites and grazes, thrush and 'crutch rot', as veterans of other tropical caving expeditions so charmingly described the most embarrassing affliction. Low humidity and lack of insects at this time of the year made Ankàrana a remarkably healthy place.

Even so, some of the team worried about their health. Anxieties grew as the expedition wore on and with them concerns that some trivial pain or symptom would fulminate into a horrendous incurable tropical pox. I was as susceptible to such neuroses as anyone: on the two occasions I had some real symptoms, a long list of life-threatening diseases occurred to me. I always tried to appear cheery and confident, though, because I felt that my most important task as Expedition Doctor was to mislead my colleagues into thinking I was an expert in tropical medicine and to reassure these intrepid expeditionaries that they were healthier than they thought!

All of us got colicky twinges from time to time, warning us that our intestines were limbering up to cause a hurried dash to the latrine. The aetiology of this phenomenon (bowels were discussed at length in camp) was attributed to those little white beans which remained indigestible even after pressure cooking. Other stomach troubles usually settled in twenty-four hours if the victims had the willpower to consume only clear fluids. Then there were those bouts of extreme weariness when I would feel as if my skeleton had turned to lead. After a few days, the heaviness and lethargy would disappear and I realised that the cause must have been some mild viral affliction.

How strange it was to realise I had been ill only once I was well again!

☆

I was content to let the reconnaissance teams do the hard work of exploration, while I pottered around the camp area getting to know my lemurs. It was at its loveliest in the early morning. I was usually the first to get up, just after the lemurs, and if there was no troop close enough to study easily, I would relight the kitchen fire and have some coffee before starting work. Sunlight streaming through the canopy was thrown into shafts as it stabbed through the smoke and lit up patches around the campsite. Some spot-lighted amorphous snoring bundles, suspended in hammocks. Nick lay submerged in a bivi bag, bent into an uncomfortable right angle by his badly erected hammock. Even half-buried beneath a *lamba oany*, Christian was immediately recognisable by his yellow and orange woollen hat. He, the other Malagasy and Simon (still without his rucksack), slept on rush mats on the ground. Lack of surface water meant we were not plagued by mosquitoes, it never rained so we could sleep out under the stars, it was never too hot and it cooled refreshingly at night.

Camp and the forest around us had all that I needed, so only later did I follow the explorers along routes they had found deeper into the forest. I even found following a struggle, though, and was glad that I did not have the reputation of a tough macho explorer to uphold. I was here to 'do science' and was happy for the men (and Sheila who at times seemed even tougher than them) to monopolise that rôle. Armand and Christian, though employed as guides, got lost even more often than we did. Consequently they were demoted to camp guards and water-fetchers. Their new status suited them well, for they much preferred lazing around in camp to participating in the strenuous (and apparently pointless) jungle exploration. We thought they might also help with the cooking. Enquiries about whether they knew how to cook rice (rice being synonymous with food to the Malagasy) received a positive, if unenthusiastic response, but neither had yet shown eagerness for work of any sort. While the rest of us were out in the forest, I suggested they cook some small dried fish that we had bought in Diégo. I returned from my day's fieldwork anticipating some special Antankarana delicacy. Instead, they indicated supper in a huge blackened cauldron and I peered inside to find most of our entire supply of dried fish lying sadly stranded in heavily salted water. The least fastidious of us managed to eat two or three before the salt, fins, scales and bones scoured our throats. The rest of the fish went onto the compost heap, much to the delight of the detritis-feeding Hisperid butterflies. The fishy aroma pervaded camp for a week.

British members did the cooking after that. Simon's speciality was uncomfortably hot curries, greeted with rapturous praise by Dave and Phil, as sweat trickled off their faces. The rest of us – less enthusiastic about the need to suffer on expeditions – asked that he use fewer chillies next time. Christian and Armand were further demoted to water-carriers and rice cooks, so there was always some cold boiled rice for people returning to camp at odd times to eat. We saved more appetising instant foods (dried bananas or corned beef) for the parties who camped out.

Christian and Armand turned out to be more adept at construction than they were at cooking. After a few days at base camp, they built a dining table. The table legs were four small trees conveniently growing at the corners of a skewed oblong. To these they lashed a frame to support a lattice of dozens of branches, about three inches in diameter. Beneath, on either side, propped on cross pieces, they attached three larger trees to act as benches. It soon became the focal point of camp life and the place to exchange the days' stories of intrepidness, bravery and exploration and for Phil to regale us about 'probably the most impressive view/butterfly/flower/lizard/sun-set . . . I have ever seen' – his enthusiasm was limitless.

Unfortunately Sweat Bees liked to hang about the dining table, especially when we were enjoying some honey. These plump flying pests were less than a quarter of an inch long. They liked to hover around our faces and climb into anything sweet just before a spoonful of it was to be stuffed into a salivating mouth. If one was crushed it effused a pheromone signal which drove its friends into such a temper that they stung anything within range. Since they were so small, they should not have been much of a problem, but sometimes they became so annoying that we would be forced to eat while circling quickly around the campsite, just ahead of a small black cloud of bees.

Towards the end of the expedition, when the entomologists ruled that there was no danger of running out of *rhum* as insect preservative, the table doubled as a bar. Simon took great trouble over the preparation of evil cocktails combining *rhum*, honey and whatever else came to hand. On one occasion I discovered him using a tube of antiseptic cream as a cocktail stirrer and teased him about how his standards were slipping. He grinned blearily as he delivered a typically dismissive retort: 'What is the point of a man going on an expedition if he is not allowed to become uncivilised!'

One morning, while we were all gathered around the camp table breakfasting on cold rice and honey, we heard some manic whoops from the *tsingy* above camp. Someone had gone on an uncharacteristically early outing. Until then we had not noticed that Phil was missing. We shouted back to tell him which direction camp was in case he was lost. Half an hour later he appeared, bubbling about the amazingly impressive view he had had of the sunrise. He did not admit to being lost, only exuberant. His enthusiasm, as ever, was infectious and he soon had us all wanting to climb up.

'Which way did you go? Have you found an easy way up?'

He led us scrambling up above the gaping void of our cave bathroom and I saw how easy it would be to slip and plummet sixty feet onto the sharp boulders inside. The rest of the team had remarkable and disarming faith in the doctors' abilities to deal with any injury. Phil was particularly reckless and I wondered if he realised how impotent we would be if he was to fall. Eventually we came to a sheer, smooth, limestone cliff face, forty feet high.

'Up there!' he pointed.

'That's the easy way?'

Phil grinned his widest grin and suggested several of us went up the following morning to pose in the gentle rosy light of dawn for photographs for our sponsors; we could not imagine a stranger and more impressive background than that moonscape for advertising shots of climbing and outdoor equipment. I smiled at the idea of climbing up, knowing that there was no way I would follow him up that face. Next morning I used a longer but much easier route. Seven of us ascended for the photography session, each finding a different route up. As I scrambled gingerly up over the loose limestone, I heard the alarming sounds of rocks crashing onto the spiky pinnacles below, dislodged by someone climbing near me. It would be all too easy to fall, too, distracted or put off balance by putting a hand on a thorn or spike. I told myself that the sweat streaming off me was precipitated by effort not fear, but then my knees started to shake and my feet vibrated as fast as a sewing machine. I wished I was a more able rock climber.

The climb was worth it, though. The *tsingy* was indeed an impressive sight at sunrise. Long shadows highlighted beautiful scallops and fluted patterns in the limestone. Only from up there was it possible to begin to understand the geography of Ankàrana: pockets of lush forest sheltered by the limestone, but also hemmed in by it. The forest canopy around our camp was about sixty feet above ground level, almost as high as the surrounding *tsingy*, which provided a platform just feet from the rich and busy canopy where I could look for lemurs or watch Asitys sunbirds (representatives of an endemic bird family) flitting amongst the thorny *tsingy* vegetation. The males were a dazzling iridescent navy, while the females were dull brown. Both were tuneful and aerobatic, very much like hummingbirds in size, shape and the way they stole nectar. We searched for an area of flat ground, large enough to lay out the camera gear and equipment. The best we could find was a sharp ridge three inches wide and four feet long, which at least was not too uncomfortable to sit on. We stood around or squatted on our haunches, for there was nowhere else to sit amongst the pinnacle karst. Even moving a few yards over it took a long time, for we had to scramble over one ridge, descend perhaps twenty feet into a gully only to climb to the top of the next ridge. Photographic subjects modelled boots and protective clothing. Simon sent them to some particularly scenic outcrop and each would disappear temporarily, before emerging from some crevice a few yards further on. It was a strange landscape and not a place to be stranded at nightfall.

We also wanted photos of someone camping out in a gortex bivi bag, but it took a long time to find an expanse of flat rock big enough for even one person to lie down. Nick appeared with his T-shirt stuffed to bursting with a bulky bivi bag like a caricature of Billy Bunter: he would never use a day-sack or carry his share. Even Sheila was annoyed with him now, for she knew he would soon expect to drink the water she was carrying. This was the only time I ever saw Sheila display any kind of irritation or bad humour. She was always smiling even after the most rigorous outings; she was hard-working and the only member of the team always ready to cook, even at the end of a hard day's exploration.

# 7. Royal Clinic and Turning Bodies

To see a World in a Grain of Sand
And a Heaven in a Wild Flower
Hold Infinity in the Palm of your hand
And Eternity in an hour
                    William Blake, 1803

Maggie, Anne, Paul and, later, Sally shared the work of the
lemur studies with me, but before we could begin recording their
behaviour and collecting data for a census we had to make sure we
were all seeing the same things. At first we saw very little: a glimpse
of a fleeing furry tail, a movement of leaves or the sound of small
branches crashing as a troop leapt through the canopy just out of
sight. Our forest was teeming with wildlife, but it was a while before
we saw much of it. We were spotted long before we noticed the
animals which froze, silent and scared, watching unseen or fleeing
long before we got close: we visitors moved in corridors of silence.
Then, as we practised moving quietly, talking only in whispers and
stopping frequently to look and listen, we began to see more. Often
we would sit down in a quiet, seemingly deserted, patch of forest;
at first we heard nothing but insect calls and the wind stirring the
canopy, but then, after a few minutes, the forest would miraculously
come alive as birds resumed their songs and lemurs started feeding
again, their movements betraying them.

As the lemurs became more used to us, we were able to get
closer. Sometimes we only knew they were near when, disturbed by
our presence, they would emit a low, barely audible, anxiety-grunt
which was hard to distinguish from the rumblings of my companions'
stomachs. (Those little white beans did increasingly strange things
to our intestines as the expedition wore on.) We got to know the
area and devised routes to avoid walking over crunchy leaf-litter or

through noisy bamboo thickets. Slowly we became less clumsy and grew to recognise particular trees and rocks favoured by the lemurs or regularly visited by certain troops. Then we began to see more. The best time to spot lemurs was while they were noisily feeding or travelling in the early morning and late afternoon, but gradually we began to see them even when they were curled up asleep in the middle of the day. With time, the forest animals became used to us, too. They were shy but had not really learned to fear people, because they were protected by a local *fady* (taboo) against hunting: the Antankarana people have a traditional respect for the forest and many of its inhabitants. The lemurs soon lost most of their timidity, and unless we tried to use hides, stalk them or otherwise act like predators, they would be more inclined to come and peer at us than to flee.

We learned what we were seeing by comparing notes and through discussion. Was canopy level really sixty feet above the ground or was it lower in some places? Was that lemur a one-year-old juvenile or a two-year-old sub-adult? Was it grooming, scent-marking or did it just have an itchy bottom? What did those grunts mean? What were their responses to danger and what did they see as threatening? Anne and Maggie had only a basic scientific training and somehow they had to turn into primatologists. They were sharp-eyed and quick learners, and soon Anne was spotting more than me. After a week, the lemur study team were agreeing about most of what we saw. Then one afternoon Anne came into camp enthusing about seeing a really strange lemur. Unlike other lemurs, it scampered on the ground or low in the forest and it was red with a black stripy tail. But it was not a lemur she described, it was one of the island's few carnivores. I teased her about this misidentification, then had to admit that I had made the same sort of mistakes with my first bird observations. We were all learning.

The lemurs' shyness, combined with our inexperience and the difficulties of seeing animals in the dense foliage, meant we were slow to recognise the differences between sexes and species. There seemed to be six kinds of lemur. Most often we saw attractive grey animals with thick fur marked subtly with white underparts and brown on the head. They weighed about four pounds: small and agile. These were adult female Crowned Lemurs. Hot on the females' heels came the males: rich chestnut brown with a black academic skull cap or 'crown'. The sexes were so dissimilar that it was not until we saw them grooming each other that we were entirely convinced that they were the same species. Then we saw troops which seemed to comprise other varieties: larger, short-furred, brown or almost black lemurs, and it was not until we saw them with their mates – the males had striking bushy side-whiskers – that we were sure these were Sanford's Lemurs. These two day-active species seemed to have conspired to confuse us when they mingled together in the same tree. Initially we even wondered if it was possible to have troops of mixed species. After a few days, though, we realised that the lemurs simply liked the same liana and ebony fruits: they just happened to be tolerantly feeding in the same tree. In addition to those four very different looking lemurs, there were uniformly grey animals about half the size of the Crowned Lemurs, but long-limbed and gawky. These were one-year-old females which sometimes wandered away from the main troop. Yearling males were less adventurous and easier to recognise for they were marked exactly like the adult males. We learned to distinguish lemurs by colour and body shape and we grew to recognise their characteristic styles of movement and their subtly different calls and grunts. The Crowned Lemurs emitted satisfied, happy little grunts, while the larger Sanford's Lemurs grunted more deeply and sounded more like pigs snoring.

I made almost as many lemur observations while I was around camp, as elsewhere in the forest. Not long after we arrived at Ankàrana, a troop of Crowned Lemurs re-established their habitual resting place directly above camp. This suited me well, since I could study them from my hammock. At first the others too were pleased to have lemurs as close neighbours, but when our cooking fire or noise disturbed them, the lemurs communicated their displeasure. When camp was at its most active, and often as we were about to eat supper, they would assemble along a branch above us and a fine warm drizzle would descend while they peered down to see what effect their urine was having on us.

Lemurs spent most of their time feasting or resting in the canopy layer high above our heads. There was not much to eat down low and leaf-litter there made movements noisy; perhaps they were wary of scorpions, too. Recording what each lemur was doing every fifteen minutes was straightforward enough, if boring when the lemurs slept, but the troop structure was difficult to fathom. We found what seemed to be huge troops scattered over a large area, yet still communicating with each other. Then at other times we would see isolated individuals, contentedly browsing or resting without any other lemurs nearby. Crowned Lemurs were supposed to live in troops, so why were these solo lemurs not distressed to be separated from their friends and relations?

On 12 September, Anne found a troop of Crowned Lemurs, cuddled up in such a tight ball that she could not be sure how many lemurs were there. She needed to wait until they woke up before she could count them. A female Sanford's Lemur had chosen a branch nearby for her siesta and Anne watched to see whether the two species might squabble – as books say competitors should. Maggie and I were close by watching another troop. Anne called us over: through the binoculars she had noticed something writhing amongst the Crowned Lemur huddle. Was it a huge leech? Ankàrana's forests were too dry for leeches. The three of us settled in a comfortable pile of leaf-litter to watch and see what it was. After a long time the Crowned Lemurs moved and we realised that the 'leech' was a little bald tail. Anne had spotted our first infant Crowned Lemur. Not much more than a day old, it clung tenaciously around its mother's middle.

Anne and I conferred excitedly in whispers, then turned to Maggie to share the news of that first birth. She was fast asleep. Our giggles awakened both Maggie and the Sanford's female. The lemur roused herself to browse on little liana fruits. Her foraging took her close to the Crowned Lemur huddle which suddenly untangled, and a male shot out, screaming aggressively at the Sanford's Lemur. He chased her away convincingly, despite being so much smaller than her. Until the baby Crowned Lemurs appeared, the two lemur species had tolerated each other's presence, but the responsibilities of parenthood made troops nervous and we saw many more 'arguments'. These were shouting-matches rather than fights and usually Crowned Lemurs came off best.

We left Anne to continue observing that group while Maggie and I went in search of others. I asked Maggie to show me the path that Dave and Sheila had recently cut to the *Canyon Forestier*. She had been this way on the strenuous exploring trip with Phil. She led me into deep forest, away from the main track running the length of the *Canyon Grand*. In we walked, looking for where Dave and Sheila had marked the trail by cutting notches on tree trunks and bending saplings over until they broke. The rich diverse forest seemed to be full of lemurs. Moving slowly, we scanned the tree-tops and spent perhaps ten minutes with each lemur we encountered, until we were sure we had counted all its troop mates. One troop had found a *Strychnos* liana heavy with little green fruits. The lemurs, acting as if they had been starved for a week, frantically gobbled the fruits or stuffed them into their cheeks. Then, suddenly, as if several misaligned circular saws had been started up, we were assaulted by a grating noise like metal rubbing on metal. Cicadas were trying to outdo each other.

After ten minutes the path forked: another party had chosen a different route. Uncertain which way we should turn and distracted again by another troop feeding above us, we took a rest. I was new to jungle exploration and did not want to go further without a compass; we decided to return. I waited for a just-hatched lizard – less than an inch long – to climb off my boot and, as I stood up, I alarmed what I had taken for lichen, so that it scattered from the branch it was growing on. The 'lichen' had legs and was actually a huddle of *Fulgoroidea* nymphs: immature colonial Flatid bugs which had no confidence that their extravagant camouflage would prevent me from eating them. They are sap-suckers, like giant aphids, and Day Geckos, ants and lemurs feed on their honey-like secretions, but carefully avoid eating the nymphs. Their waxy white 'lichen' coats were probably distasteful as well as camouflaging.

Meanwhile Maggie had set off, determinedly heading deeper into the forest. 'Isn't camp back the other way?' I asked.

Maggie was sure she was going the right way and I was equally convinced that home was 180 degrees in the other direction. I felt uneasy with no compass and no machete. We tried my way, but soon lost the trail of marked trees. At first I thought it would not matter for I expected that we would break out onto the main track where Anne was working; it could not be far. But the vegetation grew thicker and, more alarmingly, the ground became steep and we began climbing. Surely we must be going in the wrong direction: on the way in the ground had been almost flat. When we retraced our steps, the terrain was no more familiar. Then we could not find the way back to where we had watched the greedy troop. There were still no marks on the trees. Was I right or was Maggie? We tried again along the first route. As we scrambled around, confidence in my sense of direction diminished rapidly and I felt more and more foolish. Back and forward once more, then I wondered if Anne would hear us if we shouted? She did. We plunged through thick vegetation towards her shouts and emerged on the main track. We had been less than fifty yards from her. She laughed at the tousled mess we were in.

The small pointed rufus face of a Vontsira poked out of the undergrowth on the far side of the track as if to see what all the noise was about. Anne pointed and said, 'Oh, that's the funny ground-lemur I saw before!' It was a Madagascar Ring-tailed Mongoose. They were shy at first, but it was not long before greed overcame any fear they had of us and they became regular visitors to camp. They loved the compost pit. They were hyperactive animals like true mongooses, but with the short retractile claws of cats, webbed feet and a pair of udders between their back legs, they cannot be classified as cat, ferret or mongoose; they belong to an endemic subfamily. Their scientific name *Galidia elegans* is well chosen, for they are indeed elegant creatures with beautiful russet fur and foxy brushes decorated with black rings. Their habits were not so charming, though. Not only did composting vegetables and coconut shells attract them; they also spent a lot of time squabbling over the maggots in our latrine!

As the 'mongooses' got used to us, they became increasingly cheeky. Often we found them with their little webbed feet perched on the edge of a saucepan, craning in to see what goodies they could steal; they even ran off with entire eight-ounce blocks of chocolate. Two *Galidia* families vied over whose territory contained our kitchen and compost heap. High-pitched whistling announced when competitors met over a coconut shell and there were frequent tumbles of rufus fur and ring-tails. The battles never resolved the question of territories, though; there were ample pickings for both families. Books say that *Galidia elegans* only give birth to their young singly, but one visiting family had two identically marked half-sized young and the other had four. Clearly the species was more fecund than the experts realised.

They were delightful to watch, but we felt slightly queasy about them feasting in the latrine and then searching for dessert in our kitchen. We also became increasingly nervous of perching precariously over the deep latrine pit as it filled up. There was not much to hang on to, so Armand constructed a rather insubstantial frame. Particularly when ominous noises came from beneath, users of the facility imagined sliding sedately into the hole. But the noises were not structural, they originated from the 'mongooses' which would pop up from the pit, maggot in mouth, cheeky and smily-faced, as if acknowledging the new contribution to the latrine.

☆

Two-legged visitors to camp were rare. We were too far into the forest and there was seldom a reason for people to walk such a long way, although a few came to sell us things. One day a dozen dogs trotted confidently into camp. Dogs always heralded the arrival of villagers, but this time they were not followed by the usual salesmen from Matsaborimanga. It was Abdulla, the *aide sanitaire!* I was surprised to see him again and wondered why he had walked all the way from Ambatoharanana. He had brought the King. At the end of our audience with him in Ambilobé, when he had promised he would visit, we had thought he was only being polite. His huge entourage included Simagaul and other leading figures from Matsaborimanga. Suddenly our campsite was overrun: forty-nine adults plus innumerable children. They were hot and parched by the long walk across the savannah in the midday sun. We brought water and the hordes emptied a gallon jerry can. I wondered if they expected to be fed as they squatted down amongst the trees.

Prince Tsimiharo III was a tall well-fed man in his mid-thirties. He was confident and easy to talk to and he led the conversation, starting with the usual introductory platitudes, then smoothly going on to the point of his visit. I had offered his people medical help, and he asked what diseases we could cure. A little on the defensive, I asked what they had got. Unhesitatingly he listed malaria, tuberculosis, gonorrhoea, arthritis, skin problems, worms, headaches, stomach troubles . . . I should have guessed he would say VD, since in Diégo one tenth of consultations are for gonorrhoea. I told him that this at least was easy to cure. The King turned to his entourage and said something like, 'Hands up all those who have got gonorrhoea!'

Every man raised his hand. Eagerly, and grinning broadly, they formed a long queue to collect two little packets of antibiotics: one for him and one for her. This baffled the men. Why should the women get treatment? This, they announced, was not a disease which afflicted women! We explained that by treating the women too, they would avoid catching the disease back again. They went away looking extremely pleased with themselves and still impressed with this revolutionary idea. Nevertheless, Simagaul and some of the others were back again three weeks later for another course of treatment.

Women and children then queued up with a great selection of symptoms and more complicated complaints. Jean Radofilao interpreted for us. Mothers said that their pot-bellied children had no appetite, they had stomach-aches and they passed worms. Some had nasty eye and ear infections. The women themselves were troubled by abdominal pain from their VD, as well as stomach troubles, infected cuts and backache. We treated as much as we could and then we had more time to talk.

The King spoke so convincingly of his respect for the forest that I felt that Ankàrana's wildlife would be safe while he was alive. He was preparing for a great ceremony to honour his Ancestors interred in caves in the south of the massif. All Malagasy people are preoccupied with the influences of the Ancestors. The *Hauts Plateaux* tribes go in for lavish parties when Ancestors are exhumed and brought out amongst the living. Here at Ankàrana the dead would be left undisturbed in their cave tombs, but there was still to be an extravagant week-long party to entertain the Dead and bring the Ancestors closer to the living. Prince Tsimiharo III invited us to walk down for the initial ceremonies. These would not be the real celebration to honour his royal Ancestors, but a preparatory feast to inform them of the rich party that was planned for the following year. I was sorely tempted to desert my zoological research to witness this ceremony to honour the Ancestors, but making the trip would take too many days away from our tight schedule of fieldwork. While in Tana, though, I had been privileged to attend a Mérina exhumation party, a *famadihana*, and had to content myself with the thought that most foreigners do not get the opportunity to witness even one of these unique cultural practices.

The *famadihana* had been arranged after a spell of bad luck and the appearance of a dead family member in a dream had been interpreted as a complaint of neglect from the Ancestors. There were long consultations with the *mpanandro* about the most auspicious day to hold it, since if it is performed in the right way, an Ancestor placated by exhumation will look after the living for years. When we arrived at the large old three-storey house on the outskirts of the city, the party had been going for many hours. Someone was making a long speech. As ever it was three-quarters apologies and the rest self-deprecation. Style is always more important than content. Everyone was engrossed: the Malagasy love speeches. Our host offered drinks and told us to stay in the courtyard, for the bones would soon be turned. There was increased activity around the tomb.

Believing that so much more time is spent in the tomb than in any earthly dwelling, the Malagasy make these substantial structures. Often long abandoned villages can be located thanks to the tombs which remain years after the flimsy huts for the living having disintegrated. This tomb was a low, grey and white, undecorated structure made from granite and cement, fifteen feet square and five feet high. The massive stone door had already been rolled away by specialists who knew how to placate the tomb's thirst for death. Typically, Mérina tombs have an underground chamber usually about twenty feet square and this was no exception, so the six relatives of the deceased did not need to stoop as they descended the steps and went inside. They reappeared carrying the dusty dry bones of our hostess's great uncle on their shoulders. The bones were now held together by a polythene bag, for the old *lamba mena* burial shawl had disintegrated long ago. They brought him into the midst of the guests, putting him on a bamboo table sheltered with a leaf-thatch awning, and wrapped him in a vastly expensive, beautifully embroidered new white *lamba mena*. Above the body hung a photograph of the man in his youth: waxed moustache, straw boater and European clothes, high fashion of the 1920s. The bones of his wife joined him and also those of our hostess's father.

A Catholic girls' school choir started to sing hymns in beautiful harmony, their faces glowing with pleasure. Then a Christian priest said some prayers and delivered a short sermon before the Protestant girls' choir took over the singing. This incongruous mixing of religions is not peculiar to Madagascar. In Indonesia, mosque officials conduct ancestral rituals as well as Islamic rites, and in Sulawesi an anthropologist concluded that Ancestor worship was the religion of the women while the men followed Islam!

There were around two hundred guests. Men wore their Sunday best suits and the ladies, with their long straight hair plaited into the traditional oval bun, wore chic Western clothes with fine embroidered white *lambas* draped around their shoulders. These neat Mérina white *lambas* should not be confused with the *lamba mena* burial sheet, or even the everyday *lamba oany* (like a sarong);

they are worn like a Western stole. Priest and choristers dispersed and our host showed us around his house. An entire room was filled with zebu carcasses for the feast. *Rhum* started to flow and bands set up electric guitars, drums and microphones on the temporary stage. Their version of 'Ot Stuff' and an Eagles rock album seemed sure to make the Ancestors turn in their tombs and it soon got everyone disco-dancing. The *famadihana* is not an occasion to mourn but to be loud and happy: to cheer up the Dead and remind them of the good times they enjoyed when they were alive. Later I was invited to a Mérina wedding which was a quiet and modest affair. The church service was followed by a subdued gathering where we were offered dainty savoury nibbles and 'punch' – a potent concoction based on local rum. The bride and groom left after just an hour. What a contrast to the lavish, days-long *famadihana*, deemed auspicious every five years. Frequent exhumations, along with the building and maintenance of the tomb, are an enormous drain on the resources of even a rich Malagasy family.

Traditionally, people believe that their Ancestors thrive in the spirit world so long as they are remembered by the living. Beliefs and ceremonies concerning the Ancestors vary throughout Madagascar, but the respect for the Ancestors and a belief that they influence the destiny of the living is common throughout the island and also in South-East Asia. The people who first populated Madagascar came from what is now Indonesia and in traditional Indonesian communities burials and exhumations strangely echo the Malagasy ceremonies. Every August during the *Ma'néné* ceremony in the Toraja valley of Baruppu in Sulawesi, deceased relatives are brought out of their tombs and rewrapped in red or white shrouds amidst feasting and chanting. In Madagascar the *lamba mena* is also usually red, but can be multicoloured or even white – white being the mourning colour in much of Asia. In Kalimantan, burials have a great party atmosphere with raucous gambling parties and much feasting; as in Madagascar, many cattle are slaughtered. The tombs there are strikingly similar to those of the Mahafaly tribe of southern Madagascar and both are decorated with superbly carved wooden posts, called *alo-alo* in Madagascar. The wooden posts feature people, animals and sometimes a *taxi-brousse*, or perhaps even an aeroplane if the deceased had travelled in one. They are topped by carvings of zebu horns.

Several more bodies were surreptitiously being taken out of the tomb, quickly paraded seven times around it and returned to their resting places. A few people close by covered their mouths with handkerchiefs for fear of catching something. The guests were cautious of the power of the bodies since sickness is believed to be passed on by displeased Ancestors. Near me was my Mérina Quaker friend, Suzanne, elegantly dressed in a fashionable European suit, but wearing a *lamba* and with her hair in a plaited bun. I asked her what was going on. She explained that the Government taxed *famadihana* according to the number of bodies that were being turned. Our hosts had declared only three and were working a tax fiddle on the others! When we left late that evening, the party showed no signs of ending. Suzanne said that the celebrations would go on for a couple of days. 'But isn't it primitive?' she said.

It was long after dark by the time we walked home from the *famadihana*, through Tana's deserted streets. Nightjars swooped and dived as they hunted insects attracted by street lamps. As silent and eerie as spirits, they disappeared and reappeared as they flew in and out of pools of light. Perhaps they were Great Uncle Pierre and his exhumed relatives, revitalised by the *famadihana*!

☆

That first Royal Clinic at Ankàrana impressed the locals. Subsequently our services became so much in demand that we had to settle on only one clinic a week, otherwise we would not have got any other work done. People always came with some significant problem and never merely with an excuse to gawp at the doctor or to sell us eggs, tomatoes and jackfruit. Each jackfruit lasted a very long time – they reminded me of dissected brains, but did not taste as nice.

The people of Matsaborimanga had another chance to ask for medicines when we were working on our medical project. This also allowed Roo a further opportunity to tease me about my obsession with poo. The prospect of examining fresh stool samples, even in the cause of parasite eradication and improved health, was far from attractive. After breakfast one morning, five of us walked to Matsaborimanga. The first hour was along the familiar logging track through the *Canyon Grand*, then we were out onto the rolling dry savannah. We wandered between sparse bushes, our feet throwing up little clouds of dust. I paused to look back at the forest: such a rich habitat so close to such unproductive land. At one point I saw smoke rising from inside and I asked Armand whether it was an accidental fire. He smiled at my naïve question and explained that it was people taking out a tree. The best trees are too big to cut down so people burn through the base with a small fire. It is a lot of work to remove one tree, so they take only what they need.

The villagers were delighted to see us back again: we were the best entertainment they'd had in months. Everyone came to the 'worm clinics'. Parents, older siblings and our pot-bellied wormy subjects surged into the school room and perched on cases of Three Horses beer (what was beer doing in the school?). Some children clutched half-eaten unripe mangoes. I was surprised that our clinics were so well attended, for I had been warned that the Malagasy were suspicious of outsiders. But we had a royal patron and this, as well as Armand's presence, had encouraged people to come. I had read that the Malagasy have an array of herbal medicines and there are at least eight anthelminthics made from native plants (including ebony leaves). It seemed, then, that they thought Western cures might work better.

Armand and Jean-Elie translated explanations and instructions to parents and guardians, while we doled out anthelminthics and sweets. Armand enjoyed playing medical secretary, but Jean-Elie clearly felt the whole process of discussing paediatric excrement was beneath him. He was a Mérina and these were backward unsophisticated people. He was no less unimpressed when I explained how useful it would be to know how much disease parasitic worms caused, and how they affected the children.

After we had finished, Armand explained that some people wished *une visite*. Anne deciphered this as a request for a consultation. The first woman had a scarf tied around her head and under her chin: toothache. Anne was delighted, for she wanted to see me use my dental pliers. I was not so keen. To extract a tooth, some of the socket has to be broken, and the bone-crunching sensation is amongst the most unpleasant experiences of medical practice. I had once been forced to pull the tooth of a woman in a remote part of Ladakh. She had been suffering for weeks and begged me to help even though the only anaesthetic available was barley beer. The rotten molar came out intact but left both patient and doctor in a cold sweat. Next day, to my horror, there was a queue of new dental patients. When I suggested that the Matsaborimanga lady took some aspirins and went to see a proper dentist in Ambilobé, Anne was most disappointed, but Madame Toothache looked relieved. We sorted out miscellaneous medical complaints in the villagers, who all went away happy and seemed willing to help with our strange requests for poo samples.

No one came to the follow-up clinics.

The following week we found a further nineteen children to deworm and we arranged to see them again after the anthelminthics had done their work. We arrived at the school and set up laboratory in the dusty playground under a tree. Some mothers had already dangled small plastic bags of excrement from a tree, like Christmas decorations, and then retired to the shade from whence they giggled at us with their hands over their mouths. None had brought the complete 24-hour sample that we needed. We explained again, but never did collect any useful results – although we did cure a lot of wormy tummies.

In the lads' eyes our outings to Matsaborimanga were a great success – we brought back beer and even this warm watery brew lifted everyone's spirits! After a few bottles (*grande modèle*, of course), camp would become noisier and that warm drizzle of urine would begin to descend, but by that time people no longer cursed the lemurs, but laughed at their temerity.

☆

Outside Madagascar, calls of related birds sound surprisingly similar: Indian robins and tits sound remarkably like English ones. At Ankàrana, though, all the sounds were unfamiliar and frequently I found it difficult to distinguish noises of insects from those of reptiles, birds and mammals; even this crude level of identification was often beyond me. At first I labelled each according to the sounds they emitted: the billiard-ball bird, the cowboys-and-indians bird, the marble-bouncing-on-concrete bird, the scratchy-sounding-*wee-eee* bird, the wolf-whistler, the metallic-buzz bird (which turned out to be an insect!), the plopping-water bird, and so on. There was another which sounded like a squeaking gate, the squeaks always repeated five times. The bird which annoyed me most sang a convincing impression of the theme of the *Blankety Blank* television programme. I loathed the theme tune because of its associations. It reminded me of a seedy hospital flat and the semi-stupor of being too tired to sleep

after a long Easter weekend on call: three days and nights working
without sleep.

Malagasy birds are relatively poor in numbers of species – only
about two hundred breed on the island – but are remarkable in their
uniqueness and specialisation. Four bird families and forty-six genera
are endemic. With Jean-Elie's help and his (now out-of-print) book,
we named all we saw and most of what we heard. We identified
seven of the fourteen members of the endemic *Vangidae* family. Each
*Vanga* species has a bill of different size and shape, designed for
different feeding strategies. One turned out to be the wolf-whistling
bird, and another consistently had Anne and I in fits of laughter. It
was a striking black and white bird, the size of a raven, with a long
curved slender beak which gave it its common name, the Sicklebilled
Vanga. They flew around in disorganised rowdy flocks, often egged
on by an attendant Drongo. When at their most excited they broke
into paroxysms of *Caw-caw-caws*, followed by a disgusting noise like
someone vomiting. If we imitated their call, they became all the more
excited and every member of the flock of twenty or so Sicklebills
would all start to *Caw-caw-caw* . . . puke! So, until we had matched
them to their more respectful and scientific title, we called them
Pukebirds. One morning a rabble of Sicklebills landed in a tree close
to a troop of resting lemurs and an amazing shouting match broke
out. The lemurs became terribly agitated and all started grunting
frantically and penduluming their tails. The Sicklebills stayed put, so
the lemurs let out a shrill volley of ear-piercing shrieks which upset
the Sicklebills enough to make them fly away.

Boffins at the International Union for the Conservation of Nature
in Cambridge had asked us to search for Mesites; we agreed to look,
but hardly expected to find any. The White-breasted Mesite has
only ever been found in three small forest pockets in Madagascar,
including one record in 1931 from the 'Ankarana cliffs'. Only a
couple of days after arriving at base camp, while looking for small
mammal resting holes, I was tentatively climbing on the low *tsingy*
close to camp. Perched up on a knife-edge of limestone, I was unable
to turn and wondered whether the others ever got themselves stuck
cat-up-a-tree-like. Then a characteristic *whoo-oop* came from Phil.
'White-breasted Mesite!' he shouted. Spasms of indecision grabbed
me as, finely balanced, I realised that one boot was firmly wedged
between two limestone spikes. By pulling my foot out of my boot,

I managed to turn, but then could only get my boot free after a perilous struggle balanced on the toe of the other boot. Amazingly, the White-breasted Mesites were still there by the time I got down.

They were brown, clumsy, thrush-like birds, about eight inches long: strange birds whose closest relatives outside Madagascar are uncertain but may be the rails. 'Incredible!' announced Phil. 'These are probably the rarest birds I have ever seen.'

After that first sighting we often saw them near camp. They were surprisingly abundant in undisturbed forest. But, for all their rarity, they were dull, uninspiring birds, distinguished only by a royal blue eye-stripe, and did little but wander around in pairs, rhythmically flicking their beaks, side to side, and turning over the leaf-litter. They had the typically low intellect of Malagasy endemics and their only remarkable feature was impressively strong pair-bonding. Couples became agitated if separated and, making a distressed hissing call, would take crazy risks to get close to their mate again. Once reunited they circled each other in a mate recognition ceremony, before setting off a-litter-flicking again. They were most reluctant to fly and, if cornered or threatened, would only flap chicken-like away. Alternatively, they would simply freeze, a response perhaps evolved to avoid the eagle-eyes of aerial predators. Neither seemed particularly healthy responses to danger and might explain why they have become so rare.

White-breasted Mesites had not been photographed before, so we wanted portraits for posterity and to prove our rediscovery; a close-up of the bird in the hand would be ideal. One morning Phil and Paul left camp with two mist nets, each ten feet by forty long, and set them out in a V shape, intending to herd the birds in. The Mesites, which we had credited with intellects of chickens, were not so stupid as to enter the trap and, after a whole day chasing the birds, our budding ornithologists came back Mesiteless, cursing and harrassed. We would have to photograph them in the forest. Phil, Paul and I all tried independently to capture them on film, but just before we got close enough, they always moved into thick shadowy scrub where they became unphotographable. No wonder this species was never-before-photographed. One morning, while lemur-watching, I heard the familiar rhythmic litter-flicking noise and went in pursuit with my camera, telephoto lens and flash-gun. Half an hour later I was lying flat on my face, scratched, stung and exasperated, with my hair full of twigs and my shirt full of leaves, having not quite got close enough for a photograph. I laughed at the state I was in and looked up to meet the intent and perplexed gaze of a Crowned Lemur, sitting in a low branch not six feet away from me. His chin was propped on the backs on his hands. He must have been watching me for some time, but scampered away as soon as we made eye contact.

Although Paul's main responsibility was the crocodile study, he worked on many projects. He was an excellent all-round naturalist, observant and full of interesting ideas, and it amused me to realise that this 'youngster' was teaching the more experienced team members as much (if not more) than we were teaching him. This was not at all as the Royal Geographical Society had imagined. Paul thought that the Mesites were worthy of a special study and resolved to watch them continuously for several days. After the first day, though, he returned to camp complaining: 'Mesites are so boring! The most exciting thing they ever do is make thrushy trilling noises.' Phil, who had been watching them intermittently in a different part of the forest, agreed. 'Yes, probably the most boring animal I have ever tried to study!'

Eventually I got a photo of a Mesite head poking out from behind some leaves and later Phil photographed the whole bird – the IUCN ornithologists in Cambridge would be impressed. By following various pairs, Paul and Phil also learned about the territory each bird needed. The area available to them at Ankàrana is dangerously small – less than a couple of square miles – and further felling would probably wipe them out. Their two other precarious refuges (forest near Morondava and in the Ankarafantsika Reserve) are similarly threatened and are perhaps in even worse condition. Later we were to search in vain for signs of them in the dry forest near Morondava.

The Mesites can only live under unbroken canopy and so would be especially sensitive to exploitation of the forest. Wherever tree extraction has been too extensive and the canopy broken, there have been great changes in the forest. Unappetising bamboo begins to sprout opportunistically, swamping more nutritious plants and excluding Mesites and many other smaller animals. The tracks cut into all the most extensive areas of forest by commercial loggers in the 1940s still allow vehicle and bullock-cart access to some areas, which means that villagers and small-scale commercial timber cutters can continue to take trees one by one. This slow exploitation seemed to be tolerated by the Mesites, because although few large and no valuable trees remained in these accessible canyons, the all-important canopy was intact in most places. The deep litter underneath is a foraging ground not only for Mesites but also for a wealth of other species and the richest vertebrate fauna known anywhere on Madagascar. At least eighty-three birds (that is more than a third of Malagasy species) live at Ankàrana and eighty per cent of these are endemics. Some are rainforest species, so they should not have been present at all! Ankàrana is rich in reptiles, too – thirty-seven in all – and includes at least six species endemic only to Ankàrana. There are also at least fifty-five butterfly species: thirty-four of these are endemic to Madagascar and many of the less spectacular invertebrates were new to science. The diversity of habitats within Ankàrana's small area allows a remarkable range of animals to live alongside one another, indeed this is the richest vertebrate community known anywhere in Madagascar. But its small size and discrete populations make it very vulnerable to environmental change, and exploitation of even a little more forest could upset the delicate ecological balance and spell disaster for innumerable species.

# 8. Caves, Chamaeleons and Leaping Lemurs

I could tell you . . . about those sacred apes of Madagascar. Living
in groves and never worried by man. . . . That monkey gallops along
quickly, six or seven feet at a bound. . . . Short arms, and never uses
'em for locomotion. The man-monkey, so-called. Half the size of a man,
but he has side-burns and a white face. . . . What about that monkey
at Btsimsarak? An egg-scooper! Provided by providence with a forefinger
twice as long as the other digits. Could scoop an ostrich egg if necessary.
No doubt a relic of the old days when the moa was part of the scenery. A
world-beater for egg measurement, that bird. But no wings. His size being
his natural weapon of defence . . .

Alfred Aloysius Horn, 1928

As dusk gathered, the familiar Crowned Lemurs melted away and
the mood of the forest changed as new animals emerged and made
eerie sounds. The first noise-mongers to start up at dusk were the
Madagascar Coucals. Chicken-sized birds, they look similar to the
litter-skulking birds of Asia, but are, predictably, a species endemic
to Madagascar. Their evening song (if you can call it that) is a
descending scale of nine *boo-boo-boo-boos*, or at least it was usually
nine. Sometimes they would annoyingly stop in mid-scale and the
suspense of waiting for them to finish the sequence would be broken
by them starting at the top again. One would call, a second would
reply from another part of the forest and others would pick up the
chorus and try to outdo everyone else. Then, as if awakened by the
Coucals, the other forest animals would join in a cacophony of
shrieks, squawks, whoops, caws, chirrups, buzzes and humms.
Even two hundred yards from the lights and clatter of camp, forest
sounds betrayed innumerable busy creatures. For their size, scorpions made the most noise, as they stomped through the leaf-litter,
pugnacious and looking for someone to eat. Small bats whispered by.

The underbrush was aquiver with a host of small animals. Quietest was an attractive grey rodent, *Eliurus myoxinus*, which looked like a slim chinchilla; ignoring the spot-light, it confidently scaled branches and trunks. Other eyes shone back at me beyond the chinchilla-rodent and I was startled to discover that I was being watched. Pairs of eyes reflected back, every twenty yards, themselves like little torches. Lemurs possess a highly reflective layer behind the retina which helps them see at night, and it is this which shines back so brightly. The eyes watched for a while, unblinking, then disappeared with a slight shiver of leaves. There was a thud as the Lepilemur landed on another tree trunk from where it would turn again to regard me with yellow torch-eyes. I empathised with superstitious Malagasy who believe that the Ancestors constantly watch – spirits in the form of lemurs, bats, butterflies, even crocodiles and snakes. The Lepilemur's call was unnerving, coarse and grating, like a Tawny Owl. Individuals shouted loudly at each other from the edges of their territories, angered if others of their species came too close.

In daylight the owners of those disembodied eyes and the originators of those grating aggressive squawks revealed themselves as innocent little lemurs weighing a pound and a quarter. These Lepilemurs subsist on leaves which have such low food value that they need to eat a great volume and they are, as a consequence, rather pot-bellied: a Fozzie Bear of a lemur. Lepilemurs are also called Sportive Lemurs yet they are amongst the least energetic of lemurs; their calorie-poor diet makes them incapable of sustained effort and even when they are at their most active at night, they sit around or gently browse, and seldom move far. Nevertheless, they are stylish jumpers, leaping elegantly from trunk to vertical trunk, unhampered by their paunches. Their distinctive upright posture made them look superior to the two day-active true lemurs we saw scampering around less stylishly like spring-loaded squirrels.

During the day the Lepilemurs were surprisingly difficult to spot. They dozed in some hollow trunk or crook of a tree, sleepily surveying the forest, their soft brown fur helping them to merge into the shadows of the forest. Paul took me to see one but, even standing fifteen feet away, I was unable to spot him, until I was told which tree he was clinging to. He had a shorter muzzle than the Crowned Lemur, with the most captivating, huge, bush-baby eyes. He was not at all timid of us; he would let us approach quite close, yet he ducked and anxiously scanned the skies when branches above him rustled. Such behaviour suggested that Madagascar's birds of prey were his most feared predators. Each evening for a week I watched him leave his daytime sleeping place – until Phil, in photographing him, got too close and frightened him away. Whether the skies were dark and overcast or bright and moonlit, he became active at exactly four minutes to six. He first had a two-minute wash, then would spring away into the forest, sometimes pausing at a wild coffee bush for a few breakfast leaves. As soon as Anne saw him jump she named him Zebedee-the-Leapilemur. Until then we had not appreciated the length and power of his hind legs. When resting he kept them flexed, tucked close to his body half out of sight, but when he wanted to move he effortlessly extended his legs and sailed upright through the air with an artistry and control that even an inspired gymnast would envy.

The night forest was so very noisy with unidentifiable calls that we wondered what other species were hidden by the dark. We noticed gnawed conical holes in tree trunks in several forest pockets, but did not know what had made them. They were three inches across and two inches deep with tooth marks just over a tenth of an inch wide. Were these connected with the woodpeckery tappings and bangings I kept hearing? Was this the work of the elusive Fork-marked Lemur? It has long robust teeth to scrape away bark, but a gum-eater would not need to chisel so deep. I could think of no animal which might make such holes. Phil contended that the only likely candidate was the Aye-aye, but I dismissed this as another of Phil's potty overenthusiastic ideas. The enormously rare Aye-aye, a rainforest species, could not possibly be at Ankàrana.

It is such a strange-looking animal that it has baffled biologists, who argue about what its closest relatives could be. For nearly a hundred years after its discovery in 1780, it was grouped with the rodents, since like a rodent it has continuously growing chisel-shaped incisor teeth. Only much later was it recognised as a weird kind of primate, tenuously related to other lemurs. The Aye-aye was so rarely seen that it was presumed extinct by about 1930. Then for a long time after it was rediscovered in 1957, the Aye-aye was said to be the rarest lemur on earth. Weighing six pounds, it is dog-sized and unique among lemurs for being grotesquely ugly. Its head is far too big for its body and its face is pinched around its buck-teeth and

staring yellow eyes, so that even the living animal looks as though it
has suffered at the hands of an inept taxidermist, and its emaciated
black fingers, greying pellage and thread-bare squirrel's tail make
it look incredibly old. It fills the empty woodpecker niche in
Madagascar, detecting insects in galls or within trees using its large,
highly mobile, bat-ears; it then chisels in with its beavery incisors
and uses its elongated skeletal middle finger to extract the grubs. In
addition to insects and grubs it also takes frogs, tree gum, coconuts,
bamboo and bananas. It gets its name from its closed-mouth *ha-hay*
call, which sounds like someone hammering on a piece of tin.

Back at Bristol City Museum (where he worked at the time),
Phil measured the teeth of a stuffed Aye-aye and they fitted exactly
the dimensions of the Ankàrana tooth marks. I remained incredulous
that the Aye-aye could be responsible for the conical holes in the trees,
until I got home and found a paper describing an Aye-aye gnawing a
similar sort of hole in a tree at Périnet and later even a reference to
sightings of Aye-aye near Ambilobé, less than fifteen miles from where
we saw these holes. So Aye-ayes could be living at Ankàrana . . .

Later, when Anne returned to Ankàrana with the 1987 expedition,
she was given the thankless task of feeding the team and often went
on lone shopping trips to Diégo. One evening, while still a long way
from villages or forest, she saw in the headlights a strange misshapen
dog with a bushy coat and overlong back legs. Anne is sharp-eyed
and an accurate observer, yet because she has no formal ecological
training she had no credibility with the biologists in camp. They said
she was seeing things. A few days later she saw another 'dog', noisily
gnawing away at bark in the canopy above camp. It took her several
evenings to persuade anyone to get out of their sleeping bags to look.
Then finally she showed them all a very unshy Aye-aye.

Recent sightings of the Aye-aye and its characteristic nests suggest
that is more rarely seen than truly rare. It is not nearly as restricted
in its range as the Crowned Lemur and it is probably less threatened.
Although they are still seldom seen, it is not uncommon to find
dead Aye-ayes. The fleshless middle finger, which consists of little
but skin and bone, is prized as a charm, and many Malagasy
believe that if you see an Aye-aye you must kill it or you
will die.

☆

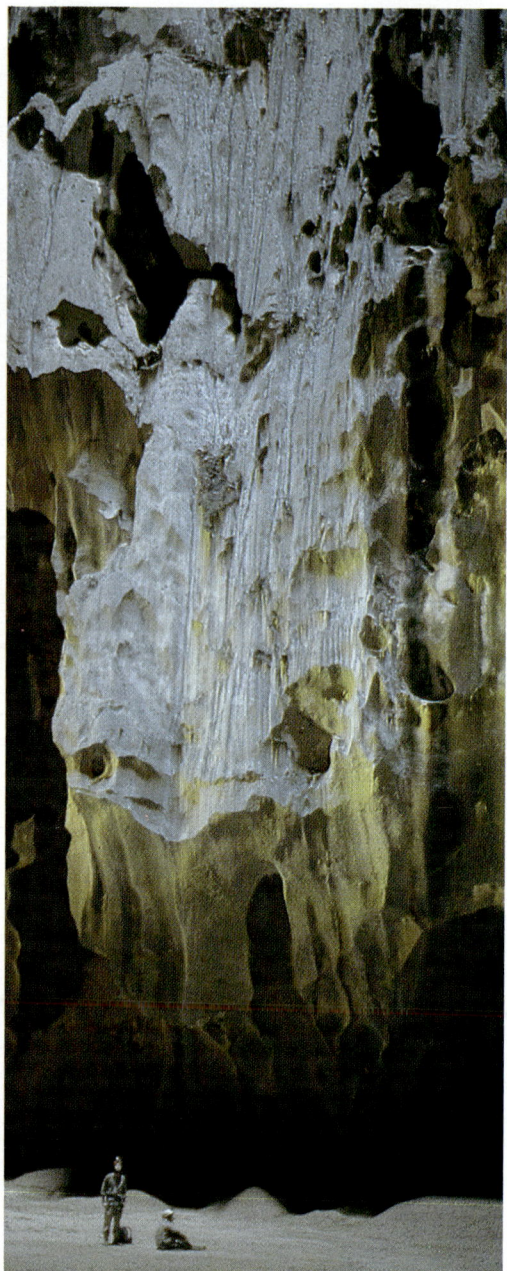

*previous page:* White Sifaka of Southern Madagascar
*below:* Bullock carts in front of Ankàrana Massif
*right:* Ankàrana Caves (Note Catherine Howarth for scale)
*far right:* Daylight filtering through a hole in the roof of Andrafiabé Cave
*bottom:* Guano dunes in Andrafiabé Cave

*far left:* Female Crowned Lemur
*left:* Nocturnal Lepilemur
*below centre:* Two Ring-tailed Lemurs trying to steal the author's lunch at Berenty
*below right:* 'Dancing' Sifaka
*right:* A huddle of Ring-tailed Lemurs resting

*below:* Baobab tree and
zebu near Ankilivalo
*right:* Alluaudia tree of
the Spiny Forest of
Southern Madagascar
*far right:* Chamaeleon
*below right:*
Chamaeleon resting at
night
*below:* Day Gecko

*above:* Lepilemur
*right:* Chamaeleon

Though the men were interested in the animals around us, they
talked constantly of the huge unexplored caves. They studied aerial
photographs which showed disappearing or emerging rivers and
shady forest-filled depressions which looked like collapsed caves.
The largest isolated forest was Manzihy: six hundred feet deep and
half a mile across and all that remained of a subterranean chamber
large enough to accommodate fifty St Paul's cathedrals. The cavers
dreamt of discovering a complete chamber just as large. At the
extreme south of the massif several large subterranean branches of
the River Mananjeba spew out onto the savannah. The cavers went to
investigate and found very large entrances, but so much debris-laden
water surges through the massif during the rains that most of the
caves were blocked with boulders or thick curtains of stalactites
which are deposited so fast in the tropics.

The scarcity of drinking water was the problem at the front of
all the explorers' minds. Many otherwise perfect campsites could not
be used because they were miles from water. When there was water
it was often hardly drinkable or else there was nowhere to camp
nearby. One group stayed away for ten days, had more luck in finding
caves in the east of Ankàrana, but had to drink from a stinking green
pool with little to take away the taste except for thrice-boiled coffee
grounds. They could never carry enough drinking water to quench
their thirsts so they were ever hopeful of finding big subterranean
rivers. Following one wide dry riverbed took them to the rim of a vast
pothole which, in the wet season, swallows the entire Besaboka River.
They abseiled inside, but the cave was dry and totally blocked by
debris after only sixty yards. Nearby was Ampondriampanihy-north
Cave. The entrance, hidden in a huge steep-sided depression, was
over 150 feet across. It narrowed to an impressive gallery, sixty feet
high by fifty feet wide. Half a mile into the cave, they found water:
so much water that they had to take to the boat to negotiate a deep,
half-mile-long canal. The cave continued for a further mile until the
passage was choked with boulder collapse. Jean again reported: 'Ze
cave she was blocked wiz bolsters.'

We all became pessimistic about ever reaching the big isolated
forests in the centre of the massif. The lads would never be able to
show their faces in the cavers' pubs back in Britain after travelling
thousands of miles in search of 'caverns measureless to man' only to
have found a couple of miles of new passage. They were ever hopeful

of discoveries even exceeding the scale of Mulu: the vast caves in Sarawak that Phil, Dave and others had explored.

Trips out were frequently uncomfortable, but the explorers always returned to base camp full of tales, new information and sightings of more animals. And Phil had yet more material to describe as 'probably the most impressive . . .' he had ever seen. We all began to tease him about so much hyperbole. Even in my most enthusiastic moments, I felt like a wet blanket in comparison.

There was a lot of discussion about how dangerous a bite from the hairy Mygale spiders might be. These were real Granny-frighteners, too large to sit in a saucer. They lurked on the walls of the smallest cave passages; usually they hung about in twos and it was not until after squeezing past one that we would notice its mate, much closer, on the opposite wall. Jean, overhearing our conversation, said that they were fatal and I tried to diffuse the alarm that his casual remark caused by saying that there are very few animals capable of killing a healthy adult. No one seemed cheered by being told that the deadliest animals on earth are the *Anopheles* mosquitoes, yet the *falciparum* malaria it transmits was deliberately given to patients earlier this century – to cure insanity! It was said to have worked, too. I did not tell them that there was little I could do if anyone was bitten by a noxious arthropod – as I was later to find out to my cost.

As well as their stories, the explorers brought animals back with them, so camp became a repository for an ever-growing collection of live scorpions and other large unpleasant creatures; we were confident that the director of the Zoo in Tana would be pleased to have so many new exhibits. The largest and most impressive specimens were given names and a particularly ugly and hirsute spider was called Belinda to spite someone's ex-girlfriend.

When Paul brought the first chamaeleon back to camp, Roo was fascinated, saying 'Isn't it Wonderful!' He described a lot of things at Ankàrana as Wonderful. At first the chamaeleon was purple with rage at being dragged from its favourite tree, and inflated itself threatening anything that moved near it. Its eyes made it look really weird. They were the shape of little volcanoes from the centre of which some trapped being peered forlornly through the crater peephole. The volcano eyes were surprisingly mobile and, rather unnervingly, moved independently of one another. As I picked the creature up for a closer look, it peered with one strangely disembodied eye at my hand, and with the other scanned around for an escape route. Its colour darkened as its frustration heightened and I was amused at this harmless reptile trying to frighten me by hissing and gaping open its toothless mouth. Then to my surprise it seized a chunk of flesh on the back of my hand and its sharp tooth-like outgrowths of the skull and jaw drew blood. As I struggled clumsily to get it to let go, Paul came to the rescue. His concern was not for me, however; he chastised me for the inept way I handled the chamaeleon and warned me to be careful not to injure it.

It settled down to a more natural brown colour soon after it had been installed in its new home: a sleeve of mosquito-net material surrounding the top of a sapling. Each of its feet had two thumbs which were opposed to three other digits and there was a sharp little claw on the end of each. The two thumbs and three fingers were so fused together as to look like mittens covered in chain mail. Reptiles keep evidence of gender discreetly tucked out of sight, so I never discovered whether our chamaeleon was male or female.

Chamaeleons do not change colour according to their surroundings. Their colours darken when they are angered or amorous, and they also change colour according to light intensity: a chamaeleon left in the dark fades to a ghostly pale grey but darkens wherever light reaches the skin. If an object throws a shadow on the chamaeleon, a ghostly image of the object, even one as complex as a doily, will remain on its skin for a short time. Pigment cells are arranged in layers under the transparent epidermis. The outer layer contains yellow and red pigment cells and underneath are two reflecting layers. One reflects blue light and the other white. Beneath them are black pigment cells which send up tentacles towards the skin surface. Changes in colour come about when the red and yellow cells expand or shrink and the resulting colours are further modified by the reflecting layers. Concentration of the black pigment into the bodies of the cells lightens the colours, but if pigment spreads along the tentacles, the chamaeleon tends towards dark brown.

After dark we would sit around the camp table eating, organising our field notes or writing up the expedition log. The candle flames acted like homing beacons for a variety of chamaeleon food. Until they began crash-landing in our bean stew supper, I would not have believed that the heavy three-inch dung beetles were capable of flight. But in they came, droning like an approaching helicopter. The lights

also attracted shiny black water beetles. Had they got lost in their
search for breeding grounds or were they just too early? Would
Ankàrana's canyons become waterlogged when the rains came? The
chamaeleon completely ignored unpleasant or distasteful insects, like
Digger Wasps, Stink Bugs and similarly smelly beetles. The bugs
were half-inch, shield-shaped insects, which let off a pungent and
pervading smell when disturbed or attacked: veritable skunks of the
invertebrate world. If one landed in a cup of coffee it was rendered
undrinkable in seconds. One did a kamakazi dive into my cleavage
one evening and, on finding itself trapped, indignantly let off its
unsociable smell. Fortunately the nauseating odour had gone by the
following morning.

The chamaeleon ate as many insects as we could catch and soon
it was obvious that there was no basis for the literary reputation – on
no lesser authority than Shakespeare – which chamaeleons have for
needing no food. Our chamaeleon soon became thin and dehydrated
when we failed to provide enough insects. Its tongue flashed out
towards the prey and there was an audible soggy splat as it stuck
to the insect. Once the meal was secured, the tongue – which is as
long as the chamaeleon itself – was carefully pleated back inside the
mouth. Madagascar boasts fifty-one species of chamaeleon; but they
are also found in Africa, one species in India and one as close to home
as southern Europe. The Spanish used them to control houseflies by
placing one in a song-bird cage with a little meat. The flies attracted
to the meat fattened up the chamaeleon and ceased to be a household
nuisance. We needed such a cage above the camp table.

Superstitious Malagasy are scared of chamaeleons. A proverb
says you should be wise like the chamaeleon, by keeping one
eye on the future and one eye on the past. Ours peered with
one wrinkled volcano-shaped eye at anyone approaching, while
regarding his surroundings with the other. The only time he would
fix both protruberant eyes on a subject was just before his tongue
would lash out to catch some insect. If his prey was beyond
the range of his foot-long tongue, he would slowly move towards
the insect, swaying forward and back as he moved. This seemed
an ineffectually tentative way of stalking, but in fact he was
disguising his advance; insect prey mistook his slow movements
for a leaf swaying in the breeze. Praying Mantises use the same
kind of motion to confuse their victims, yet they are often fooled by

chamaeleons: ours munched the largest insects as noisily as someone
eating crisps.

☆

We had been in camp for over two weeks now and Jean Radofilao
had to return briefly to the University. The others decided that Mick
and I should volunteer to go to Diégo with him. We had two tasks. The
first was reasonably easy: to buy another consignment of carbide to
fuel our caving lamps. The second drove me to despair and set Mick
mumbling '*stressant*' again. Where was our equipment? Trans-7, the
shipping company, apparently had less information than we did. The
man in charge seemed to be hiding and when, after a couple of days,
we found him, he was drunk, incoherent and giggly. The *Emilia* was
the only ship on their blackboard and yet they did not know when it
would arrive. Even if he had been sober he could not have told us
much, since the telephone lines were down between Diégo and the
rest of Madagascar and telegrams were taking a fortnight to reach
Tana. The only way we would find out about our gear was to fly back
to the capital. Later, after some heated discussions back in camp,
Phil volunteered to fly back to Tana on what turned out to be a wild
goose chase.

   We met the palaeontologists in Diégo as arranged. Most of
their team was going to look for fossils south of Ambilobé, but
Martine and Raobivelonoro (Doctors Vuillaume-Randriamanantena
and Ralaiarison-Raharizelina) were joining our group at Ankàrana
to look for remains of extinct lemurs. In 1981 we had found some
strange skeletons which I gave to the Natural History Museum in
London. They caused great excitement there: they were bones of
the Broad-nosed Gentle-lemur and only twelve other skeletons of the
species existed in the world's museums. Martine had heard of our
discovery and asked me if I would take her to search for more lemur
remains. I rode back to camp in the palaeontologists' overloaded
Land-rover. There was no room for Mick so I abandoned him,
unchaperoned, to fend off the attentions of the gay *patron* at the *Hotel
Fiadànana*. He hitched and walked back early the following day. We
had an anxious moment when we drove past an expanse of scrubby
savannah which was being burned to stimulate new grazing for
zebu. The flames briefly licked right over the Land-rover, dangerously
close to the drum on the roof containing spare petrol. We stopped at

Anivorana on the way, famous for the crocodiles which are said to be incarnations of mean villagers, drowned when they refused to give water to a thirsty traveller. This would have been an unforgivable crime to the hospitable Malagasy, but the local people still regularly sacrifice zebu to the crocodiles. The three ten-foot crocodiles that I saw at Lake Anivorano certainly looked well fed. They cruised around close to the bank waiting for sacrificial zebu or for some meat provided by tourists. It is *fady* to kill crocodiles in some parts of Madagascar and also in parts of Indonesia (the Land of the Malagasy Ancestors) they are still protected and Makassar people even bring them to the village where they are fed rice, eggs and meat.

Just beyond Anivorana, we turned off the main road and onto a dirt track. After a while, when it took a dog-leg between two huge orange volcanic ash-cones, I realised that we were coming close to the northern tip of the Ankàrana Massif. The savannah was deeply rutted by bullock carts and rice lorries, and littered with black boulders. The closer we came to camp, the slower our progress became, for we had to stop frequently to roll boulders aside or drag fallen branches out of the way. From this part of the savannah, forest masks the canyons and I was uncertain exactly where to enter. The palaeontologists asked a group of women who replied, in Malagasy, 'Just go in there, the forest is seething with foreigners!'

By hacking down low branches with machetes we got about a mile along the track, but eventually were halted by a substantial fallen tree. The palaeontologists looked unhappy about the prospect of walking and I sympathised when I saw how much luggage they had brought with them for their ten-day stay. Raobivelonoro sat herself down on her huge mound of bags and announced that she would wait for the porters to arrive! I picked up as much as I could and set off towards camp, thinking that perhaps I had been wrong in recruiting these women to the team. Fortunately there were people in camp, so six of us returned to porter the rest of the luggage. Raobivelonoro, carrying only her handbag, walked with us, as Anne, Maggie and I struggled with her luggage: I had rather hoped she might be shamed into helping when she realised the 'porters' were mostly women. But no. At camp the palaeontologists set about clearing a large area of scrub and small trees; half of their luggage was a vast frame tent, large enough for their table and camp beds and with a little veranda attached. Supper that evening was rice, as usual, with pumpkin, almost rehydrated dried fish and cabbage, and then (luxury of luxuries) French bread and bananas that I had brought from Diégo. Everyone enjoyed this, but the cold rice for breakfast and lunch received an unenthusiastic reception from the new arrivals. The palaeontologists wanted to look for bones in some of the small rock shelters in the canyon walls and I enthused about some I had seen a few hours' walk away. That was too far. Simon suggested starting with the *Canyon des Anglais Perdus*, the nearest small side-canyon to our camp. We soon lost him. When he did not reply to my shouts, we began searching the left canyon wall for small caves. Martine, Raobivelonoro (still with handbag in hand) and Jean-Eli (who had appointed himself guardian and bag-carrier) strolled along the canyon bottom, while Maggie, Anne and I clambered around poking our heads into crevices or scrambling along ledges and shelves in the canyon wall.

One rock shelf took Maggie and me onto the *tsingy*; we got tangled in the vegetation and spikes and thorns soon forced us to scramble back down. The only plants which thrived up there were armoured to prevent herbivores puncturing the plant's thick waxy skin and allowing vital fluids to evaporate. The Sausage Tree, *Euphorbias*, as well as having horrendous thorns also has an additional defence: if its waxy cuticle is damaged the plant oozes a highly irritant and toxic white latex. This discourages most animals from feeding on it – but it is used to caulk *pirogues* or as a glass cement in some parts of Madagascar. Many *tsingy* plants have taken on cactus-like forms, although, typical of Malagasy species, they are not remotely related to cacti. Drought-resistant species, Bottle-vines, Screw-palms, straggly figs and others, managed to grow in cracks in the bare limestone; their roots, searching for water, penetrated more than thirty feet or sprawled from their bulbous water-storing bases out over the parched limestone. Roots sprout out half-way up the little *Pandanus* trunks as if the plant, triffid-like, had begun to pull up its roots to walk away. In some places a few small trees grew, providing habitats for now dormant stags-horn ferns and orchids. Some were endemic to Ankàrana. Orchids manage to grow half-way up trees or perch on some rock ledge through a complex interdependence with fungi which live in orchid roots; these nourish the orchid by liberating sugars from organic matter. Vanilla is an orchid, though not one of Madagascar's thousand native species. It was introduced from Mexico. Now two thirds of the world's vanilla comes from Madagascar and most is exported to America to flavour ice-cream.

We heard Anne shouting, 'I've found a good one!' She beckoned us enthusiastically from a wide ledge forty feet above the canyon floor. It was a surprisingly easy scramble over to join her. The cave entrance was wide but not quite high enough to stand up inside. It was only a shallow rock shelter but inside were fireplaces, broken pottery, animal bones and sea shells. This had been someone's home. Martine and Raobivelonoro joined us and identified some of the dinner left-overs as lemur bones. This was a surprise, for the people who now inhabit the area believe that killing lemurs would offend the Ancestors. Who had lived here then? Were the inhabitants refugees or early hunters? Most likely, the remains had been left during the late 1820s when local people took refuge from the armies of King Radama I. We collected shards and bones for archaeological colleagues who said later that the pottery was probably eighteenth century.

Part way through the excavations, Simon reappeared, asking why we had not followed him. 'What do you mean you got lost?' he said. I cut short his sarcastic remarks by putting him to work. Soon he had produced a neat sketch survey of the newly christened *Lakaton'Ny Lakozina* or Kitchen Cave. In Malagasy the name looks unintelligible, but the second word (kitchen) is merely the Malagasy spelling of *cuisine* with a definite article stuck on the front and the usual Malagasy final syllable which is hardly pronounced. The 'o' in Malagasy is long as in book. There are plenty of other borrowed words in Malagasy, although until you get the hang of the pronunciation, they are not so easy to recognise. Food words tend to come from French, sometimes with a definite article: so *lafarina* is flour, *dité* is tea, *dibera* is butter, *pitipoa* is peas and *poma* is apple. Words adopted from English are more intellectual: *sekoly* (pronounced school), *lesony* (lesson), *penina* (pen) and *boky* (pronounced book). Strangely, many of the other words resemble modern Indonesian. The only Malagasy word that has been adopted into English is 'raffia'.

Next day Phil took the palaeontologists to *La Grotte Trans-7*, a dry uninviting little cave that he had named after our shipping agents, since it was full of rat skeletons. (Phil was unimpressed by Trans-7.) The palaeontologists returned from their outing absolutely shattered. Phil again had made no allowances for femininity. It had

been a worthwhile trip, though, and they unexpectedly provided
information on Ankàrana's rodents that we had been unable to
collect since the Longworth traps were still 'In The Freight'. Unlike
caves elsewhere in Madagascar, *La Grotte Trans-7* contained bones
of rodents peculiar to Madagascar. Nearly everywhere else (including
at the nearest village of Matsaborimanga), these endemic species have
been ousted by the ubiquitous ship rats. Ankàrana's forests, however,
are protected from the invasion of destructive foreign species because
they are walled in by *tsingy*. It was gratifying to learn that we were
not the only ones to find moving around Ankàrana difficult.

I suggested we spend a few days in the southern part of Ankàrana,
searching the cave where we had found the lemur skeletons in 1981.
While the palaeontologists excavated, we zoologists could work in
one of the isolated forests only accessible through that same cave.
Martine and Raobivelonoro were keen, but first they wanted a rest
day to prepare.

# 9. The Cave of the Broad-nosed Gentle-lemur

---

The sacred river
Five miles meandering with a mazy motion
Through wood and dale the sacred river ran,
Then reached the caverns measureless to man
And sunk in tumult to a lifeless ocean:
And 'mid the tumult Kubla heard from far Ancestral voices . . .
Samuel Taylor Coleridge, 1816

---

Just before we left base camp, I divided the food for our outing
into eight lots, reserving the heavy tins, rice and onions for us
British to carry and making up two especially light parcels for
the palaeontologists. While it was still early we walked out along
the old logging trail, but before we had reached the edge of the
forest Jean-Elie was already carrying Raobivalonoro's sleeping bag
and Martine her small share of the food. Reaching the savannah
was our signal to head south, following the line of the Ankàrana
Wall but keeping several hundred yards west of it so that we did not
get tangled in the band of scrubby forest which grew in the shelter
of the massif. I was anxious to cover the next eight miles before it
became too hot, but our untidy group straggled along slowly and it
was several hours before we reached the landmark I sought. Three
narrow canyons which split the massif showed that we were not far
from the cave where, in 1981, I had found the Gentle-lemur subfossils:
the cave which the palaeontologists were so anxious to visit. The low
forest growing against the cliff was several hundred yards wide here
and it hid even large cave entrances. Christian disappeared into the
thicket to find the cave, while the rest of us slipped off our rucksacks
and sprawled out under a tree to wait. The cooling breeze moved the
huge palm leaves which soothingly pitter-pattered above us; a crash
close by was only a palm leaf falling to the ground. Madagascar was
a friendly, safe place.

Christian had not come back after half an hour, so I started off after him, thinking I might remember the way. The cave entrance was little more than two hundred yards from where we had been resting, but Christian was not there. Was he lost? I shouted. No answer. I returned to the others. It turned out that Christian had found the cave but when he got back to the others and they told him that I had gone into the forest, he followed me in again. He thought I was lost. We then spent the next hour farcically running around in circles trying to find each other and the rest of the group who by then had joined in the search.

Andrafiabé Cave has an impressive yawning entrance and the cool cave air made it a comfortable spot. We set up camp on the same sandy beach in the entrance as we had in 1981, beside two murky little pools which were our water supply. Once we had collected enough firewood, we began cooking a memorably nasty supper. Rice cooked in one small saucepan, too fast, boiled over, and all but extinguished the fire. Frustrated, we abandoned the rice to watch the endearing lemurs who had come to drink at our campsite pool. But hunger drove us back to a nauseating meal of half-cooked, half-burnt, soggy but hard rice, flavoured only with onions. Bad food can taste remarkably good if you are hungry but we left most of our meal on our plates. Enough remained for breakfast, and the following evening, after even more cooking, the rice was just as nasty.

For the past few days Christian had been swallowing pain killers for toothache and the only way I could persuade him to get the gaping black hole in his molar filled was by threatening to withhold the aspirins. Next morning, early, he set off for the dentist at Ambilobé, clutching the three thousand Malagasy francs we had given him. Even as he disappeared over the horizon, he was an unmistakable figure, wearing the yellow and orange knitted hat that he never removed.

We had camped inside the cave entrance, but going into the cave itself meant a scramble forty feet up the sandy sediments which half-fill the series of passages close to the entrance. Once on top, the going was easy, over undulating dunes in a passage twice our height and beautifully water-smoothed and scalloped. A few torpid bats were dotted about on the roof and, further on, beyond the limit of light penetration into the cave, we found the skeletons of two wild boar which had strayed inside and got lost. Here the walls were almost entirely made of fossil corals, shells and crinoid sea lilies, which had lived in warm shallow seas during the reign of the dinosaurs.

The low fossiliferous entrance passage brought us out to a much larger chamber. We climbed down ten feet and turned left deeper into the massif. The cave opened out into a huge void and we could not see to the far side of the passage. I was used to navigating in small English cave systems where landmarks, guides to the way out, can be picked out with the feeblest caving lights. Cavers manage to navigate out of Mendip caves just by the light of a cigarette. Here at Ankàrana the scale of the caverns was very different, even the most powerful of lights was not bright enough to enable us to see all around. I became anxious about route-finding; it would be easy to miss the way out, as I well knew from being lost in a Himalayan cave. That had been ten years before, but the frightening size of the Andrafiabé's galleries revived my anxieties and memories of that thirteen-hour wait, lost in an absolute blackness.

We arrived at *La Grande Axe*, the first of Andrafiabé's largest passages. This was a good landmark and I told the others to note it carefully. It was only then that I noticed that the palaeontologists had been leaving a trail of pink plastic markers. Hiding my own nervousness, I teased them about having no confidence in the 'expert' caver who was guiding them. The T-junction led into the main north–south gallery of the cave and in turn into other large passages which riddled the massif. Turning left, I recalled, would take us to a long series of blind-ending passages at the very centre of the massif. A sharp right turn led to where we had found the lemur subfossils in 1981. We turned into a passage so large that it was intimidating: 150 feet in diameter and, in places, five hundred feet high. I could hear bats twittering high above me, but my light was not strong enough to pick them out.

Continuing, we began to make out the fuzzy grey glow of daylight coming into the cave nearly half a mile away: a second entrance where fault-canyons cut right into the cave. We marched on, making deep footprints in the dry sand floor, the palaeontologists leaving their trail of pink tape. It took a long time to reach daylight but eventually we arrived at the shady bottom of a canyon less than 150 feet wide but more than six hundred feet deep. The light dazzled us. It was beautifully cool, for sunlight never reached the bottom of the canyon for long. It was an idyllic glade where birds sang and Turtle Doves roosting high in the cliffs above us cooed contentedly and offered us excremental greetings. The water in the little stream which fed the canyon's plants was deliciously cool. After we had drunk our fill, seven-inch crayfish emerged from their hiding places to continue picking over the sediments. Wild citrus trees grew here, yet we had seen none on the outside. We would collect their fruits on the way back to make refreshing lime drinks. We rested, savouring the fresh breeze, before entering the least salubrious section of cave beyond.

The acrid stench of guano poured out from the cave on the other side of the canyon. Generations of bats roosting in this section had deposited dunes of guano more than thirty feet high. It was dry, powdery, and made up of wing cases and other indigestible bits of beetles. A host of tiny crawling insects and maggots crawled in and over the guano so that it seethed. On top strolled inch-long crickets with antennae four times as long as their bodies and thousands upon thousands of three-inch leather-brown American Cockroaches: so many that we could not avoid crushing them under our boots. The guano was like a huge voracious organism which would devour anything falling onto it. Startlingly white skeletons of bats lay about on its surface.

Later I was horrified to discover that the lads had chosen this place as a campsite. There was very little flat ground, so they had to sleep on the guano. This was soft and comfortable, but anyone sleeping on it risked catching Histoplasmosis – the Cavers' Disease or, since the early excavators of Egyptian tombs probably suffered from it, the 'Curse of the Pharaohs'. Histoplasmosis is a sinister fungus. At normal outside temperatures it grows on bat or chicken excrement, but if someone inhales its spores it can cause pneumonia or worse. My spelaeological colleagues well knew that strains of Histoplasmosis acquired in Mexican and South African caves are dangerous and even occasionally fatal. The virulence of any Malagasy strains were unknown. Fortunately only one of us suffered a chest infection and that, although annoying, was mild enough not to need treatment.

I tucked my trousers into my socks before crossing the seething guano dunes, and stupid nightmarish images of being nibbled by a thousand little mandibles made me hurry through. Fortunately the section of the cave system which was so full of guano was only a few hundred yards long. Daylight was soon visible ahead again, streaming through a natural skylight, spot-lighting the cracked mud floor of a dried-up lake. Another entrance appeared ahead as we climbed up and down over thirty-foot mudbanks deposited when floods surge through the cave in the wet season.

Eventually we emerged at yet another entrance; this was five hundred feet high and three hundred feet wide and looked into a patch of superb luxuriant forest, walled in by unclimbable six-hundred-foot cliffs, with a jagged *tsingy* horizon. This was surely the perfect natural nature reserve. The isolated forest was only a few hundred yards across, but it took an hour to reach the far side. The floor was a muddle of big limestone blocks, many three times our height, and there was not only the problem of climbing over or around these, but also the dense vegetation which slowed our progress. Four-inch-diameter lianas stretched across our path, *Pandanus* screw-palms or other thorny shrubs grew out of all the best hand-holds and the Sweat Bees pursued and stung us as if to chase intruders out of their secret forest. Boots sank deep into leaf-litter, stirring up savoury smells and disturbing centipedes and scorpions. At first I imagined we could study the lemurs here, but we moved too slowly and clumsily, while the lemurs leapt so easily through the trees that we only caught tantalising glimpses of them. We even failed in our attempts to climb trees or scale surrounding cliffs and so get a view over the forest and study the lemurs from afar with binoculars.

It was an uncomfortable place, but very rich. I encountered my first Frilled or Leaf-tailed Gecko here. This belongs to another genus peculiar to Madagascar; it contains only seven species but four live in the Ankàrana area – a centre of diversity for *Uroplatus*. They are masters of camouflage. Their skin is indistinguishable from the tree bark they choose to rest upon. Even their large round eyes look like varnished sultanas, and to assist further with camouflage the eyes have no obvious pupils. To perfect the disguise a skirt of flesh protrudes from head, flanks, limbs and broad flat leaf-like tail, so that no shadow is thrown. Camouflage is the gecko's first line of defence, but it has another trick: it displays a surprising orange gape, designed to startle and distract a bird for a split second – long enough for the lizard to escape being eaten. Mantises are one item on the Frilled Gecko's menu and we saw these in the Isolated Forest, too. What poetic justice that mantises, such cruel predators themselves, so often fall prey to larger animals. Their mean little triangular faces and heartless bulbous green eyes suit them well, for they are cold-blooded killers, as insensible to their prey's slow death as a crocodile. The French call them *insectes religieux* but their hypocritically praying hands are actually wickedly barbed weapons to secure some passing insect.

Although to us this sanctuary was an isolated forest, the vertical cliffs were no barrier to the lemurs: it was easy for them to scamper down into this rich larder. At this time of the year vegetation on the outside of the massif is lifeless and dry, while inside, sheltered from drying winds and watered by another subterranean river, leaves stay green. Lemurs come here to supplement their dry-season rations. Did this explain why lemurs were so very abundant in the forests nearby? I looked in, registering lemurs and birds calling from the trees and the forest buzzing with insect sounds. How long had it taken for the largest trees to grow to their full three-hundred-foot height? I gazed in admiration at this unique isolated forest. A habitat as rich as rainforest and the most luxuriant I had seen in the dry zone of Madagascar.

☆

The site where we had found the subfossils was in another cave leading from the Isolated Forest. I took the others to an entrance in the cliff wall. Inside we slid and jumped down another silt bank, across the crunchy, jig-saw mud-flake floor of a smaller dried-up lake and up over silt dunes again. Inside the stalactites were so dry that a torpid bat had chosen to cling to the end of one. Piles of dusty boulders were heaped up along the far side of the old lake bed. I peered between the dry rocks and soon discovered some limb bones. Paul spotted a skull. Then Martine found another and another. There were lemur bones everywhere we looked. The palaeontologists were overwhelmed, and then I heard Martine saying under her breath: 'Impossible. It can't be. No, it's impossible.'

'What is it?' I asked, uncertain whether she was distressed or elated. She repeated herself, and then: 'I think this is *Meso-propithecus*.'

I tried to look impressed, for she was clearly extremely excited by her discovery. I would ask later what was so fantastic about *Mesopropithecus*, and indeed what a *Mesopropithecus* was.

Lights disappeared in all directions as we searched the cave. The chamber was well over a hundred feet high and very long. It was littered with angular blocks, thirty feet square, that had fallen from the ceiling. The fresh rock chips which were littered about everywhere made me wonder about the next boulder fall. I forgot my anxieties when Paul showed me a gorgeous grotto seemingly carved out of frosted glass with walls covered in sparkling calcite crystals. Inside were four complete Broad-nosed Gentle-lemur skulls and a muddle of limb bones, ribs and vertebrae, all iced over and securely cemented in place with tiny transparent reflective crystals. We did not have the tools to excavate such delicate skulls intact, so left them undisturbed in their secret beauty.

It was two hours before the palaeontologists were satisfied, having swept up all the bones in sight into little labelled plastic bags. Lack of funds kept them very short of equipment – we had to lend them a rucksack for this trip – but even so I was surprised when Martine simply stuffed her fragile specimens unprotected into a drawstring bag and I offered to carry them, fearful that they would be reduced to powder and tiny fragments. We returned to the Isolated Forest for water and eats. Producing a bar of chocolate induced delighted giggles from Anne. Paul then appeared and told me off for sitting on a rotting log: 'I just saw a Black Widow Spider near there.' I grinned, but he wasn't joking. The *Menavody* is dangerous: black and only a little larger than a pea, it is all too easy to overlook.

I was unhappy about being the only one able to navigate around these caves. What if I had an accident? I asked who would lead us back, and since no one volunteered I cajoled Anne and Maggie into leading – by committee. We relit our carbide lamps and headed back towards the stink of guano, with me dawdling along behind, ready to interfere if they went too badly wrong. Soon we arrived back at the T-junction where *La Grande Axe* meets the entrance passages: the landmark that I had specifically asked them to note. They went straight past and continued on deeper into the cave system. I switched out my light and made myself comfortable in the sand.

Five minutes later, but now led by Paul, they were back to where I was lying in the sand. They had noticed that the cave was narrowing right down and that they were in unfamiliar territory, and so they backtracked. I reminded them of the difficult T-junction and, although I was sitting just opposite it, they could not find the way home. I left them searching. The gallery was just too large for them to notice the small side passage which led back to the surface. I hoped this would impress upon them how easy it would be to get lost if they just mindlessly followed me. They searched and searched, unable to find even the palaeontologists' pink markers. Eventually I yielded and showed them the turning, not admitting that when we had first come here, Mike had built a huge cairn to ensure that we would not miss the way back. The next gallery ended in a sheer wall and again the party were baffled. I reminded them that we had climbed ten feet down the wall of this chamber and Paul led them up into the fossiliferous passages.

The remaining quarter mile was extremely slow going, for although this was not a particularly complex cave system it was still all too easy to mistake a side passage for the main route. Inexperience meant that it would take people a while to realise they had gone wrong. When they turned down one such off-shoot, I followed behind, interested to see where it led.

Maggie confidently led us in through a long winding corridor. We entered a large classroom-sized chamber strewn with boulders and continued on along another corridor until Maggie, unable to continue because of a sheer drop, realised we had not come this way before. A bat brushed by, and was gone more quickly than a whispered curse. It was only then that I recognised where we were. Matches Mike had abandoned five years before were still there at the top of the pitch; now they were covered in mould and tiny Springtails grazed there.

Near here, in 1981, we had found '*Visitez les concretions*' inscribed in soot. The message, scrawled by members of an earlier French expedition, invited us to descend into a ten-metre-deep, sheer, slippery, walled pit to see the beautiful stalactites that were there. I was not so interested in stalactites but the strong stink of bats made me think that there was a large roost beyond the thirty-foot drop. We abseiled down into an unpleasant little chamber. A thin layer of liquid guano covered everything and made the already smooth boulders soap-slippery. The only way to move about without slipping over was on all fours. The place exuded an oppressive feeling of doom and even my passion for studying bats was not enough to make me want to explore further. Mike was determined to find the stalactites, though, so while Mary and I prussiked back up the rope, monkey-on-a-stick fashion, he continued on with André. Four hours later Mike and André had still not emerged and we became fearful that one of them had slipped on the slime and fallen down one of the pitches. The gannetish lads had never been late for supper before. We had planned to cook chapatis and I knew they were savouring the thought of a riceless meal.

Mary and I packed pain killers and dressings and demolished one of the tents to use the poles as splints. Liz gave us a couple of carefully hoarded toffees for the lads. We rushed back into the cave, scrambling over dry boulders and cracked mud and along that same low winding corridor, hoping that they were still in this part. If they were not at the end of this passage, we would have to search miles of cave. We came to a junction and shouted, unsure which way we should turn. Mike replied. We hurried on until we could see him sitting in the dark on a large boulder at the far end of the huge classroom-sized chamber. He was exhausted and in a disgusting state, plastered with black sticky mud and bat guano. Although he was clearly extremely pleased to see us, he swore, indignant at being rescued by a couple of women. We asked after André.

'He's OK – he's waiting down at the bottom of the pitch.'

At the top was a pile of broken matches and the remains of the box. The three of us woke André by shining light down the sheer drop to where he was waiting. We lowered another light with a toffee attached.

Mike told us how they had continued in deeper by threading between boulders made black and treacherously slippery with guano and mud. The boulders were perched above another thirty-foot pitch. They had descended with ropes and, below, the passage had become a veritable wallow. There was no sign of the stalactites and it was not till later we discovered the inscription was a French joke: the *concretions* were actually three miles away, at the other end of the cave system. As Mike and André slithered and fell about, both carbide lights rolled into a muddy pool and became blocked. There was so much tenacious mud everywhere that even sucking the mud from the jets did not help. They had managed to ascend the first pitch in the dark, prussiking up the rope by touch alone. Mike continued up the second pitch to get back to his bag and the spare box of matches but, with muddy wet hands, not one would light. So he started trying to grope his way out, crawling along, crashing into boulders and occasionally using his photographic flash-gun. It illuminated the cave superbly but he could not adapt the vivid picture in his mind to the speed of his movement through the cave. In four hours he had managed to progress just a hundred yards. Then, tired and totally disorientated, he had decided to sit and wait.

There were more expletives, this time from André. Liz had mistakenly sent her boyfriend a tampon, not a toffee!

☆

With Maggie still leading, we turned back from the thirty-foot drop and retraced our steps. Not long after we had found the main route again, the smell of the cave changed, the draught increased and the friendly grey glow of daylight appeared. We emerged just as the swifts were returning to roost after their day's insect-hunting. Confused by our lights and unfamiliar forms, several crashed into us and fell to the ground. They lay there blinking stupidly until we picked them up and launched them again. The crash-landers were all juveniles, yet to acquire adult flying skills.

In contrast to the lifelessness of the cave, the forest around our campsite was a rich habitat. During the day, endemic Paradise Flycatchers daintily flitted around the muddy pools. Their elegant white tails, streaming out behind them like ribbons, were more than twice as long as their tiny bodies, yet did not handicap their masterful gyrations. All day long the little pools attracted superb butterflies, unpleasant two-inch navy digger wasps and other large insects. Then, as dusk gathered that evening, a swishing of leaves and some low grunts announced that two troops of Crowned Lemurs and a troop of Sanford's Lemurs had come to drink. As usual, a female Crowned Lemur came first, scampering down a thick liana which dangled close to the limestone cliff. She could not quite decide which way to descend. She started head down, turned and slid down bottom first, turned again and again in controlled somersaults until she was able to leap the last few feet to the poolside. The rest of her troop followed gingerly, but only two or three were ever on the ground at the same time; most waited in the safety of the high branches until their turn came.

The Sanford's troop took a different route to the water, skimming carelessly down the sheer limestone, using tree roots and shrubs to control their descent. They were even more anxious about being down on the ground, drinking quickly and thirstily and hurrying back to the security of the tree-tops. This was my first good look at this rare lemur. They were less numerous in the canopy forests around base camp, favouring the degraded forest at the edge of the massif, and the few that did inhabit the forest near base camp were shier still than these at the cave. At five pounds they are a little larger than the Crowned Lemur. The males have faces like human skulls, but enlivened by bright round eyes and fine bushy side-whiskers: they look like curious bald old men or gnomes. The females are drab brown, but although dull-looking they always lead the troop. Sanford's Lemurs have been designated an endangered sub-species. By the time I left Ankàrana, I knew that the only reason why Crowned Lemurs are not also considered in danger of extinction is that they are so little known.

We were entranced by the living lemurs, but Martine and Raobive-lonoro hardly gave them a glance, engrossed as they were in sorting their treasures. The eighteen Broad-nosed Gentle-lemur skeletons that they had found that day had more than doubled the specimens in the world's museums. The Broad-nosed Gentle-lemur is the second rarest lemur, after the Hairy-eared Dwarf Lemur. The Broad-nose was once found in western, northern and central Madagascar. Now the only known survivors live in eastern Madagascar in a patch of degraded rainforest near Ranomafana, six hundred miles south of Ankàrana. There are only about sixty individuals left. Martine explained how palaeontologists reconstruct the extinct animals and make deductions about how they lived and even what they ate by studying skeletons and teeth. The delight of studying the Broad-nosed Gentle-lemur, Martine said, was that she could make these deductions and then be able to check her theories by studying the living animal. Few palaeontologists are so fortunate.

The skeletons that Martine had just collected looked surprisingly recent. They had hardly begun to fossilise (hence subfossils). How old were the bones? Ever the cautious scientist, Martine was most reluctant to give an estimate without further evidence. Lack of sediments meant that it would be impossible to date the bones other than by the expensive and destructive Carbon-14 technique. Would I take a bone to England for dating? I persisted. Could they be tens, hundreds or thousands of years old? Finally she yielded. The bones we had seen spanned a great range of dates. Some of the bird and bat skeletons were only a few years old, but the lemurs might be two thousand. 'But couldn't they be more recent?' I probed. 'They might be as little as fifty or a hundred years old, but equally they could have died over a thousand years ago,' she replied. I latched on to the most recent figure of fifty years and began speculating. Could a second population of Broad-nosed Gentle-lemur still be living in some remote corner of the Ankàrana forests? There was certainly bamboo to sustain them and Ankàrana was so poorly known that its survival here could easily have been overlooked. Was not the Mesite thought to be extinct locally? Might we yet find a second surviving population of Broad-nosed Gentle-lemurs and help rescue an endangered species from extinction?

Amongst the subfossil finds was Perrier's Diademed Sifàka: another enormously rare lemur never recorded in Ankàrana, yet here were its bones bearing witness to the fact it once lived here. At first we had presumed that it had already died out at Ankàrana, until the 1987 team filmed it in secluded forest close to the Second River Cave. A large gibbon-faced sub-species, it has teddy-bear ears buried only just visible in the dense head fur. It is a magnificent gymnastic animal, clad in dense long silky fur, lustrous jet black on the back and shorter with a warm rosy brown tint on the belly.

Martine was not interested in these living lemurs, despite their rarity. Not stopping to look at the visitors to our cave pools, she was almost ecstatic about the *Mesopropithecus* skeleton. This is a lemur which has been extinct for at least a thousand years. *Mesopropithecus* is known only from a few incomplete skeletons collected in central and southern Madagascar more than fifty years ago. Martine was excited with her *Mesopropithecus* because it was hundreds of miles from where it had previously been known to live. More important, though, her skeleton was almost complete and even most of the handbones were present. These provided new information about the species and suggested that *Mesopropithecus* had a lifestyle different from that of any of the surviving lemurs, and that it moved more like the slow-moving sloths and lorises. It was as large as the largest surviving lemur, the Indri, three feet from nose to rump, but only medium-sized when compared to the extinct giant lemurs. *Mesopropithecus* was not the largest lemur to have lived at Ankàrana. French cavers had found an *Archaeolemur* skull. This, one of the heaviest lemurs ever to have existed, may have lived like a baboon: a powerful tree-climber that was also at home on the savannah. Before all the giant forms were wiped out, lemurs occupied an enormous range of different niches, from substantial savannah-grazing animals and arboreal species the size of a small bear, to tiny creatures feeding on grubs.

Why were there such rich deposits of lemur subfossils at Andrafiabé? How had the lemurs got there? The following day we searched for more clues. Very few bones were of lemurs still common at Ankàrana. Had conditions changed since the subfossils arrived in the cave so that lemurs could no longer get trapped inside? Was there any significance in all the lemurs being in the highest parts of the cave? The skeletons had not accumulated in corners nor were they mixed in with detritus or silt, as they would have been if washed inside, nor did they seem to have been brought into the cave by a carnivore, since the remains were undamaged and not in caches.

None of the subfossils was in a part of the cave reached by daylight. The skeletons lay amongst the boulders thirty yards above the small dried-up lake close to the cave entrance, just beyond the limit of light penetration. Considering the behaviour of living lemurs, we decided that they had come into the cave to drink (just as they still do at the Second River Cave) and were frightened deeper into the dark section of the cave. If a predator entered the cave while lemurs were drinking at the little lake, their most obvious escape route would be up over the boulder pile and deeper into the cave. This path would have rapidly led them into a maze of boulders and absolute darkness. Once beyond the limit of light penetration, they would have been unable to find their way out. Even with a light, navigating between the boulders was difficult and confusing, and later Paul got lost amongst them and feared that he too might end up as a subfossil!

☆

After supper that evening, I peered into my wash bag and let out a muffled yelp when something cold and clammy leapt out and stuck to my face. Investigating with my hand I discovered a two-inch bug-eyed tree frog. After that we were often startled by a sudden cold splat on a bare leg. We knew that they were completely harmless, like most of the endemics, but living in the forest made us constantly on edge and each time they landed my adrenalin surged.

The next morning we delivered the palaeontologists to the subfossil site and then went to work on our own projects elsewhere in the cave. Cataloguing all the animals – bats, birds and invertebrates – that lived in the diverse habitats of the seven-mile cave system would take some days. We began by exploring one of the major galleries that led from the T-junction towards the centre of the massif. Disappointingly, we could find no way to the surface there. A steep climb took us to the top of a bank of sediments as fine as in an hour-glass. The dune half-filled the hundred-foot-high passage and from its crest we looked down fifty feet to a lake so clear that we could see the ripples on its sandy bottom. Would we be able to swim across? It was only a hundred yards to the far bank but we were wearing heavy boots and carried daysacks full of equipment. Our lights were too feeble for us to see how easy it would be to climb out on the far side. I slipped off my daysack and went down, half skiing, half running. The water in this cave was so clear and still that I had already several times found myself in water before realising. I braced myself for another immersion. Suddenly I was standing on the flat lake bottom: the water I thought I could see from above was an illusion of our inadequate lights. The others slithered down in my wake and together we struggled up the next dune. From there we were able to stay sixty or seventy feet above a series of green lakes by walking along the tops of the sediment banks. As we went deeper in, the quantity of silt diminished and the galleries increased in size. We continued across low mud causeways which meandered across huge lake-filled chambers over 150 feet high. These chambers were awesome.

Attracted by more twittering above me, I craned to see a bat colony high in the roof and suddenly I found myself skidding off the causeway into deep water twelve feet below. I went right under, weighed down by my boots and heavy daysack. I floundered until I felt my feet on the bottom, stood up and grabbed a breath, but then slid away deeper into the lake and under water again. The immersion extinguished my carbide light, but by the time I had got my feet firmly planted in the mud, someone, alerted by the splashes and gasps, appeared at the top of the mudbank. I could not see who it was, but the giggles gave her away.

'What are you doing down there?'

Mumbling about people asking stupid questions, I extricated myself by kicking steps in the glutinous mud and soon joined Anne at the top of the causeway.

I had had a similar misadventure during the previous day's explorations when, having captured some blind shrimps, I ended up plastered in sticky clay. I had been enticed into water so clear I could not see its surface. Little lakes looked inviting, but as soon as I slid in they quickly turned from clear green into a sticky brown porridge and I kept losing my boots in the tenacious mud. The shrimps I pursued were eyeless, yet very adept at avoiding capture – their enormously long antennae adequate substitutes for eyes. Different parts of the cave yielded a range of shrimp species in various forms that were new to science. Some had the pigmentation and eyes of normal freshwater shrimps, some were pale with reduced eyes and others totally lacked pigment, had no trace of eyes at all and were fully adapted to life in caves.

Cave animals rely on floods or commuters like bats to bring in food. Moulds grow on such imported detritus and are grazed by glistening white Springtails. These are very small and totally harmless, their most offensive weapons being their sausagey antennae which they use to identify friends or beat the stuffing out of intruders. They never evolved wings, so their only defence is to jump and they manage an impressive eight inches – spectacular for a creature just a tenth of an inch long. Here in the cave, wherever there was a trace of mould or bacteria, they would dash around dodging ants, mites, spiders and centipedes – all of which would have liked them for dinner. Deeper into the cave, where the humidity was nearly 100 per cent, there were complex interdependent little invertebrate communities wherever there was enough detritis to feed them. The richest was beneath a colony of a thousand bats. Here blind white millepedes, diplura and bleached woodlice, earthworms, springtails, moths and their larvae feasted and reprocessed tasty excreta, insect remains and bat carcasses into digestible prey for larger invertebrates.

The bats were too high for me to identify, so I brought in Jean-Elie's butterfly net, bandaged it onto a line of tent poles and knocked five angry bats off the cave roof into the net. Two managed to escape while a third distracted me by sinking his teeth into my hand. I had forgotten my leather batting gloves and, as blood trickled, I felt grateful for the rabies immunisation but at the same time looked forward to a septic hand: it was covered in bat guano. The bats were large animals with a two-foot wing-span. I held one and it twittered inaudibly, its head scanning around, ears and nose-leaf quivering as it tried to find an escape route. The nose-leaf, which helps with echo-location, comprised minute sensitive hairs on intricately folded skin; it covered nearly a quarter of the face, making it look as ugly as a leper. These, the largest insectivorous bats at Ankàrana, were Commerson's Leaf-nosed Bats, named after the French zoologist Joseph-Philibert Commerson who, in 1771, described Madagascar as the veritable promised land for naturalists.

Returning from this site, splattered with guano and with all my specimen vials full, I paused to take another look at the suicidal climb Jean Radofilao had conquered some years before. In this part of the cave the rock was white, rotten and loose. Handholds provided about as much purchase as a handful of stale spongecake. In 1981, we had tried to climb to what looked like a high-level passage 120 feet above. Whenever we paused in our ascent, moving upwards by excavating hand- and footholds and moving on just before they slipped away, gravity would take over and we would slide down again. I did not get more than eight metres off the ground before I chickened out. I allowed myself to slither back down, my descent slowed by what looked like a bow-wave of trifle heaped up under my boots. Mike managed to get all the way up, though. He used a tree that Jean had dragged in and also a dubiously suspended forty-foot elektron ladder that he had left in place. I thought this greying mathematician must be mad to climb up there alone, particularly since the high-level passage was an illusion: it was only a shadowy alcove which closed down after a few metres.

We had already photographed stalactites, columns, translucent curtains and the miniature calcite 'pine forest', but we wanted to record the really huge passages. We returned to *La Grande Axe* where Paul and I took up positions with cameras and tripods at the top of a fifty-foot-high sandbank, close to the T-junction. From this vantage point we could look along the half-mile length of the awe-inspiring passage. At the far end, the indistinct grey glow of daylight was just perceptible.

Maggie and Anne strode off down the corridor, each clutching two of the most powerful flash-guns that we had been able to borrow. After twenty and fifty yards respectively they stopped and looked back at us. We used the lights on their helmets to line up the cameras and check how much of the cave was in the picture. Without their lights we could see nothing but blackness through the view-finder. Then it was lights out, open the camera shutters and flash. The powerful flash-guns showed us the grandeur of the passage for the first time. It was magnificent. The narrowest parts were at least 150 feet in diameter. The course of a dried-up river snaked away from us with fifty-foot sandbanks at each bend.

As soon as we had replaced the lens caps, Anne and Maggie relit the lights on their helmets and continued walking away from us. After a hundred yards more we stopped them again: lights off, uncover the lenses and flash. We continued this routine until we could no longer communicate with them but by that time they had illuminated patches all along the cave corridor. To be sure of a photographic record, we went through this routine several times trying different apertures. Work done, Anne and Maggie once more failed to find the elusive hole in the wall at the T-junction and the way back home.

That evening Christian turned up, proudly displaying his newly filled molar. We would walk back to camp the following day. We burned or buried our rubbish and I enjoyed the satisfaction of packing all that I needed to survive into my rucksack and then just walking away with it all. The savannah birds were strikingly different from those of the forest. Many gasped open-billed, to keep cool: pure white Cattle Egrets, gorgeous green Madagascar Bee-eaters, orange Hoopoes, Grey-headed Lovebirds, raucous black Vaza Parrots, Pied Crows and black Drongos. Looking like the forked-tailed birds, familiar from my Indian travels, this endemic species had a sprout of feathers where the beak meets the face so that, in profile, it looked to be wearing pince-nez spectacles.

There were occasional meandering lines of green trees, growing in dry riverbeds and standing out in stark contrast to the surrounding yellowed vegetation. Underground rivers maintained these evergreen streaks. Legend tells of the great fire which destroyed Madagascar's forests and this was taken as evidence suggesting that the island was once entirely forested: that the savannahs were unnatural habitats created by forest clearance. Recent research, however, has revealed that even before Man's arrival, some areas of savannah existed and, as at Ankàrana, they were dotted with clumps of trees and patches of scrub. Fire may have destroyed some forest and regeneration is limited by grazing and burning to stimulate better grazing. Fortunately, though, goats (those Genghis Khans of nature conservation) are not kept in the area. At Ankàrana the luxuriance of the forest is controlled by water availability and the small number of people living locally cannot be entirely to blame for the absence of trees. Blaming villagers for all forest clearance and subsequent environmental problems allows the biggest criminals, commercial timber merchants, to continue destroying forests.

Continuing north, we walked as far as a dry river bed and followed this until it stopped abruptly at the Ankàrana Wall. During the wet season, water surges out of Antsatrabonko Cave and along the course we had just followed. Even so the cave was difficult to find, since tons of rock piled up at the base of the cliffs completely hid the entrance. I found a strong up-draught and led the group, squirming down between the muddle of boulders. There was so little room that I had to wriggle through, dragging my daysack behind me. After a few minutes I was lying flat on my stomach, looking ahead at a slot eight inches high and two feet wide. By this stage in the expedition, I had lost so much weight that it would have been just possible for me to get past this squeeze, but the passage beyond was even smaller and turned a right angle bend. This was surely not the way on. I was too firmly wedged to be able to look behind, so I started to back up. My boots met someone's helmet and its owner cursed me. 'Sorry, can you back up? This doesn't go anywhere.'

Anne was able to turn a little to give the same message to Maggie behind her, and she to Jean-Elie. After a few backward shuffles I was in a passage sufficiently large for me to turn around. Paul had entered the cave last and quickly found the passage that I should have taken. He led us down into a wide, low chamber, fifteen feet high, where a deep fast-flowing river had eroded along the plane of the limestone beds. Everything looked so dry and parched on the surface, it was strange to see such a big river only thirty feet beneath the savannah. The floor of this main passage was scattered with thousands of polished black basalt boulders, one foot in diameter. The river had smoothed them, making them glisten in our lights.

Paul and Jean-Elie collected white crabs from the river, while the women – having been reassured by Paul that crocodiles do not like rapids – monopolised the best bathing spot. A section of thigh-deep bubbling water made the perfect jacuzzi, though the water was flowing so fast that I soon lost the soap. Refreshed by the bath, we then got a good coating of fresh mud on our clothes as we slithered back out between the boulders. Raobivelonoro and Christian had made the right decision in staying above ground! We still had a lot of walking to do and I certainly did not want night to fall before we had found our way back to the start of the track into the *Canyon Grand*.

On the savannah, shadows were lengthening and the day was cooling. The birds, no longer gasping to keep cool, were busy at their late afternoon feeding. This was a lovely time of day. We reached the *Route Grim* and the end of the forest track just as dusk was gathering and the lemurs were out in force to welcome us home. They peered at us all along the two miles of forest that led back to camp. The palaeontologists were so relieved that their trial-by-expedition was nearly over that they even seemed to enjoy the bean curry and rice. Over supper I told Martine of all the places where we could search for further bone deposits during her last day at Ankàrana. She looked weary and said she would need a day to pack up her fragile subfossils.

## 10. Snow-White Lemurs of the Spiny Desert

> The forests were unpleasant places. . . . The spines of the Didierea trunks
> and the thorn bushes that grew between them caught in our clothes and
> tore our flesh. In many places our way was barred by half-fallen stems
> so entangled in the under-brush that it was impossible to either step over
> them or stoop beneath them.
>
> David Attenborough, 1961

Ankàrana was the perfect place to study true lemurs, but my
favourites, the Safàka, were not in evidence. They are very rare
in the north of Madagascar, although a few large black Diademed
Sifàka live near Ankàrana. The smaller White Sifàka is much more
common and widespread, living in the dry south and west. Sifàka
are delightful, athletic and the most graceful of lemurs.

I first saw Sifàka in 1981 with the Southampton University team
when we visited the Berenty Reserve. Our weeks in the forest with
them more than made up for the six long days we had spent on the
five-hundred-mile bus journey from Tana to the reserve. The first
*car-brousse* (a full-sized bus) took us half-way – to Fianarantsoa,
'Where-there-is-good-learning', the main hili town of the south. We
spent the night with friends of friends who were not expecting us
but, in typical Malagasy style, accommodated us as if we had been
long lost and much loved relatives. We hoped to reach Berenty the
following day, but had to wait two days for a bus in sufficiently good
condition to cope with the awful roads further south. At four o'clock
on the morning that we left Fianarantsoa our hosts walked with us
down to the bus station. We passed a queue of a hundred people,
waiting to buy a meagre ration of rice, sugar and a tiny piece of
soap. The shops were empty and there were shortages of everything
– even in the major cities. As students we were poor compared to most

tourists but by local standards we were rich and privileged: we never had to queue all night for rice.

Despite our early start and our great eagerness to continue the next leg of our journey, we had to wait for the bus. It left, not at 4.30 (as we expected) but at eight. By this time it was packed with an unbelievable number of people and livestock. Someone strapped a bicycle to the roof rack, having first let the air out of the tyres so that the lowland heat would not burst them. This was going to be a hot uncomfortable trip, but fortunately we had no idea then that we would be crammed inside the bus for three days. We made good speed along the smooth metalled road, even though the *car-brousse* needed to be bump started every time it paused to pick up more passengers and the grating engine stalled. As the road descended from the *Hauts Plateaux* moorlands, though, the temperature climbed and the road deteriorated rapidly. The bus crawled mile after mile in first gear over appalling dirt tracks through the rutted, brick-hard savannah. Yet this was the best time to travel. The 'road', which was little more than a clearing in the course scrub, was impassable in the wet season.

None of the people within shouting distance of where we were wedged spoke more than three or four words of French, but everyone smiled a lot and gave us infants to hold. Amused at our revulsion, they laughed loudly when the children started vomiting and we hurriedly gave them back to their mothers. The infants were constantly sick, yet they seldom cried. Each time they vomited, another handful of dry stale French bread would be stuffed into their mouths so that they would not be sick on an empty stomach. Spending all those days so close to our fellow travellers induced a real feeling of cameraderie. I wonder what they thought of us.

Inside the bus it was stiflingly hot and smelly; outside the scenery was monotonous. The bus broke down for the first time just north of Betroka, about half-way between Fianarantsoa and Berenty. When it finally limped into town at eleven at night, we chose to stay in a hotel, rather than sleep in the open beside the bus, as we had done the previous night. A strange tall thin man appeared out of the darkness to show us where we could sleep. Wearing nothing but a blanket and a raffia hat, but carrying a sharp spear, he beckoned to us and called out '*Chambres?*' in a deep sinister voice. The beds in the hotel were all full, but the occupants invited us to climb in too. We chose to sleep on the floor on clean rush mats instead. The toilet was a very full slop bucket on the balcony overlooking, and in full view of, the main street. Using this at night was bad enough; next morning I followed the directions to the 'Water Closet'. The little brick hut had been waterless for months: now the bowl was writhing with maggots. No wonder the locals suggested that I relieve myself in the bush.

Repairs to the bus took many hours and we did not set off again until early afternoon. The monotonous scenery continued and there was little sign of life, except for an occasional car or bus heading north. Around ten-thirty the next night, we stopped to snatch some sleep. We were hot and thirsty and baffled a *hotely* owner by refusing to have ice in the evil lukewarm *Bon-bon Anglais*: the only drink on offer. With that smug self-assurance that medical students have, I was convinced that only by abstaining from ice would we sidestep giardiasis, dysentery, worms, cholera, typhoid and hepatitis. Despite my health evangelism, we got sick anyway – but fortunately not on the bus. We spent the third night of this bus-ride stretched out on the roadside again, our sleeping bags stimulating more mirth and delight in our fellow passengers. Unabashed, they pointed and laughed as we squirmed into our bags, like competitors in a sack race; we were non-stop entertainment.

At three in the morning, we wedged ourselves back inside again and dozed until dawn. Once the sun had driven away the thick morning mist, we realised we had arrived in a very different habitat. Six days after we had left Tana we were driving past plants like nothing on earth. We were in spiny forest and our journey was nearly over. Then the people around us started slapping us on the back, shaking our hands, grinning and triumphantly shouting: '*Arrivé! Finis!* Amboasary!' We had finally arrived at Amboasary Sud: the town nearest to the Berenty Reserve, home of the Sifàka. The bus that we had been jammed in for so long was awash with paediatric vomitus, chicken excrement, fruit skins and egg shells, and still it had a further half-day's journey before it would reach its final destination, Taolanaro.

The bewilderingly palatial Scientists Lodge at Berenty was already occupied, so we found somewhere to camp, washed off three days' grime and headed into the reserve. Dusk was gathering. Beckoned by the characteristic high-pitched call of Mouse Lemurs and the owly squawks of Lepilemurs, we headed for the spiny forest to search for nocturnal lemurs. From a distance, the spiny forest looked thin and sparse. There was no canopy, and we were confident that we would be able to explore this exciting new habitat with ease. But progress was painfully slow as we threaded between the thorny scrub, under or over fallen *Didierea* trunks, and never in the direction we wanted. There was a sound quite close and I shone my torch up. Two dazzling pink spots looked back at me, blinked, and were gone with a slight shiver from the tree that it had been in: my first Mouse Lemur. These are one of the most widespread and common of all lemurs, but, at Ankàrana they had been asleep in their communal hiding places emerging only when the rains brought out their insect food. We saw others at Berenty but seldom caught more than a glimpse of a fleeing shadow. They were extremely timid, fast and very small. Indeed these lemurs, which weigh only as much as a hen's egg, are the smallest of the world's primates. We returned to our tents to attend to our scratched skins, resolving to look for the Mouse Lemurs' daytime resting sites the next morning.

Early next morning we returned to the edge of the spiny forest. Some of the strangest plants on Madagascar, and perhaps in the world, grow here: 95 per cent of the plants are found nowhere else on earth. The most bizarre of these are members of the endemic *Didiereaceae* family. The largest are thirty feet tall, yet hardly resemble trees: they look more like a handful of gigantic pipecleaners, or scrawny elongated octopuses with tentacles frozen stiff. Most resemble cacti, but are unrelated; also, they are more useful than cacti since the trunks provide wood for building. Some *Didiereas* have tangled thorny branches like monkey-puzzle trees, but lemurs leap about in them unscathed. During the dry season the plants look dead and shrivelled, being covered only by whorls of vicious thorns. When the rains start, though, sinuous branches and insubstantial trunks turn bright green as they sprout masses of tiny waxy leaves no bigger than pennies. Then, in early September, the tallest *Alluaudia*, looking like emaciated green squid, sprout a surprising white bouquet on their tentacle tips. Other *Didiereas* become almost totally covered in yellow-green blossom so that they look like giant catkins. Occasionally, towering over the short spiny forest, was a huge baobab tree. Ideally adapted to desert conditions, their gross trunks are distended enormously by stored water as if afflicted by the botanical equivalent of dropsy or gout. Like a diseased leg, there are even varicose veins on the trunk. The baobabs and all the other strange plants give the ambience of a science fiction set rather than an Indian Ocean island.

Soon we disturbed a small group of Sifàka basking in the morning sunshine. Again we tried to pick our way slowly and quietly through the ferocious thorn scrub, but the twigs under our feet cracked like gunshots and our clothes snagged on spines and rattled the desiccated shrubs. The Sifàka fled before we had moved more than a few steps towards them. There was no shade and by nine the sun glared down on us and sweat trickled into our scratches. They stung unbearably. This was not a good training ground for novice primatologists.

Berenty Reserve comprises five hundred acres, roughly half deciduous and half spiny forest, and it is hemmed in by a monotonous spiky green sisal plantation. We were relieved that the deciduous forest was a much easier place to work; if we had had more time, we could easily have spent it there idly watching the lemurs' enchanting antics. But we had little time for our work. Soon we had to start the scientific study of the graceful White Sifàka and the comical Ring-tailed Lemur. Food is often crucial in controlling wild animal populations, so we started by looking at what plants the lemurs chose, then how they used the forest. André was keen to look at faeces to find out what the lemurs ate. He noticed a mucky-looking tree and went to collect the droppings littered beneath. A Sifàka troop lounging in the tree peered down at him and helpfully contributed further samples, as André fled from the rain of urine and excrement. So began the collection of information which helped us understand how such large numbers of healthy lemurs continued to thrive in a reserve which seemed far too small to sustain them.

The reserve borders the Mandraré River and the richest forest is closest to the river. Here grow massive ancient Tamarinds, and other leguminous trees with seed-pods nearly three feet long. Just as at Ankàrana, the forest type is determined by water availability. The further the forest is from the river, the drier and scrubbier it becomes and the large trees thin out until the vegetation merges into the impenetrable spiny tangle. Close to the river, the deciduous forest was an ideal place for studying the Ring-tailed Lemur. Unlike Crowned Lemurs, the markings of the Ring-tails are the same in both sexes. Previous researchers recommended determining sexes by manoeuvering into such a position as to observe the genitals through binoculars. This was easier said than done, but while craning to see we did get good views of the strikingly marked coat. It was grey on the back, merging into pure white on the belly and throat, face and ears. The black rings around their eyes and nose, with the black and white striped tail, made them look clownish. The animal's Latin name, *Lemur catta* (the cat lemur) seems inappropriate, until you hear its cat-like miaow. They purr, too, when they are particularly pleased. The miaow-call is used by the Ring-tails to keep the troop together: a contact call to keep in touch when the dense foliage of the forest canopy hides them from their troop mates. Lemurs, especially those feeding at the edge of the group or in a neighbouring tree, would call miaow as if to say, 'I'm over here. Are you still close by?' Other members of the troop would miaow back, 'Yes, we're here.'

We learned to whistle the descending tone of the miaow-call, and nearby Ring-tails would reply to us. We were delighted to be able to communicate with the lemurs, and the whistling trick was not only amusing, but useful too. We were trying to make accurate counts of the numbers of lemurs in each troop, but this was difficult where the forest canopy was thickest along the river; particularly when the lemurs were actively browsing, we could never be certain whether we had counted one individual twice. Often it would take more than half an hour to be confident that we had an accurate count. Once we had learned the whistle-miaow contact call, though, we had a double check. We noted where each lemur was, and would then whistle an enquiring miaow. Replies would come back from the troop we had just counted, but often another lemur, feeding a few yards away, would respond, as if teasing us, saying: 'I'm over here; why haven't you counted me!'

During the mating season, when troops defend territories and males vie for females, the Ring-tails become quarrelsome. But even when at their most aggressive, lemurs often avoid fighting. Ring-tails smear scent from wrist glands onto their tails, which they then vibrate vigorously, wafting threatening personal smells towards their rival. This usually provokes a retreat, but if it does not, then the males attack with their tusk-like canine teeth. Ring-tailed Lemurs have a great sense of fun and sometimes have time to play. One troop inhabited a tree which was also a roost for hundreds of huge Red Fruit Bats – *Pteropus* again, an Asian genus not found on mainland Africa. These were much larger than the flying foxes at Ankàrana, with wing spans in excess of a yard, and had a set of very sharp teeth – though these did not deter the lemurs. The Ring-tails visited the tree roosts, but not to feed there, for the bats had long stripped all the leaves from the branches. They delighted in scampering out to where the bats hung, just to tug at a wing or poke them. The bats would squawk in frustration and try to bite the lemurs, but they were too slow and clumsy to retaliate and could only fly away to another roost.

Within a few days we were beginning to predict the Ring-tails' movements, which made it easy to locate troops, map territories and work towards estimating the size of the Ring-tail population at Berenty. They had civilised behaviour patterns and, like us, slept all through the long sub-tropical night. They settled down in their favourite sleeping tree about half an hour before sunset and usually did not move until an hour or so after dawn, staying together in their tree until they had dispelled the night chills. Each morning they indulged in a sun-bathing ritual which allowed time for us to take a leisurely breakfast before starting work. They warmed up by what primatologists call 'sunning' – sitting upright, thumbs pointing skywards, chin up and white belly towards the sun, as if in ecstasy. Some interpret 'sunning' as sun-worshipping, an additional piece of evidence proving to the Malagasy that Ancestors can be reincarnated as forest animals, and that these lemurs are intelligent and have human souls. Consequently, the lemurs are protected from hunting.

Tamarind trees, probably first introduced to Madagascar by Arab traders, are the Ring-tailed Lemurs' most important dry-season food source, though we also saw them eating other foreign species, climbing the flagpole-like sisal stalks to feast on the flowers. They also took *Raiketa* or prickly pear. These were introduced by the French in 1770 to strengthen the defences of their slave-trading community at Taolankarana which they renamed Fort Dauphin in honour of Louis XIV. The town is now known as Taolanaro. The colonists had reason to be nervous: the first French settlers had been wiped out in their chapel one Christmas Day a hundred years before by disgruntled Antanosy – 'People-of-the-Island' – whom they had double-crossed. The new settlers were also massacred, but the prickly pear survived and spread rapidly from Taolanaro, especially once the Antandroy – 'People-of-the-Thorns' – discovered how effective its vicious spines were against cattle thieves. The lemurs, too, well used to the thorns of the spiny desert, were delighted with this exotic addition to their diet.

One lunchtime, while sitting cross-legged in the sand near my tent writing up the morning's field notes and eating my lunch of rice pudding and sliced bananas, I became aware of movement near me. Looking up I saw a female Ring-tail confidently approaching me. She was momentarily flummoxed when I looked at her and she paused while the rest of the troop watched from the trees. Sitting down, she casually looked around, avoiding eye contact and acting as if she had not noticed me at all. She and a friend circled behind me. Suddenly the female darted in and grabbed a piece of banana from the mess tin which was on the ground in front of me. Moving to defend my lunch did not scare them in the slightest and when I cradled the mess tin close to me, she climbed up onto my knee so that she could reach more banana pieces. Bananas were scarce locally and, tired of our rice diet, I tried to distract the lemurs from stealing this valuable half-piece. I offered them a handful of rice pudding, but they were as unimpressed with it as I was. They scampered around me, often pausing to stand up on their hind legs, straining to see if there was any banana left. Soon it was all gone and the couple cantered away and up into the trees to scan around for more titbits, while the hen-pecked males of the troop continued to look on dolefully.

Two troops were habituated to taking bananas from tourists. Several times a week a minibus load came from the airport at Taolanaro, driving quickly through Amboasary, their attendant dust-cloud hiding its ugliness. They arrived at the neatly landscaped little garden at the reserve entrance, near the model Antandroy village and purpose-built restaurant where they would enjoy lobster and rare delicacies. They brought armfuls of bananas to feed to the Ring-tailed Lemurs. Local people never ate bananas: they could afford only sweet potatoes and *brèdes*. The tourists, festooned with expensive cameras, would stand in a wide clearing in the forest, shout '*Maki! Maki!*' and wave bananas enticingly. The greediest troop in the forest would appear from nowhere and approach to snatch bananas in ever-increasing numbers, dancing about until all were gone. The greedy troop was the largest at Berenty with twenty-seven adults, but – strangely – when other troops were giving birth, they did not produce any youngsters. Could the almost pure-starch banana diet, with insufficient protein, have rendered the females less fertile?

Bananas did not tempt Sifàka. Animals of the semi-arid parts of Madagascar, they have no taste for fruit, preferring to browse only on leaves or chew on bark. They peer down aloof and disapproving of people and Ring-tails beneath them. They are long-bodied like gibbons, but while gibbons swing from especially long arms, Sifàka use powerful hind legs to propel themselves through the air, leaping from trunk to vertical trunk with arms used only to steady themselves. Completely at ease in the canopy, they move with fluid grace. They rarely descend to the ground, but if they have to cross an open patch, they perform an astonishing sideways dance. Swinging their short arms, they progress like galloping country-dancers. Surprisingly, they find this easier than cantering along on all fours like true lemurs and monkeys. The Sifàka gets its name from its alarm call, which sounds like a loud indignant sniff followed by an obscenity: '*siff-Fak!*' The '*siff-Fak!*' exclamation is accompanied by a loud snoring sort of noise and an abrupt movement of the head when the chin is jerked upwards.

The White Sifàka does not drink water and survives best in poor dry habitats. It is difficult to spot against the glare of the sky for it is mostly snow white, except for a dark brown fur beret and naked black muzzle, and on the chest where the white fur is so sparse that the black skin underneath shows as a darker breastplate. Their intelligent round yellow eyes are misleading, since an animal which spends its life browsing on leaves does not need a great intellect. They are certainly not as quick and adaptable as the true lemurs: Ring-tails, Crowned and Sanford's. But they are peaceable, affectionate creatures and perfectly delightful to watch. Being folivores, they need to spend much more of the day browsing than their fruit-eating cousins but they still find plenty of time for a long midday siesta. They spend this rest time sitting on a horizontal branch, propped up against the trunk or against each other. Sometimes they squat on a branch with their knees drawn up looking like thoughtful gnomes. Often they sit sleepily with an arm flopped casually over a mate who may occasionally turn to offer an affectionate lick of an ear or touch of noses. Others slump face down on a branch, limbs dangling as if the morning's eating has been too much for them. The Sifàka attract such glib anthropomorphisms, but perhaps it is the very way they seem to mimic humans which makes them so appealing – and which in some parts of Madagascar protects them from hunting.

Whenever we needed to shop, we hitched a lift into Amboasary Sud in the sisal factory ambulance; an ailing 2CV. After the delights of watching graceful lemurs and beautiful forest birds and butterflies, Amboasary was a stark ugly place. It had been decimated the previous year by floods and there was no work. People lived in tiny temporary shacks, some fortunate enough to have a rusting piece of corrugated iron or some flattened oil drums to keep out the rain. Women collected water from the mud-brown river, loaded with sediments and bacteria. Everything was dusty and decaying. Amboasary was a scant market: there was usually no more than sweet potatoes, cassava and spinach-like *brèdes*. Occasionally there might be a few spring onions, tomatoes, tiny river fish, green coffee beans and prohibitively expensive rice. One morning we also counted three eggs, eight bananas, two pounds of cauliflower, a couple of beetroot and about ten pounds of onions; only rarely were luxuries available and there was never much for an entire town. Who would not be tempted by an occasional lemur steak when subsisting on such an unappetising, unnutritious diet? We were beginning to appreciate the terrible conflicts between conservation and human survival in Madagascar. In a country where people are starving and medical services are inadequate, setting up nature reserves is one of the lowest priorities. Even when they are established, there is no money to protect them from hungry poachers. Travelling by *car-brousse* had shown us how slow and expensive it was to move about the island and how difficult to transport food and medicines.

Time was getting short and we now needed to travel the length of the island (the same distance as between London and Naples), so we decided to fly back to Tana from Taolanaro. It took only a couple of hours to reach Taolanaro by *taxi-brousse*, but those few miles took us from behind the shadow of the mountains to where frequent rains watered rich agricultural lands. The city market was full of fruits, vegetables and sea food and it seemed odd to find such diversity so close to the poverty of Amboasary: transporting foods to the impoverished is never a commercial proposition. We feasted our eyes and while we were indulging ourselves with fried savouries and mangoes we realised we were being watched by a *vazu* i family. A man asked in the drawl of the southern States whether we spoke English.

'We *are* English!'

'Oh my! What are you all doin' here?'

Full of self-importance, we said that we were doing zoological research. He was not as impressed as we would have hoped,

saying that he had heard there were some interesting animals
in Madagascar. He explained that he was from America (why do
Americans always think you do not know?) and he was here to teach
dentistry – a Born Again missionary dentist. He invited us to spend
the day with him and his family at their weekend beach cottage.
Mike looked anxious – missionaries frightened him – but the rest of
us could not resist the invitation to lunch. How greedy and obsessed
with food we had become!

At the bungalow, we were offered green *syrop* – a sweet, minty,
iced cordial. 'Do you drink the water here?' I asked. 'Yes Ma'am;
the water is potable from the faucet.' (He had asked *us* if we spoke
English!) 'There was some typhoid here a couple of months back, but
not now.' The health evangelist in me felt moved to preach but I could
not match his Born Again fervour and meekly sipped my *syrop*. Dan
and his wife entertained us royally, fed us hugely, showed us where
the best snorkling was and educated us on the dangers of scorpion
fish. I asked of his work, saying how good it must be to be able to
take people's pain away.

'Yes Ma'am. We go out into the villages and sometimes pull two
hundred teeth in a day. Praise the Lord! But we can't do much work at
the moment – we've run out of local anaesthetic. I just fit dentures.'

Transport and supply are perennial problems in Madagascar: I
had heard of people dying for want of antibiotics, while medicines
lay unused in the ports. Surely Dan could fill teeth while he waited
for the anaesthetic? 'No Ma'am, not till the local arrives.'

I winced, knowing that he was training local counterparts and
the dental equivalents of *aides sanitaires* who would have to work
with intermittent supplies. Dan was dedicated and well-meaning but,
isolated by language, he had no real appreciation of the problems.
He criticised Romanian aid to Madagascar: they too were teaching
dentistry but with very primitive techniques, he said. But perhaps the
Romanians, well used to improvising to cope with supply problems
and shortages, might give a more useful training? Valiantly, and in
great isolation, Dan had worked for three years in Taolanaro and
pulled thousands of teeth, praising the Lord with each extraction.

On the way to the airport, we went back to the market to
buy some treats for Suzanne in Tana. The air-hostesses did not
even glance at the basket, heaving as the lobsters moved about
inside. Nor did the large tentacles belonging to a seven-pound

smoked octopus protruding from a bundle of newspaper cause them
to take a second look. Other passengers brought on as hand-baggage
sacks and baskets containing tens of lobsters, bundles of pineapples
and fresh fish.

☆

After the Ankàrana phase of the 1986 expedition, I returned to Tana
to report our findings and to plan the medical projects. This process
proved to be a more relaxing interlude than the fraught negotiations
in August. Perhaps by then I had settled down to the Malagasy pace
of life. The distressingly emaciated woman with her face eaten away
by leprosy was still asking for money outside the bank, but I
was cheered by meeting the sparkling-eyed beggar-boy again; his
impetigo was healing.

We had planned to follow the ecological work at Ankàrana
with some medical research in the villages around the massif,
or in Sambava, a town not far to the south-east. Sambava was
of special interest, for it lies at the supposed southern limit of the
ranges of Crowned and Sanford's Lemurs, the same rare species that
we were to study at Ankàrana. During weekend breaks from medical
work, we would be able to add to our Ankàrana lemur observations
by watching members of the same species a little further south in
a different habitat. The Malagasy medics, not sharing our interest
in lemurs, suggested instead we work in Betroka, that desperate
savannah town in the far south where the suspension of the bus
had finally collapsed in 1981. My two overwhelming memories of
that place were of sad unemployed drunks slumped around in the
main square, and of the hotel slop bucket and waterless WC full of
maggots. Betroka was an unattractive place. Half-heartedly I tried
to suppress my hypocritical disinclination to go there. Eventually we
compromised on Morondava in western Madagascar, a good long
way from Betroka, and where the public health chief was *très
dynamique*. There was useful research to be done there, and, almost
as important, some primary forest survived close by. The White Sifàka
is found over a large part of south and west Madagascar and here we
had a chance to see them in another part of their range.

By this time Anne, Maggie and I had been joined by Simon
Howarth, a public health engineer, and Sally Crook, a zoologist with

post-graduate degrees in both entomology and human nutrition. The Malagasy Ministry of Health had asked us to collect information on Bilharzia and other diseases in rural peoples, and so the five of us flew out to Morondava, a region notorious for its range of parasites and mosquitoes, half way up the island's west coast.

Dr Razafindrakoto, *Médecin Inspecteur* and local public health chief, met us at the airport and drove us straight to Ankilivalo: 'Place-of-eight-Tamarind-Trees'. Our first task was a courtesy call on the *président* of the *fokon'òlona*. We discovered him driving sedately around the village at ten miles an hour, his little piggy eyes only just above the level of the steering wheel of his ancient Peugeot. He was less than five feet tall but with a magisterial paunch; he wore shorts, American army jungle boots, pink shirt and yellow baseball cap. Later we were to notice a remarkable number of the local children with his piggy eyes who claimed to be sons of the *président*. He made a fine speech of welcome, thanking us many times and saying how fortunate they were that we had chosen to work in Ankilivalo. When I failed to respond with a similarly long flowery and excessive speech, Dr Razafindrakoto bailed me out, saying how honoured but unworthy we were to accept the president's lavish hospitality. He explained how conducting the clinics would help the people of Ankilivalo and also how our research would contribute to the understanding of ways to control parasites in other tropical countries. It sounded all very impressive and I wished I believed what he said.

Ankilivalo was a pleasantly small village with a population of two thousand, sitting in a rich alluvial plain. There were five shops and something approaching a market where women sat beside the dirt road selling vegetables and small river fish. The original inhabitants of the area were the Sakalava, the 'People-of-the-Long-Valleys', who are traditionally pastoralists. Completion of a large irrigation scheme (which had precipitated the present Bilharzia epidemic) encouraged the traditionally rice farming Betsileo ('Many-Invincible') to move in from the *Hauts Plateaux*. The Antandroy ('People-of-the-Thorns') had settled here too, after fleeing from droughts in the Spiny Desert further south. Traditional lifestyles had altered with migrations and frequent inter-tribe marriages so that now all tribes both kept cattle and cultivated rice.

Even close to the village, gouty baobabs dominated the scenery. Around Diégo in the north the baobabs are small and scattered, but here in the dry west of Madagascar there are so many large baobab trees that they give the horizon a strange, out-of-this-world appearance. Madagascar has seven species, while elsewhere there are only two: one species in Africa and one in Australia. (Baobabs growing in Peninsular Malaysia and north-western Sri Lanka were planted by Arab traders.) These baobabs had disproportionately fat water-storing trunks with a diameter sometimes as much as half the tree's height. Their vast trunks distend enormously during the rains. Spindly leafless little branches stuck on top give an impression of an upside-down trunk with elephantiasis, more like a child's drawing than anything real. Legend says that some god was angry with the baobab, ripped it out of the ground and planted it roots skywards. The rains bring the funny little straggly branches into leaf. Baobab wood is spongy and easy to cut into. Scars around the base of the trunks show where people take material to build the walls of their houses and where animals have been encouraged to drink. Scabs in the pattern of a ladder all the way up to the tree-tops, reveal how people scale the hundred feet or so to the first branches by banging pegs into the trunk. They climb up to collect the edible fruit or the seeds from which oil can be extracted.

Dr Razafindrakoto suggested that we stay next door to the local *aide sanitaire*, Emile Andrianjafy. His wife was volunteered to cook for us. We would sleep on the dusty concrete floor of a small, unoccupied, unfurnished house, which should have been allocated to a worker on the sugar estate that never was. Emile's dazzlingly seductive smile, tight denim jeans and loud tropical shirt made him appear an amiable rogue, which indeed he was. Dr Razafindrakoto was bewilderingly dynamic and wanted us to start work that afternoon, but we stalled and began setting up clinic on the school veranda at seven next morning. The teachers lined the children up into long straggling lines. They giggled excitedly, all eager to be interviewed, weighed and measured. Each child had been primed by the teachers to bring a stool sample in a matchbox. At the interview we swapped the matchbox for a specimen pot which they were asked to fill with urine. Some passed urine so thick with blood that we were in no doubt that the child had Bilharzia. So this was why it has been called the disease that makes men menstruate. In fact about three-quarters of the Ankilivalo school children were infected with Bilharzia, half had other worms and one sixth were grossly malnourished, partly because of the debilitating effects of the parasite.

Emile breezed by from time to time and although he wanted to learn about what could be seen down the microscope, the urine and stool samples did not hold his attention for long. He excused himself saying that he had work to do at his basic little clinic and reappeared at dusk in time for us to buy him beer – if there was any in town. Our presence in Ankilivalo was a great novelty and we were constantly pursued by a comet's-tail of laughing children. Our house had no toilet so we had to devise ways of distracting the children so that we could relieve ourselves unobserved. Often it was only possible to escape into the undergrowth close to the school, when the teachers would prevent the kids following. On one necessary excursion, I found a large black and white chamaeleon; he had fallen out of a mango tree and was heading back towards the safety of its trunk. He was two feet long including his rolled tail and must have been *Chamaeleo oustaleti*, the largest chamaeleon. Madagascar boasts two thirds of the world's chamaeleons ranging in size from this one which is recorded as reaching a length of well over two feet, to the world's smallest reptile. Obligingly, it climbed onto a branch and I carried it triumphantly back to the school veranda. Appearing with the chamaeleon caused the children to scream and scatter, then turn to laugh and point from a safe distance. Why the mass hysteria? One teacher explained that chamaeleons were poisonous (which they are not); another said bad luck befell those who touched one.

Ermone Ranaivoson, a greying parasitologist lent to us by the *Institut Pasteur* in Tana, had come to help us with a survey of the snails which are intermediate hosts of Bilharzia. He led us to an area of paddy-fields close to where women did their washing, saying that this would be a good place to collect snails. It was very hot and he stood in the shade of a tree, apparently with no intention of doing any more work that day. I looked around trying to suppress my impatience. Within five minutes about thirty children had caught up with us, excited by the prospect of more entertainment. Ermone explained that they were to collect snails. Enthusiastically, they scoured the fields, irrigation canals and drains. In an hour we had hundreds of snails, including many of the species capable of harbouring the parasite. Back at the house we put each suspect snail into a separate specimen pot and watched them to see how many would shed the miniscule immature Bilharzia parasites.

Unlike at Ankàrana where we were fit and healthy most of the time, at Ankilivalo we took turns to be ill, as if the bugs that we were here to eradicate were trying to drive us away. During my worst attack, I decided dispassionately that I had meningitis. I lay vomiting with a thumping headache and photophobia, being tormented by circling whining mosquitoes, and briefly regretted that I had ever come to Madagascar. My illness proved to be only some strange short-lived tropical fever, presumably a gift of one of the mosquitoes. Next day I was still weak but back at work. Illness and poor food made life miserable; the work itself was unpleasant too because of the heat, the flies that the samples attracted and the tedium of peering down the microscope all day. It was all too easy to be distracted by the delightful lizards which skimmed across the sand of the playground. Stool samples prepared by the others would pile up as I watched the slim, fast moving little *Zoonosaurus hazofotsi*, one of the ten endemic *Zoonosaurus* lizards. They had elongated froggy back legs with huge feet and had enormously long tails which enabled them to run at amazing speed back to their burrows. *Zoonosaurus* possess a black eye-shaped spot on the top of the head – a third eye which can detect changes in light intensity and perhaps heat, too.

Food was bad and Anne had a recurring dream about owning a chocolate factory. Morale would have been desperately low but for the diverting weekend trips. Our first excursion was back to Morondava, to languish on the white sand of the palm-fringed beach, soothed by the cool fresh sea breezes and freedom from the clamouring children. The *Hotel de la Plage* had running water, fans, and sometimes electricity to power them. In the mornings we surveyed the sand-strewn streets from the hotel balcony and watched women walking back from the beach carrying unwrapped on their heads fish two or three feet long. The Urdu-speaking Muslim owners of the hotel sold imported sweets. Anne ate Mars bars for breakfast: they cost a thousand Malagasy francs, the equivalent of several days' wages for a worker on the sugar or cotton estates close by.

Just north of Morondava, towards Belo and Tsimafana, dry western forests still survive and the baobabs emerge through the canopy like misplaced giants, twice as high as the other trees and truly deserving their title of Mother-of-the-Forest. The baobab forests had their own unique fauna. Most unpleasant were the selection of particularly voracious mosquito species, many of which had been implicated in transmitting various nasty parasitic diseases and odd viral fevers. There was also the strange-looking *Oplurus* lizard, one of the six endemic species, with a spiky cheese-grater tail resembling the reamer that orthopaedic surgeons use to rasp out the centre of the femur before inserting a replacement hip joint. Iguanid lizards such as these have a bizarre worldwide distribution, like boas, they are found only in South America and Madagascar – something biogeographers are still puzzling over.

The forest was disappointingly open and degraded, but two diurnal lemurs survived here: the White Sifàka and the *Gidro, Lemur fulvus rufus*. This is a red unwhiskered form of Sanford's Lemur but nowhere near as distinguished. The male is dull red-brown with the same round eyes and foxy face as its northern brother but larger, at six pounds. They have black noses, as if they have put their heads in a coal bucket. Sadly, they were not protected by *fady* here. Emile remarked that *Gidro* were good to eat – although fruit bats, which have very fatty meat, suit Malagasy tastes better! Apparently the best time to eat lemurs is around May when they are fat after feasting on the lush vegetation stimulated by the rains. But they are easiest to catch in September, at the end of the dry season, when they are forced to seek food close to villages, congregating in the few trees which remain in leaf. No wonder they grunted with alarm whenever we saw them in the forest. The thought of people killing these placid gentle animals saddened us and we were pleased our Ankàrana lemurs would not suffer a similar fate – at least in their lifetime.

One Saturday Emile took us to some forest near his home village. As we drove past abandoned paddy-fields, Emile explained that the fall in rice prices had made it uneconomic to grow rice on this government land. Yet a few hundred yards further on, lizards fled from the blazing forest: more land was being cleared for subsistence agriculture by private individuals. A picnic of barbecued water-buffalo hearts and French bread lifted our spirits. Not far inside the forest, we encountered a troop of six White Sifàka with two-month-old infants riding piggy-back. Adults browsed in trees overhanging a dry riverbed. These were the same species we had studied in Berenty. When I met the snowy-white Sifàka again in 1986, I was startled to realise just how small and vulnerable they looked.

These animals had so delighted me in Berenty that my memory had exaggerated their size. They weigh only about one pound: a fraction of the size of the great Indri which they resemble in posture and body shape. Thinking that we wanted to see them jump, Emile shouted and threw rocks at them and they soon fled into deeper forest. I marvelled at the strength the babes had in their young fingers to be able to cling to mum's fur while she leapt five metres or more between the trees. I had hoped that Emile would have had more respect for the Sifàka and asked whether they too were hunted for food. Emile said that there was no local *fady* against killing them, but I was uncertain whether to believe him: educated Malagasy are often embarrassed to admit that anything as primitive as *fady* might still influence their lives. Even so, many worry about offending the spirits and perpetually bear a profound sense of guilt, superstition and apprehensiveness. Emile explained that people would not eat Sifàka, because they behaved so like people that it would be cannibalism. Their hands looked remarkably human and, when wounded, Sifàka even chew particular leaves to apply as a poultice. We hoped that it was not only Emile who felt bad about eating them.

I recalled the pair of Sifàka at Tsimbazaza Zoo in Tana. Whenever people visited their small cage they would say 'Mmm, Mmm' rather approvingly and leap effortlessly over to see whether the visitor had brought leaves to eat. The couple sat together on a horizontal branch, the female with her back propped against her mate's stomach. A helicopter flew over and, mistaking it for some predator, she let out an alarmed '*siff-Fak!*' and jerked her chin upwards, in so doing bashing her mate on the nose with the top of her head. She anxiously scanned the skies for the bird of prey, while he, rather dazed, blinked and looked around bemusedly, wondering what all the excitement was about. When Roo met this couple, he declared, 'They are Wonderful . . . but they have faces like ET!' I berated him for being so disrespectful to these the most graceful of lemurs. I looked at them again, trying to ignore the fact that, close up, their bare black wrinkly muzzles were not really very attractive. I told Roo why they were called Sifàka and did my best to imitate the '*siff-Fak!*' alarm call. The couple turned their heads sharply in my direction as if to ask, 'Who said that?' But, seeing no other Sifàka, looked indifferently past me.

# 11. Ranomafana Rainforest

The Province of the *Madecasses* is pester'd with a vast number of
Monkeys of several sorts. There are some . . . the colour of Bevers, their
Hair Downy, the Tail long and broad, which they turn up on their backs
to defend them from the Rain and Heat of the Sun, sleeping thus cover'd
on the Boughs of the Trees like the Squirrels . . . they have a snout like
the *Martin*, and round ears. . . . There are some as white as Snow, of the
same bigness with those above, long snouted, and grunting like Swine.
They are no where but among the Malegasses, on the red Mountains,
by the natives call'd *Amboimenes*. The natives believe the Monkeys can
speak, but will not for fear of being made to work as men do.

F. Cauche, 1651
(Translated by John Stevens, 1711)

When we had finished the ecological studies at Ankàrana and the
medical work at Morondava, I was very tempted to visit Bernhard
Meier, whom we had first met in Tana in August. He was studying
the rare Broad-nosed Gentle-lemurs in rainforest around Ranomafana
on the east coast. I wanted to visit this rainforest anyway, but after
finding the subfossils I was particularly keen to meet the last living
Broad-nosed Gentle-lemurs. I was daunted by the prospect of travelling
350 miles along bad roads, but the man at the bus station said that the
roads were much better now and the *taxi-brousse* would take just
twenty hours to drive from Morondava on the west coast to Ranomafana on the opposite side of the island. The Toyota pick-up would
leave at 6am. Having completed the medical projects, I was feeling
ready for a holiday. Simon was also keen to go. He had not experienced
Malagasy roads yet and thought I exaggerated how bad they were.
Nor had he seen many lemurs in the wild, since by the time he
arrived we had already left Ankàrana. After the heat and discomforts
of Morondava, the reputation of Ranomafana as a beautiful spa resort
in attractive forested hill country was irresistible.

Having spent so long travelling on the buses in 1981, I did not believe that the journey would take only a day. Some of the roads had been repaired and vehicle spare parts were more readily available now, but even so I doubted that the bus services would have improved that much. Sally, Simon and I booked seats and, confident of Malagasy unpunctuality, turned up at the bus station at seven-thirty. The *taxi-brousse* did not look about to leave, so we had a leisurely breakfast back at the hotel and were still able to return in plenty of time. The owner of the pick-up wanted to delay the journey for a day – or three – in order to get more passengers. Two men going to Tana and we three were the only passengers. I gently insisted that we had to travel, and to my surprise three '*chauffeurs*' prepared to leave. If we were to have three drivers, it was going to be a tough journey. We finally began the usual pre-departure tour of the town, touting for more passengers, and left, surprisingly punctually by Malagasy standards, soon after nine.

By the time we reached Mahabo, only thirty miles east of Morondava, the two co-drivers had demolished a whole bottle of rum and were giggling like schoolgirls. We waited more than an hour to refuel. Ahead of us in the queue was a lorry and all the petrol had to be pumped by hand. The drunks took the opportunity to buy more rum and press-gang more passengers. After only ten more kilometres the reasonable, if potholed, metalled road degenerated into a deeply rutted track, terribly deformed by heavy lorries. This was National Highway 35. It could have been worse: it had not rained for a few days so the mangled road was at least negotiable. We were grateful for this since there was no alternative overland route and the planes out of Morondava had inexplicably been cancelled for a few days. Anne and Maggie had opted to wait for the next flight and in the event did not reach Tana much before us, despite our tour of the rainforest en route.

The baobab horizons gave way to monotonous unproductive grasslands, dotted with palms. The road meandered miles and miles across the great flat western savannah: through the kind of habitat that covers nearly three-quarters of Madagascar. Sometimes we slalomed between telegraph poles, teetering at forty-five degrees, the wires half-supported but mostly lying across the rutted savannah. Often we had to drive over the wires and sometimes they became tangled amongst lorry wheels. We were amazed that our medical colleagues in Tana and Morondava had been able to communicate by phone when we first set up the medical projects. Surely this line was not still working?

The grasslands were strangely devoid of animals: there were just a few cattle grazing close to the infrequent villages. All the indigenous wild grazing animals were wiped out by the seventeenth century: the baboon- and deer-like Lemurs, the Malagasy Jumping Aardvark, Pigmy Hippos, two species of Giant Tortoises and the ostrich-like *Aepyornis* were all dead. The *Aepyornis* may have inspired tales of the ferocious *rukh*: the elephant-eating bird of *A Thousand and One Nights* and Hindu legends. Marco Polo, who never actually ventured as far south as the Great Island of Madagascar, wrote a fanciful account of some Malagasy animals. His *rukh* resembled a huge eagle; its feathers measured eight paces, quills two palms in circumference and its wingspan sixteen paces. Large as Madagascar's *Aepyornis maximus* might have been, it did not measure up to the *rukh*. It was nearly twelve feet tall, very powerful, and the largest bird ever to have lived. Since it weighed nearly half a ton, it comes as no surprise that it never flew.

The suspension broke. The trio of *chauffeurs* went into a huddle to discuss what to do. More giggles. Eventually they settled on the usual local solution to this problem: binding the suspension leaves together with inner tube. Further discussions, games of tag, and the repairs took an hour and a half. Wherever did these drunks find their energy in heat like this? Continuing along the appalling road, the two drunk *chauffeurs* got drunker and we nodded off, until we were woken by attempts to bump us out of another huge boggy hole in the track. Often we stopped to survey the best way through waist-deep pools that blocked the way. In places, we could drive around, but in others scrub and trees forced us to drive straight through. Perhaps the extra 'chauffeurs' were really just cheap substitutes for four-wheel drive. They often had to push the car out of the mud and thoroughly enjoyed wading and falling around in the muddy sludge. The sober driver then took great delight in driving off at top speed, spraying his drunk colleagues with soup-thick brown water, pretending to leave them behind. The giggles became even more hysterical, tears rolling down their faces as they became helpless with infectious laughter and fell back into the water.

Only about sixty miles of the road was in such bad condition but it took all day and half the night to negotiate. It was a long time after dark before we finally reached good tarmacked road and stopped at a *hotely* for some food. We were so hungry that we even enjoyed the usual lukewarm rice and thin chicken stock with fat globules congealing on the surface. We washed the fat coating from our palates with mugsfull of *ranovola* – 'golden water' made by burning some rice onto the bottom of a saucepan then boiling some water in this. We then had to make a huge detour north, almost as far as Tana, in order to join the only road across central Madagascar: the direct route had deteriorated so much that it was completely impassable.

The contrast of being on a normal road was such a relief that the sober driver decided it was now safe for him to start drinking. The other two drunks never did take over the driving, and by one in the morning the sober driver was so intoxicated that he had to pull over for a sleep. We too dozed but after a while even the ever-diplomatic Simon grew uncomfortable enough to dig the driver in the ribs to suggest we should be on our way again. Tired and tetchy, I empathised with the early etymologists who linked travel and travail with the *trapalium*, a Roman instrument of torture. Just after dawn we arrived in Antsirabé', the 'Place-of-much-salt', named because of the thermal springs. We were back up at nearly five thousand feet on the *Hauts Plateaux*. Rickshaws are in great demand in the resort of Antsirabé, to convey Malagasy and other tourists. The predatory scrawny underfed rickshaw-wallahs operate in pairs, one pulling and one pushing from behind. It seemed to be the only way to get their often hugely overweight burdens up Antsirabé's steep hills. Hence rickshaws are known as *pousse-pousse*.

We breakfasted on sweet black coffee and greasy doughnuty *mofo 'gasy*, and then squeezed aboard a Peugeot 505, to speed for three uninterrupted hours along unbelievably smooth, newly tarmacked road. Fianarantsoa, Madagascar's intellectual capital, looked livelier and richer than it had in 1981. We did not pause long there but crammed into another Toyota pick-up which took us down along the forested Mananjara River valley to Ranomafana; I spent most of the last leg of the journey having an incoherent conversation with a recumbent drunk who intermittently surfaced from between passengers' knees to tell me what a terrible place Madagascar was. Fortunately he lost consciousness at frequent intervals. Our fellow passengers alternately laughed at him, kicked him or used him as a foot rest. We had now entered Madagascar's wet zone and it was raining torrentially. The drunk did not notice that he was sleeping in water, but the rest of us all fidgeted around trying to avoid the various streams that were soon flowing through the leaking tarpaulin roof and sides of the pick-up.

The rain had eased by the time we arrived at Ranomafana – literally, 'Hot-water' – named after the geo-thermal springs which made it a fashionable French spa. Dusk was gathering and the air was beautifully fresh after the rain. The tiny scruffy village nestled in a deep, forest-clad river valley. I was almost resigned to the fact that there were no large expanses of primary forest left on Madagascar, but here there was forest as far as the eye could see. Little more than a line of shacks, Ranomafana is dominated by the huge but decaying *Hotel des Thermes*. We checked in, exhausted and filthy, but anticipating the luxury of a thermal bath and a real bed after a whole month of sleeping on a concrete floor. Sadly, the thermal bath arrived in a bucket in a vast draughty bathroom, icy cold after the sizzling temperatures of the western lowlands, but the superb food more than made up for the hotel's other deficiencies.

Next morning, much refreshed, we walked up the road towards the part of the forest where Bernhard was working. The vegetation was quite unlike the deciduous forest at Ankàrana and very different from the degraded scrub with baobabs that we had just left in Morondava. The endemic Traveller's Palm, *Ravenala madagascariensis*, was the most striking plant here. The two-dimensional, fan-like arrangement of the huge leaves make it unmistakable. It is now a distinctive feature of gardens all over the tropics: there are even life-sized plastic Traveller's Palms in Singapore Airport's shopping plaza. The name is a misnomer; it is really a fruitless banana and not a palm at all. It is even less use as a guide to travellers: the trees are supposedly aligned east-west and can thus be used as a natural compass – but in fact they may be ninety degrees out. A more convincing explanation for the name is that the boat-shaped bases of the leaf stalks, which are lined up on two sides of the trunk, hold three pints of rainwater: enough to quench the thirst of any traveller, provided he has a weapon to penetrate the leaf bases (though unfortunately this reservoir also provides a breeding ground for armies of mosquitoes). The tree has other uses, too; it has a useful woody trunk, and the banana-shaped leaves provide thatching material. There are few Traveller's Palms in undisturbed tropical forest but they spring up as soon as trees are cleared. We passed many newly cleared patches of hillside, already planted with their first crop of bananas or hill rice. These clearings were dotted with *ravenàla*. The hard blue seeds are fire-resistant, so they survive the slash-and-burn agriculture. Here the land is really too steep for cultivation and, deprived of its essential forest cover, topsoil inexorably slips away. Traditionally, land was left for ten or twenty years to regenerate and the secondary forest was home to an array of lemurs. But now, with increasing population pressure, the forest is given no chance and so soon it degenerates into barren wasteland which is good neither for agriculture nor for wildlife. As well as protecting the soil, the forest is an irreplaceable resource of innumerable valuable species.

The endemic Madagascar Rosy Periwinkle, *Catharanthus roseus*, well illustrates how useful such rainforest species can be. It is a pretty weed which is so easily cultivated that it is now found in gardens all over the world. Traditionally, it is used to cure numerous ailments and in 1949 it was tested as a possible treatment for diabetes. Far from curing diabetes, the *Catharanthus* extract actually killed the rats that were being tested by destroying their defensive white blood cells. This normally lethal side-effect was then put to good use to treat leukaemia: cancer of white cells. Now, for the last twenty years, Vincristine and Vinblastine – two of the seventy alkaloids yielded by *Catharanthus roseus* – have been used in the treatment of this and other cancers. Sadly, however, Madagascar makes no money from its life-saving native plant, since the medicines are extracted from periwinkles grown in the States. Madagascar's annual income from sales of all medicinal plants totals only about £650: world sales of Vincristine and Vinblastine in 1980 totalled £60 million. The *Catharanthus* genus contains eight species, five of which are only found on Madagascar and at least one of these is likely to become extinct before anyone investigates its pharmacology. Another is Snakeroot, a relative of plants which provide Reserpine and Rauwolfia, the powerful antihypertensive drugs. There are undoubtedly many other potentially valuable plants which are disappearing with the rainforests and with them some crucial medicines will be lost for good.

The vivacious, fashionably-dressed manageress at the *Hotel des Thermes* talked fondly of Bernhard and gave directions to his hut.

Once we were close to his patch of forest we asked after him again. Everyone smiled when we mentioned his name: clearly he had charmed people here, too. A couple of miles from Ranomafana we were directed down a path which led to a substantial wooden bridge over a fast flowing river that had cut deep into the igneous rock. Orange water, loaded with topsoil, boiled between the rapids. We crossed into the forest. The further we went in, the more we noticed that there were more differences than similarities between the flora of the Ankàrana forests and that of the eastern rainforest. Most striking were the unmistakable tree ferns. Looking like giant English bracken plonked on a tree trunk, this is a plant which is hardly different from its ancestors which grew in primeval coal forests. They have straight regular trunks perhaps a foot in diameter and fifteen feet high, and are crowned by a top-knot of fern leaves twelve feet across. Unfolding young leaves, curled in the centre of the leaf crown, looked like beckoning fingers. We emerged from the gloom of the forest into a grassy clearing. A boa was curled up and sleeping unconcernedly in the sunshine. Boas are another Malagasy oddity since they are generally considered to be South American reptiles. In Africa and Asia the big snakes are egg-laying pythons, but Madagascar's constrictors have live-born young.

As we started up a steep path made slippery by daily rainstorms, it clouded over. The dry season on this part of the island lasts only for a month. The forest was a maze of small paths and we asked directions from two women who were walking out to the road. Each carried a tree trunk on her head, but stopped to point towards Bernhard's hut. We came out into a track about thirty feet wide, savagely cleared by heavy plant as access for the imminent clear-felling. We were lost and asked for further directions. Bernhard's name once again provoked smiles and nods of approval. The rain started again just after we found Bernhard's hut. He had built it entirely from secondary forest timber: a wall–less open shelter, thatched with *ravenàla* leaves.

He suggested that one of his local helpers, Michel, take us out to see the troop of Broad-nosed Gentle-lemurs which were habituated to humans. By now rain was tipping down, but Bernhard, well used to visitors ill-equipped for the rainforest, produced oilskins and wellington boots. I declined the wellies, which were five sizes too big for me. The little forest tracks which were already muddy and slippery had turned into streams and we slithered clumsily, Simon and Sally in their over-sized boots and all of us blinkered by the hoods of our rainwear. The forest canopy was much denser than at Ankàrana but, although it was quite dark, the layer of shrubs growing beneath the trees was abundant: much of it was tangled with lianas. I tripped over several. Not far from the hut, our guide said '*Avàhy!*' and pointed up at a pair of Eastern Woolly Lemurs; an infant peered over the shoulder of its mother. Like miniature nocturnal Sifàka, they sat sixteen inches tall, with an intelligent look and an upright, trunk-clinging posture. Like the Lepilemurs at Ankàrana, they spent the hours of daylight propped in the fork of a tree sleepily surveying the forest. We watched them delightedly but they regarded us with calm indifference. As we peered and pointed enthusiastically they turned away, closing their eyes in an expression of feigned disgust. These lemurs are unusual amongst primates for being monogamous: not promiscuous like their diurnal cousins.

Becoming ever more like a stream, the path brought us into a patch of mature bamboo forest, growing thirty-feet high. I scanned the vegetation eagerly, knowing this must be the feeding ground of the Gentle-lemurs. There was movement high above me and a bamboo leaf fluttered to the ground. Suddenly I was returning the interested stare of a pair of huge round brown bush-baby eyes. They belonged, I then assumed, to a Broad-nosed Gentle-lemur, also known as the Greater Bamboo Lemur. True to his alternative name, there he was sitting upright on a thick horizontal piece of bamboo, holding two twigs, one in each hand, and looking for all the world like someone wondering how to use chopsticks. He then proceeded to eat the chopsticks, having decided that eating was a far more interesting occupation than watching me. He turned to select another bamboo morsel, nibbling the stem carefully and letting the leaf flutter to the ground. All four troop-members were busily nibbling bamboo stems, their long thick bell-rope tails dangling beneath them. They reached out and pulled the bamboo towards their mouths, bit off the best part and, feet firmly grasping the bamboo they squatted on, sat back on their haunches to enjoy their snack. Sometimes a couple would come together and break off from their feeding to groom and massage each other affectionately. Both males and females were the same attractive yellow-brown colour. They had black faces with a halo of beautiful golden eyebrows, cheeks and throat fur which extended down to the belly. The luxuriant lamb-chop sideburns made them look as if they had cheek pouches and added to the impression of being slightly too-well-fed teddies. Typical of leaf-eating lemurs, they were far from lively. Rather bear-like, they shambled around the bamboo, only rarely troubling to leap across gaps in the vegetation. The indistinct early photographs of this Gentle-lemur had failed to convey what a handsome species it was. Long thick coats, hardly wetted by the heavy rain, made them appear much larger and heftier than my athletically-built Crowned Lemurs, yet they actually weighed a little less. I threw back the hood of my cagoule and watched them for an hour as the rain continued to pelt down, running off my hair and down my back. Most of the time the lemurs browsed lazily or sauntered along bamboo branches searching for a more succulent place. Occasionally, like dogs, they shook the water from their golden coats.

Shouts came from another of Bernhard's helpers and Michel asked if we wanted to see a *Tandraka*. Yes, I said, not knowing what a *Tandraka* was. The squealing indignant beast that had been captured looked like a cross between a tiny hairy pig and an exceedingly large spineless hedgehog. The *Tandraka* sunk its teeth into its captor and, as he yelped in pain, Michel and Bernhard's other helper roared with laughter. More exclamations of pain, and the others laughed until all three were creased with mirth. The *Tandraka* is another Malagasy peculiarity; it is tailless, has a hedgehog's piggy snout, triangular face and short legs, but is quite distinct from it. Again, like most Malagasy animals, it is not related to the non-Malagasy species it resembles. It has adopted an insectivorous lifestyle and so has evolved to look like a hedgehog. This is the largest of the many endemic insectivores of Madagascar, the size of a small rabbit, and edible: the large chewing muscles are a delicacy. These Malagasy pseudo-hedgehogs belong to a group only well represented in Madagascar, but which also exist as relicts in West Africa and in the Caribbean. The shrew-like New World relative is resplendently named the *Hispaniola Solenodon*. The tenrecs were one of the earliest mammalian colonists of Madagascar, arriving long before the lemur ancestors. They range in size from the *Tandraka* to a species which weighs less than half an ounce and is just over two inches long. Tenrecs are remarkable for several reasons. They communicate with each other by rattling their spines and, since their sight is poor, they echo-locate using tongue clicks. One species boasts forty-seven vertebrae, more than any other mammal. One stores fat in its tail. Another is the most fecund of mammals: a Common Tenrec has given birth to and successfully reared thirty-one babes. This is rather poor family planning, since the maximum number of nipples recorded in this species is only twenty-nine. The smallest tenrecs are protected by detachable spines, so you will have an hour or more's work removing spines if you want to handle them.

Sally nudged me to ask what to do about the leech which was attached to her eyelid. Unsympathetically, I suggested that if any of us smoked – which none of us did – we could use the *African Queen* method of removal: applying a lighted cigarette. Simon – equally unhelpfully – volunteered that in Nepal people tied a muslin bag filled with salt onto a long stick so that the leech could be detached with a dab of the bag without the victim needing to slow their walking pace. We had no salt either and Sally was clearly unimpressed by such irrelevant suggestions, so eventually I told her that any attempt to remove the leech risked leaving bits of it behind which would cause infection. It would fall off anyway once it had finished feeding, by which time it would be so fat and bloated that it might take two hundred days to digest its meal. Until then we had hardly noticed the leeches. In some places there were none at all, but in others, tens of them beseechingly waved their revolting black bodies in the air: miniature elephant-trunks sniffing around for breakfast. They had taken up positions on vegetation near paths ready to drop onto anything warm-blooded that passed. In places, the leaf-litter writhed with them. Whenever we paused, they feverishly made head-over-tail towards our feet, climbed up over our shoes and started feeding as soon as they encountered naked flesh. I tucked my trousers into my socks after spotting the first one, but this did not keep them all out. Since they inject local anaesthetic, we did not notice the bites until our socks had grown slimy with blood and our feet were slipping around inside our shoes – the anticoagulant they secrete ensures that the painless itchy little wounds bleed long after the leech has finished feeding.

Leeches climbed over our shoes and dropped from the trees: one even fell into my cleavage. I told myself that leeches were neither painful nor dangerous: they do not even transmit disease. Yet I grappled to get it to let go, until I noticed Michel grinning broadly at me. Simon, also amused by my discomfort, assured me that Malagasy leeches were trivial in both size and numbers compared to Himalayan varieties; he described writhing anklets of bloated black bodies and large leeches attached to faces and necks, in ears and irretrievably up noses. As the rain eased we walked back to Bernhard's hut; blood was dribbling down Sally's face and our socks were pink – sodden with blood diluted with rainwater. I could feel blood dribbling down to my navel. When I removed my socks I found three leeches had squeezed between the fibres of my socks and were still feeding voraciously.

'They have had enough!' Berhard leaned forward, flicking the leeches one by one into the cooking fire. Each exploded with an impressive little *phutt*. Leeches were not the only penalty of working in the rainforest. Everything is perpetually sodden; clothes, notebooks and feet rot. Fungus grows on lenses, rendering binoculars and cameras useless in a month. Bernhard brushed such discomforts aside with a smile and talked about his work with the Gentle-lemurs. Apparently this area of forest had once been the site of a village and he pointed out South American guava trees and bamboo which so often indicates disturbance of the forest. He talked on enthusiastically. A visitor interrupted his account by whistling with delight at finding a banana, left to attract lemurs. The whistle came from a Madagascar Ring-tailed Mongoose, the same species as at Ankàrana, but duller in colour and with seven black rings on his rufus tail while at Ankàrana they had only four. A pair of magnificent Red-bellied Lemurs arrived next, lolloping along to a shrub that Bernhard had decorated like a Christmas tree with slices of fruit. The Red-bellies were a species only ever studied by Bernhard and had never been photographed in the wild. They were heavily-built animals, looking half as big again as our Crowned Lemurs and a beautiful russet colour; the male had striking white triangles beneath his eyes. We snapped away with our cameras while Bernhard fed them from his hand, being careful not to worry them by making eye contact.

There is no *fady* against killing lemurs in this part of Madagascar and I expressed fears that the habituated lemurs would be in great danger when he left. Bernhard explained that, through his local assistants, he was making good progress with conservation education. Michel and the other helpers had grown to love the lemurs and were persuading people from their villages that it was wrong to kill them. Bernhard had also shown locals how similar lemurs are to people. Just looking at the hand was enough to convince them. 'If by chance you should eat a sick lemur,' he had told them, 'surely you risk catching its illness too? Then you might die.'

I told Bernhard of my difficulties in trying to keep track of my supposedly day-active lemurs. He struggled up out of his improvised deck-chair and went to rummage in a tin trunk. He pulled out graphs of the night-time movements of his supposedly diurnal Red-bellied Lemurs. I was impressed and bewildered. How had he managed to collect such detailed data for such a perfect behaviour profile? He had tranquillised his lemurs with a dart gun and attached radio collars which transmitted signals about their movements; by operating in shifts with his assistants, he had managed to 'observe' them from the comfort of his hut and draw detailed graphs of activity for complete 24-hour cycles. I envied him his equipment.

He did not need such sophisticated techniques to study the Diademed Sifàka: the black species of the eastern rainforests. Bernhard demonstrated the pose they took up when they went to sleep at dusk and then the way he found them the next morning – with his legs crossed the other way. 'Sifàka do not have insomnia, nor do those who study them!' When I told him how much I liked Sifàka, he said that I was welcome to take over his research on them. Studying them was no challenge: they were just *too* stupid. I was mortified and felt compelled to defend the intellect of the most delightful of lemurs. Bernhard broke off his story-telling to pour out some tea and to flick another leech into the fire. It popped in a most satisfying manner and Bernhard grinned with malicious pleasure.

As soon as the Red-bellies had eaten their fill, they leapt off into the forest again and Bernhard told us about the work which had brought him to Madagascar. He was surprisingly unchauvinist in his praise of the French, describing the excellent research that had been done by French ecologists and their students. They had recognised that the Broad-nosed Gentle-lemur was in great and imminent danger of extinction; its highly specialised diet made it particularly sensitive to ecological change and forest destruction. Already it had become so rare that they wondered if there were enough to avoid the disastrous consequences of in-breeding. In the upheavals of the newly independent Malagasy Republic, the dangerously small population was thought to have died out. Then when foreigners again came to work in Madagascar in the 1980s, a population was rediscovered in Kianjavato, and then a second at Ranomafana. Its survival then seemed assured . . . until a logging company planned to decimate their forest home.

Patricia Wright from Duke University (and a team of scientists which included Martine) had come to Ranomafana and habituated four Gentle-lemurs. Thus they began a long term study to learn how best to conserve them. Later Bernhard joined the team, to continue the behavioural study, but when he learned of the felling plans he became obsessed with a rescue mission. He invited local farmers, timber merchants, a National Geographic photographer, bureaucrats, financiers and even an International Monetary Fund official to meet his lemurs and he inspired everyone with his passion for these enchanting animals – he was desperate to convince the authorities and aid agencies of the need to protect them and to establish a reserve. Dr Wright, too, began to mobilise the American conservation agencies and soon Ranomafana should become Madagascar's third National Park.

The Ranomafana Gentle-lemurs were the first that Bernhard had ever seen, and they seemed to resemble the animals featured in the few very indistinct early photographs. Bernhard and his four local helpers studied the habituated quartet and established that they ate nothing but bamboo. This was odd, for previous workers had said that the Broad-nosed Gentle-lemur ate flowers of Traveller's Trees, palm and fig fruits and leaves of other plants as well as bamboo. It would be remarkable if the Ranomafana population had different eating habits from the Broad-nosed Gentle-lemurs of Kianjavato.

Having collected a great deal of information on the habituated Gentle-lemurs, Bernhard then visited Kianjavato, setting out to survey the forests to see how common the Broad-noses were in that area. Few had ever been seen, but this was difficult country to move through and few competent scientists were capable of penetrating far into the rain-forest. He camped out – never alone, with leeches for company – and found more Gentle-lemur troops. He was puzzled by their appearance, though, for these were much larger than his habituated Ranomafana quartet and their faces were bulldog-like: almost ugly. They had huge chewing muscles and flat snouts and gave alarm calls quite unlike Ranomafana lemurs. Surely these deep rainforest animals, which he now knew were the true Broad-nosed Gentle-lemurs, were different from the Ranomafana lemurs? He realised that those four lemurs he had been studying must be something else, as yet undescribed: a new species. Three completely different Gentle-lemurs existed in the forests near Ranomafana, yet only two Gentle-lemurs were then known to science. It was no surprise to find the Grey or Lesser Bamboo Lemur, for this species is one of the most widespread throughout Madagascar: it even occurs as far north as Ankàrana. They are the smallest of the Gentle-lemurs, the size of a kitten, and they feed mostly on bamboo plus an assortment of other plants. The largest species was the true Broad-nosed Gentle-lemur which ate substantial mature bamboo stems. They were the most specialised feeders of all lemurs. Grasping four-inch diameter woody stems, they peel and shred them with their especially adapted incisors and powerful chewing muscles, leaving the bamboo in ribbons. Leaves get different treatment. They strip the indigestible fibrous outer layer away by pulling the leaf sideways with their hands, thus exposing the tender interior which they can then savour. It was no wonder that these lemurs needed to supplement their diet of indigestible woody bamboo with fruit and foliage.

Each Gentle-lemur species avoided competition with the other two Bamboo Lemurs by feeding on different parts of the bamboo. The middle-sized lemur that we had seen fed exclusively on bamboo, taking young shoots, stalks and tiny leaf stems. Bernhard called his new species the Golden Bamboo Lemur, *Hapalemur aureus*. Discovering a new species of lemur certainly seemed compensation enough to Bernhard for battling with the nightmarish leeches for so many months, but I felt sure they would have driven me mad. How thankful I was that there were no leeches at Ankàrana.

## 12. Cave Crocodiles and Trident Bats

> . . . see the havoc they [the French] have wrought in a quiet spot like
> Madagascar! Exiling a handsome woman like the Queen [Ranavolona
> III] to Algiers to fade away in homesickness. A dignified gentle woman.
> Why I've seen her disrobe and bathe amongst the crocodiles. Strip and
> swim like a web-foot! 'Twas a yearly ceremony to show her royalty to
> her people. The crocodiles, being sacred creatures, knew better than to
> touch the Queen of the Malagassies.
>
> Alfred Aloysius Horn, 1928

While my main obsession both at Ankàrana and further south
had been with lemurs, Paul had the less attractive task of studying
the Ankàrana cave crocodiles. Without boats, which were in the
missing freight, though, there was little he could do safely. Yet,
from the discussions we had had before we left Britain, I knew
he would not be put off by minor obstacles. Paul talked of the
necessity of discovering what the cave crocodiles were eating: food
and faeces are the two things that most obsess ecologists. My tales
of stomach-pumping patients inspired him to suggest that we
stomach-pump crocodiles too! He said this would be safe as long
as we (and I did not like his use of the plural) attempted this on
small individuals. Yet he was keen that the medical kits contained
plenty of strong antiseptic to clean up wounds inflicted by crocodile
teeth. Was it from bitter experience that he knew that crocodile bites
always become infected? I suggested that a dose of emetic might be
marginally more practicable, but even this would surely put Paul
(and his helper) too much at risk. In the event, Paul was reduced
to peering closely at faeces to determine what the crocodiles had
been eating.

While our little inflatable boat was still water-tight, Paul packed it
into his rucksack and, with Nick and some of the others, battled all

the way to the far end of the *Canyon Forestier* and the Second River Cave. Nick was rather an unknown quantity: he was very quiet and had not worked with any of us before. We had recruited him on the strength of his reputation and encyclopaedic zoological knowledge. Paul had great respect for his abilities and they planned to explore the cave together. As they put the boat into the water, though, Nick lost control and panicked. Splashing, talking loudly and paddling frantically, he shrieked that he would not stop paddling until they were on dry land again. Paul had no chance to watch and listen for crocodiles. Inevitably, the men teased Nick mercilessly and he withdrew deeper into his shell, becoming more and more reluctant to work.

Paul left the Second River Cave fairly sure there were no crocodiles there. Next he wanted to look in the southern caves. Base camp was ideally situated for the forest ecology projects, but it was a long way north of the large river caves rumoured to be full of crocodiles and also far from most of the massive limestones with the best caving potential. Paul joined a caving group exploring several of the large rivers which meander under Ankàrana. The team hired Simagaul's *chariot-aux-boeuf* again to carry enough food for a few days down there. With Christian as guide, they first headed south, intending to strike into the massif along the furthest of the three narrow canyons that cut into Andrafiabé Cave. Once again Christian had difficulty finding his way through the forest and so to the canyon and its stream. Tempers were frayed by fatigue, thirst and a growing tiredness that rest never quite cured, and Christian was attacked with a stream of abuse. Other cavers, embarrassed by this tirade and better appreciating the difficulties of navigation, tried to defend him and soften the insults, but the outburst caused a rift in the group. Though there were enough people for those who now loathed each other to avoid working together, bad feelings remained until all the cavers had left Ankàrana.

Just before dark, they finally found the canyon and followed it to where the impressive River Andranotsisiloha crosses it at one of its narrowest points. The river emerges from the north side of the canyon, and crosses barely fifty feet of open ground to re-enter the massif by flowing south into a beautifully smoothed arch thirty feet high and sixty feet wide. It was cool and shady and one of the most luxurious subcamps. The clear wide green river filled the entire

width of the water-worn passage and looked inviting – especially
in the shade of the cave mouth. Yet this was one cave where no
one swam. Jean had seen crocodiles there, crocodiles who would
have had nothing to eat for the whole of the six-month dry season,
and who would soon be waking – very hungry. French cavers had
cryptically renamed this river the Styx, perhaps because, at 27°C, it
was the hottest in Ankàrana. It does not of course descend into hell,
but meanders three miles through the massif until it surfaces near
Ambody Pont as the River Ankàrana: the river that Anne, Maggie
and I had waded across when we had first walked to base camp.
Despite the crocodiles, the cavers were keen to explore the entire
subterranean course of the river, expecting it to lead into new cave
systems and more forests. Roo and Mick set off in the tiny patched
yellow inflatable boat. Dwarfed by the intimidating size of the huge
rounded passage, they soon disappeared around a bend in the
river. The others busied themselves with camp chores or teased
the lethargic six-foot-long Ground Boa which shared their campsite.
Minutes later the boat reappeared with Roo and Mick paddling
frantically. The boat was deflating rapidly and they thought they
were fleeing for their lives. Perhaps they were. No one saw
crocodiles there, but then you seldom do . . . until it is too late.

They repatched the boat and Simon made another attempt
to explore. The boat deflated again and this time he was
terrorised by large aggressive eels. These were frightened of nothing,
even, Simon claimed, rearing out of the water to attack when
sufficiently provoked. They were four-foot-long muscular animals
with ferocious teeth. The lads tried to catch some. They tied a bent
nail into some strong nylon rope and baited it with dried fish. An
eel took the bait enthusiastically and, in the struggle which ensued,
the rope broke (bitten through?) and the eel made off, having
swallowed bait, nail and a length of rope as well. Despite using
increasingly larger and stronger fishing tackle, spears and hooks,
the lads never managed to secure a specimen. Fortunately we were
never aware of the eels while we bathed, although there was one in
every river cave we explored.

The inevitable noise of the ten people at the Styx subcamp
made the crocodiles too wary to show themselves. Paul, reasoning
that he would need to work alone to see any, left the others and
headed further south to search the big rivers which resurge at that

end of the massif. He wanted to determine how large the Ankàrana crocodile population was, whether they were adapted to life in caves and how threatened they were by hunting. This research would not be easy, deprived as he was of a decent boat. The leaky little inflatable did not now stay up for more than five minutes and sturdier boats Paul had intended to use for his crocodile research were In The Freight.

Simagaul, thinking Paul's project beyond reason, gave the lone explorer a load of cooked rice. Paul took it to be polite, but was then grateful for Simagaul's thoughtfulness when he discovered that his one matchbox contained only spent matches. By the second day, however, the rice, although still just edible, had fermented, and this – combined with fatigue and dehydration – induced surreal hallucinations. By the third night, the rice had turned blue-green and smelt strongly of old socks, so Paul dined on cold soaked noodles. During three miserable days alone, he searched most of the southern river caves. Following one modest-sized river upstream led him into a subterranean chamber mostly occupied by the river. He scanned around with his light and was alarmed to see tens of unblinking pink eye-reflections shining back from what little dry land there was. The wide spacing of some pairs of eyes told him that some very large individuals had taken refuge here. Was the twenty-foot-long crocodile that Jean had seen in here too? Paul made a hurried population estimate and left.

Crocodiles are cold-blooded creatures, but maintain a fairly constant body temperature by spending nights in rivers, basking each morning and evening, and retreating to the water or shade at the hottest time of the day. Most cave waters were well below the temperature at which crocodiles become inactive. If their body temperature fell below 26°C they would be too sluggish to feed, even if there was anything for them to eat. Temperature is crucial for breeding, too: if crocodile eggs are incubated at too low a temperature only males hatch. What were they doing in the caves, then? They could not raise their body temperature by basking here unless roofs had collapsed to allow the sun to warm places suitable for basking and egg incubation.

The reptiles that Paul saw were ordinary Nile Crocodiles, not at all suited to a cave-dwelling existence, but forced to retreat into the caves to keep cool when the marshes of southern Ankàrana dry up each year. The crocodiles fast until October when the rains make the marshes good feeding grounds again and they can emerge to breed. People living around the south of Ankàrana were very frightened of crocodiles: all the footpaths avoided rivers and marshes that were good wet-season crocodile habitats. Paul returned the following year, equipped with good strong boats, and looked for nesting and basking sites along the river banks. The Mananjeba River, which resurges from the massif, has gouged a deep course out of the savannah. Paul was navigating this in a small boat when he heard a sound above him and a huge crocodile suddenly appeared on the bank ten feet above. She launched herself from her nest site, rocking the boat as she hit the water.

The Antankarana claimed ignorance of crocodile-hunting, although we heard that there were annual hunts in October and November. Yet they warned that crocodile fat is poisonous: a fact that would only be of interest to those who eat crocodiles, or else to people like the Sri Lankans who say that reptile fat (extracted by hanging a Water Monitor over a fire and catching dripping), smeared on a plate or glass, is enough to dispatch an enemy. At Ankàrana, the crocodiles were not used to poison people, nor were they protected by *fady*, and people brought crocodiles to sell. Just fifteen miles away at Lake Anivorano, though, taboo keeps them safe from hunting.

We had read that crocodiles were all but extinct on Madagascar and that their only remaining refuges were a few regions where access is difficult, such as the subterranean rivers of Ankàrana or the sacred lakes like nearby Anivorano. However, the abundance of crocodile products in Tana's *zoma* had already made us doubt this. When we asked a stall-holder where his stuffed hatchlings and crocodile skin handbags came from, he told of rivers full of large crocodiles around Mahajanga. Indeed the original site of this ancient tribal capital was at Morovoay ('Where-there-are-Many-Crocodiles') further up the River Betsiboka. People in the Morondava region also talked a great deal of the dangers of crocodiles. A cartoon painting on a Sakalava tomb explained why: it showed a crocodile which had a hold of a man's leg (presumably how one occupant of the tomb had died). Dr Razafindrakoto, the local public health chief, also told us of a woman who had been taken by a crocodile that same year, not far from the tombs, while she was washing near Tsimafana in the River Tsiribihina (which so aptly translates as 'Where-one-should-not-dive' for fear of crocodiles). Crocodiles were certainly being over-exploited, but perhaps they are not yet quite as rare as the experts think.

☆

As September wore on the freight became a sick joke. Whenever anyone asked for anything, there would be a chorus of 'Sorry, it's in the freight!' It explained anything that went wrong and was the perfect excuse to avoid unpopular work. Although we did have equipment in the freight, what we really missed was the biscuits, milk and other goodies. Paul's crocodile work and Mick's bat study were the only projects which really suffered. While waiting for his harp traps to arrive, Mick spent many '*stressant*' evenings tangled in what looked like forty-foot hair nets, which caught trees, him and even passing zebu more effectively than his intended quarry. He only ever caught one forest-flying bat. Relief came on the eighteenth: the day that Dave Checkley and Sheila departed and the last four biologists arrived – Ben, Sally, Dave Clarke and Guy-Suzon. Ben brought a harp trap and Sally, knowing all about the miseries of expedition life from her experiences on the Sarimanok Expedition, brought Mars bars from England and fresh fruit. By now food fantasies were pestering us. We had grown tired of our rice-and-beans diet and longed for some culinary treats. I dreamt of crisp green apples and freshly ground black pepper and the lads discussed chocolate and beer at length. Ben, a bat boffin who made his living from organising fireworks displays, brought with him specialist equipment including a huge half-plate camera, tripod and a battery of big flash-guns and – just as important – Darjeeling tea and real English biscuits. Greedy eyes soon fell on Ben's biscuits.

Ben had already done nine months' fieldwork in the jungles of Sulawesi and had been on another expedition to Ecuadorian rainforest, so I rather assumed he would come better equipped than he did. He and his girlfriend, Jessica, had to resort to sleeping on a heap of leaf-litter and borrowed mosquito nets.

When he appeared for breakfast the first morning in a blue silk dressing gown and slippers, I feared that he would not be staying with us for long. He was a dedicated scientist, hopelessly impractical and ill-equipped for expedition life. Straight away, though, he settled down to work by putting his equipment together. We watched as he placed his harp trap across one of the newly cut forest trails. This, he said, was a likely flight path for the smaller bats. We were doubtful, for although we had seen innumerable bats flying low through this clearing, Mick had failed to catch any there with his mist nets.

But the trap was spectacularly effective. The first the bats knew of it was when they hit the spring-loaded wires which knocked them into a cloth bag below, without damaging their delicate wings. Once in the cloth bag, each bat would crawl to a place where it could hang up, until released. The bats Ben caught in his trap were different species from Mick's dull cave-roosting 'evening' bats. The most attractive were two-inch Rufus Trident Bats, with rich red-brown and white armpits, and delicate, extremely complex, nose-leaves in the form of a splendid three-pronged fork plonked on their noses.

Ben and Jessica next became preoccupied with the construction of what they called a photographic studio for bats. They made a simple wooden frame lined with reflecting silver foil scavenged from our chocolate bars (we watched suspiciously as he unwrapped our coveted rations). The close-up portraits of even the tiniest bats that he produced with the frame, his bank of flash-guns and half-plate camera were stunning. The photos highlighted all the grotesque details of the bats' lepromatous faces and wrinkly nose-leaves. Concerned that Jessica might get bored while Ben was engrossed in his bat work, I asked her what she would like to do. 'My one ambition,' she said, 'is to climb a tree and write a letter! It would be inspiring to be able to write up there with the lemurs.' She was content swanning around camp, eyeing up various unclimbable trees, but never fulfilled her ambition.

Once Ben had collected a good range of forest bats, he asked about suitable caves where he might find other species. The First River Cave was the longest nearby and was in one of the most densely forested parts of the *Canyon Forestier*. When he heard that it was only an hour's walk from camp, Ben agreed to visit it with us. It took three attempts to find the way into the narrow canyon, despite the marks left by previous parties. We scrambled up and down over basalt hillocks and squirmed between tangles of thick woody lianas. Soon the canyon narrowed and we were guided by its sheer walls –

even the incompetent could not get lost here. The original limestone floor of the *Canyon Forestier* had been buried beneath huge waves of lava that had surged in and cooled into basalt. Our route took us to the top of a basalt wave, 150 feet high, then down into a trough and up and down again. The ground dropped away so steeply in places that we swung on lianas or grabbed branches to slow our descent. The eruption which produced all this larva had cracked the limestone into segments, and spurted molten rock under such great pressure and with such high speed that it penetrated well over a mile inside the massif. The forest became much darker as the canyon narrowed to less than fifty feet across, but was still a hundred and twenty feet deep. Lack of light kept the undergrowth sparse, so that we could see that some trees had spectacular buttresses and many had substantial lianas looped between them, carelessly strewn about like grotesque party streamers. Others had been attacked by strangler-figs. These begin harmlessly enough, just using the tree for support, but then slowly grow, embracing and enmeshing the trunk and finally squeezing the life out of it. Occasionally we saw that the host tree had completely disintegrated, leaving light streaming through the strangler vine like a huge, coarse, brown, rolled up doily. Scattered between the trunks were termite hills, looking like five-foot-high crude terracotta pyramids, but built by yet another group of high endemicity: seventy-one out of the island's seventy–five termite species are unique to Madagascar.

Dave was in his element and happily pottered along, telling tales which proved, to him at least, that flies and beetles have personalities, too. Then suddenly, in uncharacteristic agitation, he shouted: 'Look out!' I stopped, peered, and then focused on a spider-web, six inches from my nose. A red and black Orb Spider was at its centre. I asked Dave if it was dangerous: 'No, not really. I've got several living free in my office in London. I just didn't want you to damage her web. Isn't she beautiful?'

Continuing, we scrambled down along the left canyon wall. The ground, previously covered by undulating black basalt, gave way to limestone where different plant species dominated. This was as far as the lava had penetrated. Angular grey boulders, no longer buried under basalt, protruded from the earth. The ground became so steep that I slithered down on my haunches, lost my balance and skied down on the seat of my pants into a dry river valley littered with huge limestone blocks and dunes of silt. Ben and the others followed in a more controlled manner. In the wet season a large river must resurge from the bottom of the right side of the canyon and cross a hundred and fifty feet to disappear into the base of the cliff on the left side: at the First River Cave. All over Ankàrana the subterranean rivers flowed across the canyons, rather than along them, in a puzzling pattern of superimposed drainage. The Ankàrana caves and their subterranean rivers must have formed long before the canyons and, when the massif was cracked from top to bottom by the eruption, the new canyons thus formed must have cut into the caves, segmented the massif, and divided the cave systems. We had already emerged from caves elsewhere in Ankàrana and found ourselves in the bottom of a deep canyon from whence it was possible to enter further passages leading from the far side of the canyon.

Ben struggled along at the back slowing us so much that it took two hours to reach the First River Cave. I pointed out its entrance, a small gap in the boulders where the dry riverbed met the left canyon wall, and said that by climbing through the cave they could reach the next forest pocket, the *Canyon des Anglais Perdus*. Ben and Dave went in to explore.

'Hey! Come and look at these!'

I scrambled inside in response to Dave's enthusiastic invitation, and sat down to allow my eyes to accommodate to the darkness; the twittering of bats was just audible above the sound of moving water. Dave pointed out 'lots of lovely Orb Spiders'. I was hoping to see something more interesting than spiders and left Dave contentedly looking around, while learned 'Hmms' and 'Ahhs' came from Ben, who was now somewhere deeper into the cave – then: 'Ah, *Miniopterus major* and *minor* too!' and 'Hey, Jane! I need a six-foot stick.'

I cut a small sapling with the machete and passed it in. Ben then busied himself capturing these common bats which roost in almost every Ankàrana cave; they did not fly low enough to be caught in his harp trap. I left the two of them in the cave, and went to learn some botany from Guy-Suzon. He was hyperactive, knowledgeable, spoke French as fast as Patrick Moore speaks Astronomy and worked at such a rate that after only a week his flower press was a foot high and bursting with specimens. He was amazed at the botanical

wealth of Ankàrana and impressed by the strange forms that plants
had adopted to cope with the harsh conditions on the *tsingy*. He
would send a post-graduate student to begin some research here.

A while later Ben emerged from the cave: a startling ghostly-white
lanky form, dripping wet and wearing nothing but a disintegrating
saggy straw hat, a pair of stripy boxer-shorts and green felt boots.
He had finished peering at bats and taken a bath, but was not much
refreshed and was staggering with exhaustion by the time we got
back to camp. However would he be able to walk as far as the big
bat roosts? I wanted to show him Antsiroandoha Cave: a gaping
black gash in the Ankàrana Wall, which, at dusk, issues thousands
of large *Eidolon* fruit bats: their name appropriately meaning
phantom. They were a terrific sight and even sitting in the entrance
chamber sixty feet beneath them, their wings stir the air. During the
day the bats squabble or poke a neighbour with the long skeletal
thumb on the leading edge of the wing. Others fan themselves with
one wing to keep cool. Walking beneath them induces them to
squawk noisily or make strange squelching and clicking sounds.
Mounds of undigested ebony seeds beneath the roost make the air
fetid, but deeper inside the cave was a wonderland of glistening
white stalactites, stalagmites and columns, wafer-thin translucent
calcite curtains, sparkling crystal floors, gour pools and terraces
in passages sixty feet in diameter. My description failed to inspire.
Poor Ben could not face the two-hour walk to the cave. Life at
Ankàrana was bewildering and even a bloodied shin from a tiny
cut (the second injury inflicted by the edge of a palm leaf) caused
him great distress. The macho cavers teased him mercilessly and
someone told him to be careful of crocodiles when he went into
the cave bathroom to wash. The cruel joke back-fired somewhat
when Nick thought he saw a crocodile there. I wondered how Ben
had managed in Indonesia and Ecuador. His previous trips had
been with military-style expeditions, living in large camps or even
bungalows, with teams of sappers on adventure-training detailed to
feed and pamper impractical scientists.

Our idyllic campsite was too basic for Ben and after just seven
days he and Jessica made their escape. They hired a bullock cart.
None of us ever wanted to ride in one of these because they moved
slower than the slowest walking pace and lack of suspension made
them very uncomfortable, but Ben and Jessica did not feel up to

walking. Guy-Suzon, with a bloated lower lip from a wasp attack, left with them to sail to the little uninhabited island of Nosy Hara (where wasps got him again). There his mission was to see whether the plants were suitable to support Perrier's Sifâka and Crowned Lemurs until a real reserve could be set up to protect them. The vegetation was fine and a few months later couples were released and a small lemur colony now seems to be thriving there, safe from human interference.

Dave slotted into expedition life as if he was born to it.
He was the only member of the expedition without a formal scientific education and was full of self-deprecating remarks about how little he knew, yet he was probably the most able fieldworker amongst us. He had come to work on a Swallow-tailed butterfly, *Papilio dardanus meriones*. By Swallow-tail standards this is not a particularly attractive insect, but Dave's sponsor, Sir Cyril Clarke, needed them for his continuing research on inheritance which had led to his discovery of the treatment for Rhesus Disease in newborn babies. The butterfly had no common name and its Latin title was too long, so we called them after this learned man. People would shout: 'Look, there goes a Sir Cyril!' And Dave would sprint off in pursuit waving his butterfly net.

# 13. The Cave Waterhole

Courage is the price that life extracts for granting peace
The soul that knows it not, knows no release
From little things;
Knows not the livid loneliness of fear
Nor mountain heights where bitter joy can hear
The sound of wings.

Amelia Earhart, 1926

The others maintained that leaving base camp at five in the morning was madness. They already thought I was deranged for habitually starting work at first light, but I had to work when the lemurs were active. We had a lot of ground to cover though; they conceded that an early start would mean a more comfortable walk while it was still cool and we would be beyond a particularly unpleasant, scorched section of the canyon before it got too hot. When we finally got away at seven o'clock, it seemed very late to me. Paul was to be our guide. He had been on one of the early trips to explore the *Canyon Forestier* and he had persuaded me that the Second River Cave was *the* place for lemur watching. Anne and Maggie were keen to work where there were better views of the lemurs. Dave also wanted to come but, by now, he had various butterfly families to look after and he dared not desert them even for a couple of days. The forever smiling Jean-Elie (now sprouting a splendid white beard) also wanted to come with us. He too now had a large collection of butterflies and I wondered why he wanted so many examples of the same species. Later I discovered that he supplemented his meagre government wage by selling them to foreign dealers. So that was it – he wanted to collect from a new habitat: *'Bien sûr, Madame Jane. On y va!'* He always called me *Madame Jane* unless he was looking for a medical consultation, when I was forewarned by a *'Pardonnez-moi, Docteur Jane. . . .'*

Paul had a year's experience of jungle navigation in the Amazon and I was pleased to be following him. I had already been lost too many times in dense forest. Half a mile of easy walking along the old logging track brought us into the funnel-shaped mouth of the *Canyon Forestier*, a side turn leading off the *Canyon Grand* where we had our base camp. Initially, the forest was fairly open and we easily found the cuts on trees made by our earlier exploring parties: what was so difficult about jungle exploration? A few metres further on, though, lemurs grunted their disapproval as we crashed clumsily around, lost yet again in thick undergrowth, and we were backtracking, fanning out to search for the lost trail. Only a week before I had got lost here taking Ben to the First River Cave. We found marks again, but then realised we had walked in a circle and were almost back at the canyon mouth. We tried one more time, eventually found the place where we had gone wrong, and continued on through the forest, now hardly needing to use the machete.

The forest was alive with birds. Up in the canopy were unidentifiable small brown birds, and yellow-cheeked Northern Jeeries feasting on insects and nectar, or Hook-billed Vangas looking out for tasty lizards. Closer to the ground were clumsy Crested Couas, busy little Button Quails scuttling in the litter, turkey-sized Helmeted Guinea-fowl and the very shy skulking Madagascar Crested Wood Ibis. The local name for this rare bird translates as 'wild chicken' – it is hunted for food. Frequently the systematic scrabbling noise betrayed a pair of Mesites as they looked for insects on the forest floor. Jean-Elie pointed out perky musical Madagascar Magpie Robins, Stonechats and strange shrike-like Vangas. The canopy blotted out too much light for photographing the birds and I wondered what chance I would have of taking good pictures of lemurs in the gloom of the cave waterhole that was our destination.

This time it took less than an hour to reach the First River Cave, and we entered to refill our water bottles. Getting to the little subterranean river involved an easy scramble between boulders; there was almost enough light to navigate to the water without a torch, or so I thought until I tripped over the six-foot pole that Ben had used to collect his bats the week before. I wished I had spent more time in there, for the following year Paul found, inside the same cave, sections of upper jaw and limb bones from an extinct giant lemur, *Paleopropithecus*.

Refreshed with cool cave water, we continued, initially along the dry riverbed. The wet season floods had scoured away the trees so there was little shade. The obvious way on was straight down the middle of the canyon through a large expanse of soft, waist-high grass. The going looked easy there, but Sheila and Dave had told us that when they had taken this route innumerable barbed grass seeds had penetrated their clothes, stabbed their flesh and driven them mad: nasty irritating seeds which were so difficult to remove. Forewarned, we skirted around close to the right-hand canyon wall. Yet we could not avoid the grass completely and an hour later we looked like grooming lemurs, squatting to extract the last seeds from hair and clothes.

Before long we were back into the welcome shade of the forest. Paul led up and down over ridges, leaping easily from boulder to limestone block to boulder, despite all the heavy camera gear in his rucksack. I followed, lumbering clumsily and jumping gingerly, imagining the skin sutures that would be needed if one of us slipped. I was not feeling at all intrepid and swore under my breath at my rucksack which kept catching on lianas and spikes of limestone. Next time I would bring a rucksack without protruberant side pockets. The long-handled shrimp net that I was carrying also hampered my progress. In spite of the difficult terrain, we kept losing the middle-aged Jean-Elie, as he sped off spouting Latin names and waving his butterfly net. Lunch was hard-boiled eggs and – a great treat – dried bananas, washed down with water already warm and tasting of plastic.

A movement caught my eye; although the lizard was vivid green, superbly marked with eight scarlet flecks on its back, it was almost impossible to see until it moved. It had the flattened expanded fingertips typical of Day Geckos; this one was *Phelsumia madagascariensis*, representing yet another very geographically restricted group, peculiar to Madagascar and neighbouring islands only as far afield as the Andamans. The Day Gecko posed beautifully, meticulously windscreen-wiping its eyes with its bright pink tongue. Then, as the camera shutter clunked, it darted around to the far side of the tree trunk. I was left with a portrait of a piece of bark. I chased it and wasted several more photographs but never captured it on film.

We had not left early enough and the hottest part of the day was upon us, just as the forest thinned out again. The ground became drier, and the diversity and luxuriance of the trees dwindled until the forest comprised just one species. This was a *Mesonovum*, a leguminous twenty-foot tree, with a spiny bark. Strangely, the same species also managed to grow on bare limestone where it took on the form of a straggling thorny vine. The scanty pinnate leaves were covered in silt. Silt and sticks stranded over one hundred feet up on the canyon walls were evidence of the dramatic floods which sweep through the massif. Jean told us how, after a cyclone, whole canyons appear from the air to be completely filled with water – not altogether surprising when you consider that almost all of the 2000mm of rain which falls annually occurs in only six months. For half the year, then, plants need to survive near-total drought, but when the rains come they have to cope with complete submersion. Few plants are that adaptable and so here the vegetation is limited to one kind of tree and a few miserable shrubs. Paul spotted some lemur faeces: evidence that during the wet season, when there are buds and fruits on the trees to sustain them, lemurs expand their territories from the canopy forests far into areas which seemed dry and inhospitable now.

Eventually, even the trees thinned out and the vegetation merged into a vicious thorny colourless xerophytic scrub. We were now a long way from any subterranean rivers and there was no shade and no shadows. The sun scorched and dazzled us. Jean-Elie stayed with us now for there were no insects for him to catch. The only evidence that there had ever been life here were some empty nymph skins, left clinging to rocks after the adult bug had hatched. Even these were coated in silt. We were now in a tangle of thin but exceedingly strong lianas and spiky bushes not much taller than ourselves. They looked fragile enough to yield to the rhinoceros technique – head down and charge – but we ended up throttled with lianas around our necks, rucksacks and legs and, as we laboriously cut ourselves free, we cursed the cumbersome backpacks we carried. Crawling on all fours got us into an even worse state: scratched, stung, hooked up, frustrated, hot and very thirsty. A path had already been cut by Dave and Sheila, but we had lost the trail a long way back – in the harsh midday sun it was impossible to see where the lianas had been severed. Cut stems normally stand out as lighter than the rest of the vegetation, but now everything had assumed the same bleached hue. We noticed tracks but they could not have been made by human feet, for the lianas above were parted only a couple of feet: not enough

space even to crawl along with our bulky rucksacks. Did wild pigs
come here? We continued hacking through each liana with the blunt
machete, taking it in turns to vent our spleen on the tangle, while
someone else attempted to navigate.

Parched and exhausted, we reached the summit of yet another pile
of river silt, to be startled by a vision of lush vegetation. Waist-high
grass – almost lurid in its luxuriance – grew in a dry river valley and,
beyond, was a glade of trees. It was a strange place and after battling
through the desert of tangled, lifeless scrub it was like arriving
on another planet. We brushed through the soft grass, crushing
herbs underfoot, and were greeted by delicious aromatic smells like
lavender: perfumes to make the plants distasteful to herbivores.

Following the riverbed, we were dwarfed by spindly *Ricinus
communis* plants, over ten feet high, looking like an etiolated
cassava plantation. Prickly seed-pods exploded with a crack in
the sun and showered us with little shiny beans. Then the scene
changed as trees one hundred and twenty feet high arched over
the riverbed. Rounding a bend, the dry riverbed continued until
it stopped abruptly in a chaos of limestone boulders at the base of
a two-hundred-foot cliff. A huge block, the size of a house, teetered
on the cliff edge, high above us, ready to join many others below.
We peeled off our rucksacks and steam rose from our sweat-sodden
backs. It had taken us five hours to cover less than two miles between
base camp and this the Second River Cave. There were still several
hours before dark, however: time enough to wash, set up camp,
collect firewood and water. But where was the water? Paul led us
over the boulders to the entrance of the cave, while Anne disappeared
behind a bush.

The cave entrance looked neither inviting nor impressive but I
followed enthusiastically, thinking of cool fresh water. Inside, the
boulders were covered in mud and the smell of swift guano filled my
nostrils: this was not the idyllic spot that Paul had described. After
the glare outside, it was difficult to see, so I squatted down, waiting
to adjust to the gloom. As my eyes accommodated, I saw a different
cave. A deep still turquoise lake, looking invitingly cool, snaked away
into the bowels of the earth. Sunlight streamed in, reflecting as ripples
on the low roof. I wanted to swim, but first asked Paul about crocs.
He did not sound as sure as I would have liked when he said that he
thought there were none.

Maggie and I sent him out with full water bottles and then stripped off and slid gingerly into the water. Delicious! We had not intended to venture in very far, but could not keep our footing on the slippery mudbanks and soon slipped in out of our depth. Taking it in turns to keep watch made us feel safer, despite knowing that even if the look-out saw a crocodile, she would not be able to warn the bather in time. We became aware of Anne's voice, complaining. She pushed past me, swearing and giggling at once, and plunged into the water fully dressed. She had brushed against a strongly perfumed groundsel-like herb while squatting in the grass and had picked up a tenacious irritant oil on her skin. Quite different from the grass that had tortured Sheila and Dave, this was yet another hazard that we learned to avoid.

As we dried off, there were splashes from inside the cave. We looked at each other nervously. I tried to sound confident when I explained that our ripples had disturbed some of the mudbanks. Maggie looked unconvinced, but as the noise died away we began to doubt our senses. We sat listening quietly for more clues but nothing broke the eerie silence.

By the time we emerged from the cave, Jean-Elie had collected a pile of firewood as tall as himself and Paul was building a fireplace of rocks, with a tripod of branches to support a pot. While Paul and Jean-Elie were bathing we boiled up some noodles and onions to accompany a tin of much-coveted corned beef. Pudding of dried bananas – for the second time that day – and black coffee and we were satisfied, content and ready for our sleeping bags.

The leaf-litter rustled close by. There was as yet insufficient food for forest rodents or tenrecs, so what else would be large enough to make this scrabbling sound? It turned out that most of the noise was coming from a small scorpion, already half-eaten but still trying to escape from a larger member of its own species intent on devouring it. Scorpions are ferocious nocturnal hunters, invertebrate thugs, partial to the occasional cannibalism. Their courtship rituals make them seem more civilised, however. The male clears an area of leaf-litter where he cements his spermatophore – a sperm-containing capsule; he then grabs his lady-love in his crab-like claws and, in what looks like a barn-dance routine, tries to drag her over the spermatophore. She plays hard-to-get and drags him the other way. Once the female's genital opening touches the spermatophore, it explodes and deposits enough semen to fertilise her.

☆

At first light some crawling thing fell onto my face and I picked it up before it wandered too close to my mouth. It was a slim, half-inch-long beetle, sporting luxuriant handlebar-antennae as long as its body. Dave would like this one, but it had toppled into the leaf-litter and disappeared before I had struggled out of my hammock. Stretching, stiff-backed, I peered around to see where the others were sleeping. Jean-Elie was the only one visible. He had excavated a little shelf in the riverbank and was snoring loudly. On my way into the cave to fill the jerry can with water, I found Maggie. She had chosen for her bed an unusually flat smooth sacrificial slab amongst the boulders.

Later that afternoon a lone female Crowned Lemur, passing on her usual route to the cave, arrived on a rock level with where Maggie had slept. She, Maggie, had left her lurid red sleeping bag and bright blue rucksack out on the slab amongst the boulders. The lemur stood up high on extended hind legs to peer at this new addition to her environment. Suspiciously, she skirted it to view it from several angles but soon established that it was neither predator nor food, lost interest and continued over the boulders and into the cave. Subsequently, that female hardly gave Maggie's 'bed' a passing glance.

Maggie was waking up as I passed.

'Coffee?'

'Mmm, yes please.'

The breakfast fire was soon crackling and Paul and Anne emerged from the forest on opposite sides of the riverbed, beckoned by the thought of coffee. Although we were surrounded by forest, it was difficult to find two trees substantial enough to support a hammock. Paul and Anne had gone quite a way before finding trees the right distance apart. Idleness had made me choose two saplings very close by, but they bowed so much when I swung into the hammock that within ten minutes my bottom was resting on the ground. I could not get comfortable, bent at such a peculiar angle, but was too lazy to get up and search for a better site. My sloth was rewarded by a backache.

Sitting on the sand, tucking into maize porridge, I noticed a movement at my feet. A tiny track excavated by an invisible engineer was appearing in the riverbed. I looked closer. The minute track grew longer, meandering across the silt. Gently I probed the sand with a twig and caught a glimpse of a pair of little pincers. I scooped up a handful of sand and, blowing it away, saw the creature: an ugly obese ant-lion, determinedly trying to bury itself bottom first in a crease in my palm. The insect was a fraction of an inch long but over one quarter of it was mouth-parts. This miniature monster would hatch out into a totally harmless doodlebug: looking like a disproportioned dragonfly with wings too big for it and whose function had to be determined by experiment. We watched the ant-lions hunt, buried at the bottom of a conical pit three quarters of an inch across. As unsuspecting ants walked close to the edge of the pit, the ant-lion flicked sand at them so that they toppled down into his jaws.

Pock-marks in the silt showed where larger engineers had been at work in the riverbed. So the tracks in the dry part of the *Canyon Forestier* must have been pig tracks. I had also seen pig in the forest bordering the savannah: they were large, very shy animals standing nearly two feet at the shoulder. Later I asked Jean Radofilao whether the wild pigs were protected by *fady*; he explained that the taboos that the Malagasy call *fady* were tremendously complex. Amongst the Antankàrana, for example, some members of a family would eat wild pig while others were forbidden to do so. Whatever the *fady* ruled about eating, however, the local Antankàrana were happy to kill wild pigs to sell to us. As conservationists, we resisted the culinary temptation: some with more difficulty than others.

Although the sun appeared quite early from behind the cliff above the cave, it was late morning before it illuminated the lemurs' route to the subterranean waterhole. They rarely came to drink before midday, so I decided to look for other animals inhabiting the river cave and try to catch the white fish Paul had seen in there on his previous visit. He had found no droppings and no tracks, but he could not be sure that there were no crocodiles in the cave. In early September (when they had first visited the cave) crocodiles would still be inactive and so difficult to see, Jean Radofilao had said. But by the time we made this return trip to the cave it was late September and we could expect the crocodiles to start waking up – (although Paul had almost convinced me that this cave was too cold to be a suitable crocodile lair. The water in the Second River Cave was only 21°C – a full six degrees cooler than the Styx and the southern river caves where crocodiles had been seen. Since the lowest temperature at which crocodiles can be active is around 26–27°C, even if there was a crocodile inside, it would be too sluggish to be harmful. Jean had also reassured us that the crocodiles did not become aggressive until October. It was still September – just.

Jean was convinced there was a crocodile in the Second River Cave, although not a particularly large one. Since he had seen one 'approximatively' seven metres long, I did not want to meet even one that he might classify as small. Knowing that I planned to swim into the cave, he had commented that crocodiles could not attack while you were in deep water; but he then added, with a wry smile, that it was not possible to stay in deep water for ever. I imagined treading water in the gloom while salivating crocodiles patiently watched! Large crocodiles do not hunt in deep water but catch animals at waterholes. They swim at full speed for the bank, then just before they run aground, they use their front legs to launch themselves at their prey, exploding out of the water before the victim has a chance to realise its fate. Smugly smiling, inert and benign-looking, resting crocodiles appear incapable of such dynamism and all too easily lull people into a false sense of security. However, recalling my scarred patient in Southampton and those malign beasts at Tsimbazaza zoo revived my anxieties.

The river filled the entire width of the cave passage so the only way to keep out of the water was to use a boat. The inflatable was now useless; the thin ancient plastic punctured easily on the sharp limestone and the innumerable repair patches took it in turns to unglue themselves. I was nevertheless determined to collect the cave fish that Paul had seen inside. It was sure to be a species unknown to science. I asked if there was anything I could do if a crocodile did attack me. 'Oh, just poke it in the eye and it will let go!' advised Paul.

'Oof.' The cold clear still river took my breath away. With the rolled up Karrimat under my arm for buoyancy, I gently cruised forward trying to make not a ripple. I swam slowly, for the riverbed was littered with jagged rock spikes and ridges which would lacerate if I kicked out too vigorously. At the first bend in the river, I managed to get my feet down on a flat boulder and stand up chest-deep in water. The view back to the entrance was beautiful. Shafts of daylight streamed in through the leaves, lighting up the water to a superb turquoise. Blue-green ripples played on the flat cave roof. A silhouetted Paul asked 'OK?' Yes, I was fine, reassured there was someone close by.

Sinking onto my Karrimat again, I continued in, out of my depth and out of sight of the entrance now. Alone. The ripples made slopping noises as they hit the mudbanks and miniature land-slips plopped into the river. This was the noise we had heard when we first bathed here; I smiled at how gullible I had been to imagine this might be crocodiles. Then up ahead I saw ripples – and it was not my gentle movements which disturbed the water. I scrabbled around feeling for the river bottom with my boots, shins hitting sharp rock edges. It took me for ever to find somewhere to get my feet down. I shuffled over a flat boulder until I was only waist-deep in the water. My heart was pounding wildly. What was causing the ripples? How would I get out of the water? The only option was to climb one of the steep slippery mudbanks, but there was no time. I was trapped in the river. I cursed that once again my lack of imagination had allowed me to get myself into danger – I had nearly killed myself cave-diving in England by being too casual about the risks. Once more I wondered what I was doing in such a situation. I stood scanning the water for the crocodile but the ripples had not changed or moved. Then, as I calmed down, I realised that a little tributary joining the main river was all that was disturbing the water. Paul was right, there was no crocodile in here. I was still tense, though, and even winced when tiny toothless fish nibbled at my thighs.

A hundred yards further on, the river stopped at a wide mud beach. Then it trickled through the sediments to continue lower down. I dumped specimen pots and the Karrimat on the beach and went back into the water. Innumerable white shrimps of different sizes swam around. Many seemed blind, but orange pinpoints reflected from others, showing that some had eyes. In 1981 I had collected what I thought were three types of shrimps from Andrafiabé Cave, but an expert from the Natural History Museum in London identified them as nine species: four were new to science. These Second River Cave inhabitants were unlikely to be the same species I had found in Andrafiabé eight miles away, so I collected a few of each variety. To the naked eye, two types were easily distinguishable, but

how many species were there and how many of these were
unknown?

I tried to match Paul's directions with what I could see; the cave
was larger than I had imagined. Beyond the beach, it continued up
over a thirty-foot mound of mud and boulders. Down the other side
was a small clear pool. I crept down to peer in. It looked sterile
and there was no food to sustain fish. But no, my first glance
had overlooked ghostly transparent blind shrimps: long-limbed and
delicate, fastidiously picking over the sediments with their tiny
chopstick pincers. Engrossed, I hardly noticed a fish that emerged
from under a rock. It was white and had no eyes at all. Most 'cave fish'
turn out to be surface species washed into caves by mistake: anaemic
creatures with normal eyesight which die without reproducing there.
This was unlike any river fish; it was a strange-looking animal, three
inches long with a broad over-sized mouth. Two tiny black spots in
the sockets were all that remained of eyes. Completely lacking in
pigment, it looked pink where the blood showed through its scales
and there was a dark streak of food in its gut. This must be a new
species, for the only other cave-adapted fish known from Madagascar
was trapped under the deserts in the south-west of the country, a
thousand miles away and in much younger limestone. Excited, I
edged close to the pool. Slipping the shrimp net into the water raised
a cloud of silt and the fish calmly meandered out of sight under an
overhanging rock. I moved the net down into the centre of the pool,
rested it on the bottom and squatted down to wait.

Just as another muscle twinge was making me think I should
abandon the hunt, a second fish appeared, larger than the first.
obligingly, it swam over the net and I gingerly raised it. Again the fish
cruised unhurriedly away, just out of reach. Following slowly with
the net, I blocked the only exit from a cul-de-sac in the pool. The fish
was content to stay put. I slid an open hand into the water, tentatively
wiggling my fingers to encourage the fish towards the net; when I next
raised the net I had a catch. Straightening up to examine my captive,
I smashed my unprotected head against the cave roof and almost lost
the fish which was rapidly climbing out of the net. Rubbing my head,
I stumbled back to the beach whilst trying to flick the amphibious fish
back to the bottom of the net, and then transferred it safely to a pot.
Soon I was back in the water again heading towards the grey glow
of daylight. The outward trip was unpleasant, though. I had churned

up the silt and I could no longer see the sharp boulders. In the exuberance of my success, I hardly noticed the lacerations inflicted by the submerged limestone edges. At first the temperature in the river had seemed refreshing after the burning heat outside, but such a long immersion was chilling and unpleasant. I emerged, dazzled by the midday sun, blue-lipped, goose-pimpled, with blood trickling from cuts on my legs – but ecstatically happy.

It was wonderful to scramble out into the daylight again and the sun soon warmed me and dried out my shorts and T-shirt. It was past midday and time to settle down amongst the boulders outside the cave and await the lemurs. This would be a perfect place both for observing and photographing them, since they would have to leave the shadow of the trees and cross open ground to reach the cave entrance. It was a lovely tranquil spot, ideal for writing an inspiring update for the newsletter of the Scientific Exploration Society, one of our sponsors. Mick and Roo were due to leave Ankàrana in about a week and could act as postmen. I settled down to write, but dropped my last functioning pen which rolled away beneath the boulders. Not again! Numerous useful objects had gone the same way: notebooks, pens, films, even binoculars. We managed to recover most of them but at the cost of scratches and bruises. The limestone rocks were eroded into needlepoints so that lying on them to wriggle down between the boulders felt about as comfortable as a bed of nails. Luckily my pen had not fallen to the bottom of the boulder pile and was resting on a ledge not far below, so I wriggled down and recovered it fairly easily. Returning to my chosen boulder perch, sore and a little more bruised, I settled down again to write. I had not managed more than a few lines before a striking orange Madagascar Pigmy Kingfisher flew in and perched close by. It was about four inches long, and another species peculiar to Madagascar. It swooped on the lizards in the leaf-litter, eating six in an hour.

The first Crowned Lemur troop appeared, heralded by gentle grunting noises. As ever, a large female led her troop through the forest stretching up out of the riverbed on my right. I could not see how many lemurs were following her. Some bounded over the limestone high above the cave entrance, others were betrayed by leaves rustling in the canopy as they scampered easily amongst the small branches. Soon the leader was descending a tree growing amongst the boulders about fifty feet from the cave entrance. She hugged the trunk and bounced down bottom first, leapt onto a rock about ten feet from me and looked all around; she was aware of my presence, but was quite unconcerned.

She was close enough now to see the markings on her fur. From a distance the females look uniformly grey but they have snowy white chest and belly fur and in place of the striking dark 'crown' of the male there is a subtle light brown triangle between the ears. She held her long bushy tail erect like a flag, ready to use it to signal to her troop or balance her weight when she leapt to another boulder. Her legs were much longer and more powerful than her arms, but when she walked on all fours, she kept her legs half-flexed so that her bottom rarely rose inelegantly into the air. Her face was dog-like, her nostrils were comma-shaped, but her hands revealed her as a primate. They were slender, well padded against the sharp limestone and thorny vegetation, and resembled human hands with their flat finger nails and – the hallmark of primates – opposable thumbs. The female Crowned Lemur studied me and I watched her from the corner of my eye. Staring would unnerve her, in the same way as it frightened the children in my clinics!

Soon, the female decided that I was a harmless imbecile and warily she led her troop into the cave to drink. A male came close enough for me to see his tusk-like canine teeth, which he would probably use when fighting for females. Only about five minutes elapsed before another troop appeared. They would not enter while other lemurs were inside, so passed the time grooming, browsing on a few leaves or simply dozing. I took notes, furiously scribbling details of each lemur and trying to record indications of troop hierarchy. As they came close I could see the characteristic prosimian inverted-comma nostrils. Primates, the order of mammals which includes Man, other apes, monkeys, lemurs, bushbabies and lorises, are subdivided according to the shape of the nostrils. The prosimians' (lemurs, bushbabies, lorises) are comma-shaped, internally convoluted, complex and hairless; while simian nostrils are hairy, with a simple internal structure and circular openings. This seemingly trivial difference reflects great contrasts in the ways the two groups use their senses. The more advanced simians (monkeys) rely on good sight, whereas prosimians have an acute sense of smell, as the Stink Fight of Ring-tailed Lemurs shows. One of the most appealing characteristics of my lemurs was that for most of the year they are placid, passing their days browsing on their favourite fruits or leaves, dozing together, grooming each other or playing. This is in great contrast to the behaviour of those supposedly more advanced primates, the monkeys, which spend so much of their lives biting, sparring and bad-temperedly squabbling over who is dominant over whom. The matriarchal lemur society is naturally a peaceful and harmonious one.

Suddenly there was a piercing shriek from a male squatting half-way up the limestone cliff above the cave. Hectic anxious grunts followed and tails wagged like pendulums. There was another shriek and all the lemurs joined in a shrill, panicky chorus. Even lemurs far away in the forest were shrieking. What had upset them? This was something serious; lemurs inside the cave shot out and sped up the cliff to join in the cacophony.

They were looking beyond me along the dry riverbed leading to the cave. I turned to follow their anxious stares and saw a powerful puma-like beast with huge round eyes, strolling slinkily, cool and confident towards the cave. He had short light brown fur and was a metre long, with his tail extending another metre horizontally. This was the Fosa, *Cryptoprocta ferox*, Madagascar's largest surviving carnivore: a mischievous animal with a ferocious reputation. This one certainly acted like the king of the Malagasy jungle. The locals say the Fosa steals meat that has been left cooking by dipping its long tail in the river, shaking it to extinguish the fire, then helping itself to the meal. The Fosa is most hated for decimating chicken houses, spilling blood but only eating a few. They even take goats and sheep and are reputedly dangerous to people, too. It is no coincidence that in Malagasy *fosa* means to vilify or backbite.

We had found grey fur and pieces of crunched bone of Crowned Lemurs in some fresh faeces, and so we knew that there was a Fosa in the neighbourhood. I did not expect to see one in broad daylight, though, for the texts say they are nocturnal or crepuscular. The hullabaloo petered out as he silently sloped away, but the anxious grunts continued for a long time and it was several hours before any lemurs felt brave enough to go into the cave again.

Back at base camp, we heard chilling, almost human cries, like the call of some lost soul, which Armand identified as Fosa. I understood how the superstitious imagine the animal to have malign powers. The cries made all the sleeping lemurs shriek and grunt neurotically. And they had reason to worry, for the tree-climbing Fosa was a formidable adversary. Cat-like, they have sharp retractile claws and are accomplished hunters with acute senses. But they are not cats. They are the sole representatives of an endemic subfamily, the taxonomic link between the cats and the less advanced civets. Apart from the Fosa there are few carnivores on Madagascar. Lemurs would duck anxiously, however, even when noisy but harmless birds flew over. Some youngsters probably fall prey to raptors like the aggressive Madagascar Harrier Hawk, which is as big as an eagle. Strangely, the lemurs seemed unable to differentiate threatening birds of prey from raucous small parrots or even Turtle Doves!

# 14. The Bamboo Jungle

. . . in the forest
I often go there, to those quiet places,
To rid myself of the ugly urgent things
That torture men.
Green turf amid silent trees and soft light airs
And a spring of running water in the grass,
They freshen a jaded mind, they give me back to myself
They make me abide in myself
For is there any man can live in town,
Harried and always at white heat with some fresh disturbance and racket,
And not be dragged outside himself,
Not waste his time on emptiness
No longer privy to his own thoughts?

Marbod de Rennes, 1035–1123
(Translated by Helen Waddell, 1927)

My days at the river cave started just before dawn, but I did not need
an alarm clock to wake so early. The lemurs did a lot of travelling
around this time and my hammock was slung between trees on the
habitual route of at least one troop. I would be startled awake by a
thud as the leader landed and the impact was transmitted down the
tree trunk and through my hammock. This would be followed by
a lesser shudder as she took off again. Then there would be more
juddering thuds as the troop followed. Immediately I would start to
struggle out of my sleeping bag, a process which always took ages
for I was yet to discover an elegant way of getting out of bag and
hammock. Still half-asleep, I would rush to find my boots so that I
could set off in pursuit, laces trailing, to discover which lemur species
had woken me. At first I assumed they were nocturnal Lepilemurs,
but these early risers were more dynamic than that slothful solitary
species. They travelled in troops, too, and made the same happy

little grunts as diurnal lemurs. My clumsy attempts to follow them in the half-light took me up steep banks and crashing through tangled vegetation, with my untied laces catching on brambles. I would lose sight of them in minutes, to be left disgruntled and no wiser about their identity. It is unusual for a diurnal mammal to be active before dawn but I suspected that Crowned Lemurs were not the purely day-active species that the books say they are. I doubted my observations, though, and was uncertain which species I was watching. Here at the Second River Cave, there was less vegetation to obscure the animals, but it was still a week before I managed to stay with a group until it was light enough to be sure they were Crowned Lemurs.

After the energetic bout of travelling at dawn, the lemurs slowed down, and by eight they had all settled into browsing and dozing in a couple of trees. They became quiet and again were difficult to spot. This was an ideal interlude for my own breakfast. Collecting firewood, lighting the fire and brewing up black coffee and rice pudding or maize porridge took an hour, sometimes two on a bad day. But there was no need to rush. While I was occupied in organising breakfast, the lemurs would be resting and grooming. Once I had breakfasted, refilled the water container, washed and finished my chores, I spent the rest of the morning exploring, looking for lemur faeces and plants characteristically damaged by lemurs as they feed.

The lemurs seldom came to drink before the midday sun drove the shadows from the cave entrance, so it was not until after lunch that I settled down to the long hot vigil perched on boulders outside the Second River Cave, waiting. Initially, I thought we should conceal ourselves while observing the lemurs. Whatever I did, though, the lemurs always saw me and, by acting like a predator, I frightened them. They were far happier if we all sprawled out obviously on top of the boulders, chatting loudly and behaving as if lemurs bored us. Sometimes they would even approach to study our strange behaviour.

I learned to distinguish the approximate ages of the lemurs by their size and markings. While trying to sort out sexes, ages and troop numbers, I watched out for distinctive 'marker' individuals which would help identify particular troops. When one troop came to drink I could more or less keep track of all five or six lemurs as they darted between the boulders and in and out of the cave. But sometimes three troops would arrive at once and I would become completely confused about who belonged to which troop. I had to concentrate for long periods on a lot of seemingly chaotic and unpredictable subjects, so it was a relief when the Madagascar Black Swifts came swooping back into their cave roost, reminding me that dusk was gathering and the day was nearly over. The cave entrance rapidly disappeared in shadow at 5.30 and no more lemurs would dare come to drink until the sun returned the next day. Then I could relax and delight in recalling their behaviour and the day's amusing new tricks.

One afternoon a large female, well ahead of her troop, scampered down into the cave to drink. Before the rest could follow her inside she reappeared, dripping wet. In the gloom she had slipped right into the subterranean river. The other members of her troop gathered around to lick water from her fur. They clearly felt very threatened when entering the cave, so were quick to seize the chance of drinking from her, thus avoiding the risk of going inside themselves. Perhaps it also comforted her, for she must have had quite a scare.

The ungainly one-year-old juveniles, not long off their mothers' backs, had disproportionately large eyes which made them look even more startled and surprised than their big-eyed parents. They were half the size of the smallest adults, but much lankier and looked as if they had not quite worked out how to control their limbs. They leapt about after their parents, looking enthusiastic but incompetent, and often slipped or missed the tree they intended to land in. Around the area of the river cave, where they scampered around in the bushes and low branches, their ineptitude was amusing. But twice I saw juveniles misjudge a leap in the canopy and tumble down towards the ground seventy feet below. Fortunately, on both occasions, the youngsters managed to catch a hold of a branch as they fell. Presumably some are not so lucky and fall to their deaths.

Ring-tailed Lemurs of southern Madagascar are creatures of habit and their movements had soon become predictable enough for us to make estimates of troop and population sizes. At first the Second River Cave seemed such an ideal place to observe the Crowned Lemurs that I thought it would not take long to work out how the troops were distributed. As the days went by, though, I got more and more confused about the habits of the seemingly so disorganised Crowned Lemur. Unaware that scientists had described them as a day-active species, they were always up well before dawn, active after dark and often had feeding bouts between about midnight and two in the morning. Sanford's Lemurs had similar activity patterns. I tried to keep track of them, endlessly lamenting the fact that Crowned Lemurs did not behave as conveniently as the Berenty Ring-tails or Bernhard's Sifaka. It was impossible to follow the nocturnal activities without radio collars.

Even the diurnal activities of Crowned Lemurs were confusing, and their troop structure proved yet more difficult to fathom. Groups split up and reformed unpredictably and sometimes individuals, often solitary females, would come down to drink without the rest of their troop. One day three males appeared at the cave without females and without an obvious leader; one of them had a ring of fur missing from his tail, making him easily distinguishable from other males and my first marker individual. Perhaps at some times of the year males separate into bachelor troops? Maybe this was just the wrong time of the year to be attempting a population estimate. The three males turned up the next day in the company of the four female members of their troop: troops had not fragmented.

Having found one marker individual, I slowly began to recognise facial differences between adults. Once I could reliably recognise individuals, I would be able to identify troops, map their territories and then calculate how many lemurs each forest type could support. Only then would I have a chance of establishing accurately the density of lemurs in the Ankàrana forests and estimating how many lemurs were surviving here. Differentiating one troop from another was difficult. I thought that the dark circles or subtle stripes on the faces of some lemurs might help, but many turned out to have similar patterns. I was even uncertain of how many troops used the waterhole. I persevered, but the task I had set myself and the team semed hopeless. Without dart guns and tags or collars, I doubted if I would ever be able to recognise individuals reliably. I also wanted to record their activities for twenty-four hours a day to establish just how nocturnal these supposedly diurnal species were, but this too would be a near impossible, and certainly thankless, task without radio-tracking equipment and night-sights. We needed more time and resources.

I had hoped that the arrival of the infants would help identify some females and thus troops, but even the births were not synchronised as I had expected. In the fruit-rich forest around camp, Crowned Lemurs were born in mid-September and were already venturing off their mothers' backs. In the forests near the Second River Cave, where lemurs subsisted more on leaves than fruit, the infants arrived nearly a month later. Was the poorer diet reducing the fertility of the females? Each observation generated several more questions.

To the day-active true lemurs, cohesion of the troop is important, yet during the short time that they are fertile, the females will often accept the advances of any male who happens to be around: even a male of a different troop, if he can fight off other suitors. The season of wild promiscuity is very short, though, for Crowned Lemur females are only receptive and fertile for two or three days one month and (if they have not conceived) will be receptive again for two or three days the next month and a third time the month after that. The fertile periods are cleverly timed so that births coincide with the first rains which stimulate leaf flushes, flowering and fruiting. In 1987, when the rains came late, the infants were born later. Here at the river cave even the normally shy nursing mothers had to come out into the open to drink and I was delighted to be able to watch the infants develop. At first their little bodies were no more than three inches long and they were only sparsely covered with fur. Each crew-cut, closed-eyed, scrawny infant clung tenaciously under its mother's belly, apparently unshaken as she leapt across the boulders. They started life clinging around their mothers' waists, dishevelling fur like scrawny misshapen belts; but they grew quickly and were soon riding piggy-back: a much better position from which to survey the forest with their forever-boggling eyes and please-don't-shout-at-me expressions. Then the youngsters began, somewhat wobbily, to venture from their mothers' backs; they started by exploring branches and sniffing leaves.

One afternoon, while I was frantically trying to keep track of two Crowned Lemur troops which were milling about by the cave entrance, I heard an uncharacteristic grunt. Startled, I scanned the trees around me to see who had made the noise. There on an overhanging limb, shaded by other branches, was a lemur which looked almost black. It peered at me anxiously and I stared back with mounting excitement. What was this? Surely this was another lemur species! It moved out where the light showed its true colour. She was one of the darkest female Sanford's Lemurs I had seen so far. But what was she doing alone here? My unexpected presence, and then my reaction of staring threateningly at her, scared her off quickly and she did not return during the rest of my stay at the cave. My delight at such an unexpected sighting seeped away as I realised how little I knew of the forest and its fauna. I had had no idea that Sanford's Lemurs came this deep into the massif. We had been working in these forests for weeks now and still there were revelations: I still had only a fraction of the information I wanted and the forest clearly held a lot more secrets.

Yet despite all the problems and limitations of our research, we spent so much time living with the lemurs that we were able to piece together the best picture yet of the factors controlling their behaviour and ecology. We catalogued their food plants, their predators and the threats to their forests, and collected enough information to form the basis of a conservation package. We never did obtain accurate population counts, since any estimate was complicated by the fact that territorial sizes varied according to how rich the forest was. Highest population densities of Crowned Lemurs (in the forests of the *Canyon Grand*) worked out at the equivalent of two animals per acre, but this high density existed only during the dry season. When the rains came there were dramatic changes in the population ecology, since the new abundance of food – shoots and young leaves – allowed the lemurs to expand their ranges into the now scrubby desiccated zones, like the seemingly lifeless dry sections of the *Canyon Forestier* we had recently struggled through.

The forest that became so familiar to me was full of Crowned Lemurs, noisy with their calls or with leaves swishing as they leapt through the canopy. It was hard to accept that Ankàrana was probably the only forest left like this. Some Crowned Lemurs survive in the Montagne d'Ambre National Park, but they are trapped there and occur at much lower densities; and those forests are shrinking fast, too. Ironically, Ankàrana is better protected – despite the fact it has no warden and few people appreciate that it is a reserve – because of the traditional respect for the forest. Other forest areas near Ankàrana are now mostly terribly degraded by logging and burning and no lemurs can live in them. They survive only in a few forest pockets further north. Ankàrana has become the Crowned Lemurs' most important stronghold, and the massif's unique sunken forests attract in more primates than any forest elsewhere on earth.

How much longer will these isolated populations survive? Felling threatens them, but the *Direction des Eaux et Forêts* has no money to protect the forest and cannot stand up to the powerful corrupting economic arguments for timber exploitation. As scarcity pushes up the price of wood, it becomes profitable to offer large bribes and invest much money in getting trees out of difficult locations. I wondered if Georges Kharma, our disreputable one-eyed Abyssinian acquaintance, was still keeping his timber yard stocked with supposedly protected trees. Felling is threat enough, but Ankàrana is also at risk through the destruction of the Montagne d'Ambre forests, as they regulate the water which becomes Ankàrana's subterranean rivers. Clearance of the little remaining forest on Montagne d'Ambre would result in the demise of Ankàrana's forests and most of its unique wildlife.

An impressive list of lemurs live at Ankàrana. At least ten lemur species (representatives of all five Malagasy lemur families) survive in the reserve. This is a remarkable number for an area just twenty miles by five, and is a record number of primate species in a non-rainforest habitat. Could more species be hiding within Ankàrana's more inaccessible corners? For nine of the ten surviving lemur species, the forests of the massif are undoubtedly a critical refuge. It is an area truly worthy of conservation: home to nearly half of the world's lemur species.

☆

A couple of days later Phil arrived at the Second River Cave to capture lemurs on film. He, too, was excited by the prospect of seeing the new blind fish in its natural habitat. I suggested that he would see more if he entered the cave alone, while I kept watch at the entrance. He did not seem to like the idea of me staying behind and did not look his usual cool, cheery, enthusiastic self as we descended into the cave. At times I thought Phil was reckless. He was an accomplished caver and had demonstrated formidable climbing skills, fearlessly scaling the Ankàrana Wall. So why was he so anxious? Clearly I had not convinced him that it was safe to swim inside. I told him I would have made a succulent meal long ago if there had been crocodiles. This made him look even more uneasy as he climbed down over the boulders and into the water, with the shrimp net rolled in a Karrimat for buoyancy. He had swum no more than a few feet when the net slipped out and sank. Spluttered curses came as he tried to dive for the net. The thought of crocodiles had unnerved him a lot. There was much splashing as he tried to dive down – arms and legs flailed everywhere like a demented breakdancer. He could not find the net.

Phil climbed out, curses cascading from his mouth and water from his clothes. 'It's lost for good!' When I offered to try to recover the net, his expression changed from anger to condescension. But I had the great advantage of having seen exactly where the net had gone down. I slipped into the water, expecting to have to dive down many times and search the bottom yard by yard, yet confident I would find it eventually, for my SCUBA-dive training had taught me how to search systematically underwater. I swam out a little, folded at the waist, head under, bottom up, and let the weight of my legs send me straight down. The water was clear, but much deeper than I had imagined. My hands touched the smooth sandy bottom at seven or eight feet. I began to swim forward, hands sweeping back and forth feeling for the net. I found it on the second sweep. What incredible luck! Phil was even more amazed than I was when, after only one dive, I surfaced, grinning, with the net. 'Oh, I forgot you were a cave diver!' he said.

This time we entered the cave together. I rolled the net, collected equipment into a Karrimat, again tucking it under my arm, and led the way. Phil was more relaxed now, strangely comforted by my company even though logic must have told him it was no protection. Just beyond the first bend in the river, where I had been so frightened by those ripples, Phil noticed a side passage. There were no boot-prints in the sticky mud floor, nor had the others mentioned it. It must be an unexplored section and might open into new subterranean galleries. We climbed out of the water to investigate. The passage was small and oval in cross-section; we had to walk bent double, our boots sinking in deep and making rude squelching noises as we took each step. The end of the tunnel opened into a low chamber mostly occupied by a deep pool glazed with calcite an eighth of an inch thick. Two-inch gobies were living underneath: fish of normal pigmentation with clearly functioning eyes that must have reached the cave, just as their next meal would arrive, in wet-season floods. We collected two and searched carefully, but in vain, for blind fish.

By the time we returned to the river, the sediments we had churned up on the way in were settling again and we noticed tens of blind fish. We had been swimming through shoals of them! All the known species of troglobitic fish inhabit deep caves, but these were living within sight of daylight. Food is normally at a premium in caves and so cave-dwellers adopt strategies of energy conservation, combined with a talent for tracking down scarce food in absolute darkness. Troglobitic fish have very low metabolic rates, they do not sleep and spend day and night slowly cruising around in search of food. Thus they survive in an inhospitable environment unsuitable for sighted, fast moving, energy-wasteful fish from surface streams. Close to the cave entrance, where food is abundant (the surface of the subterranean river was littered with dead insects), I expected that fish with eyes would exclude the blind fish. But there was enough food for all and the fish were not forced to compete.

I was stiff with cold, and fish tickled annoyingly as they nibbled at my legs. Phil wanted to collect a fish to photograph. I was thankful when he captured one quickly, and we were soon warming up in the sun again. But Phil then found that his complicated camera equipment had been short-circuited by the humidity beside the cave: bad luck, or perhaps I had offended the Ancestors. He lost interest in both fish and lenses and decided that he would return to base camp with the others to continue other projects, leaving me alone to the delights of watching the Crowned Lemurs. Another group would join me in a few days to replenish my food supplies and check that all was well. I savoured the prospect of solitude, for I felt sure I would see much more when there was no one but me to disturb the animals. That afternoon's lemur-watching was a particularly entertaining one. Several juvenile males put on a special demonstration of how not to leap around in the trees. After a fall, one of them encountered a harmless two-inch-long lizard which first interested and then terrified him by unexpectedly running towards him.

I retired to my hammock an hour after dusk and drifted off to sleep feeling contented, intrepid and completely self-sufficient. Then something came rooting in the leaf-litter close by. It sounded large. I felt uneasy, telling myself there was nothing to be afraid of in the Malagasy forest. Well not much anyway. The snuffling came closer. The animal sounded larger. If I was a proper zoologist I would investigate. I lay still. Then slowly, trying not to make a noise, I started to rummage for my torch. But the sounds of me moving put the beast to flight. I lay wide awake for a long time, wondering what it was and whether it would come back. It was a long time before I felt secure enough to fall asleep.

Big rainspots, warm as blood, woke me. The moon had set and it was very dark. Watchless, I had no idea how long I had been asleep. I lay there confident that the rain would soon stop – this was the dry season after all – but it got heavier and colder. I was too snug to move. In a couple of minutes, if the rain continued, I would climb out and find shelter. The rain continued. I stayed put. Where could I go? The only cover was in the boulder-strewn cave where there was nowhere to hang a hammock and no place flat enough to sleep. My sleeping bag was soon soaked and there was no longer any point in moving anyway. I slept fitfully, wet through and shivering. Dawn took forever to arrive and I lay meditating on the morning cup of coffee which would revive me.

Once I had extricated myself from the hammock and peeled off the clinging wet sleeping bag, I emptied out my boots and squelched over to my little fireplace, shivering still and miserable. I had left the matches out in the rain and all the firewood was soaked: that would teach me to tidy my campsite! I spread the matches, wood and myself out in the sun to dry and in a couple of hours I had the coffee brewing. There was no sugar. Most of it had emptied into my rucksack on the journey here. Maize porridge was thoroughly nasty without sugar or jam, so I investigated the recesses of my rucksack and upended it to shake out the sugar into the saucepan. The porridge was not then bad at all, despite the addition, with the sugar, of a liberal helping of sand, some onion skins, two hairgrips, a few twigs, leaves and a long-lost nailfile.

Rustling in the leaf-litter in the river bank above me disturbed my breakfast and a beady red eye on an eagly head peered out of the bushes. A rather shy friend had come by to remind me that I was not alone. He turned his head to get a better look at me and to show off in profile his substantial hooked beak. This was another shadow-skulker that I had so far failed to photograph. Like the Mesite he knew that if he lurked in the darkest undergrowth he could frustrate all attempts at photography. He was a handsome bird, with chestnut-coloured back and long black tail: a raven-sized cuckoo which builds its own nest. As always, he was reluctant to fly and stomped noisily around in the litter for a while, then lazily flew up a few feet onto a low shrub. From here he glided effortlessly, wings outstretched and legs dangling, only needing to flap his wings once or twice before he reached the next foraging ground. He came by most days and continued to foil all my attempts to capture him on film. He was a Madagascar Coucal, another endemic species, though like the drongo and the mynah, difficult to distinguish from close relatives in Asia. At the end of the last century one Dr Sclater, secretary of the Zoological Society of London, ventured a theory to explain Madagascar's zoological links with Asia. He suggested that there was once a great continent in the Indian Ocean named *Lemuria*. He supposed that, Atlantis-like, this sank into the ocean, leaving a remnant which is Madagascar. He never produced much evidence for his unlikely theory, but modern biologists still find it hard to explain why the Malagasy fauna has so many relatives in far away corners of the globe or which exist only as fossils.

Breakfast failed to dispel the night chills, so I decided to get my circulation going by continuing my explorations of the area. Only a few hundred yards from the river cave, just above and right of the cave entrance, a small canyon led eastwards. Not far in, deciduous almost English-looking forest gave way to dense bamboo jungle which filled the canyon almost completely. It was strange stuff to walk through, for although it gave the impression of hemming me in and looked quite impenetrable, the graceful thirty-foot-high bamboo crashed down easily when I applied my boot to it. I particularly wanted to search here for evidence of bamboo-eating Gentle-lemurs. There were no fresh traces of any lemurs using the bamboo, except for the occasional glimpse of a Crowned Lemur hastily leaping through it, but there were old dried lemur faeces containing the fibrous remains of undigested bamboo to prove that a bamboo-eater still lived in the area. These faeces could not have come from a Crowned Lemur. Did they originate from the Lesser Bamboo Lemur, a species which is still quite widespread throughout Madagascar (although unrecorded from Ankàrana)? Or could the Broad-nosed Gentle-lemur still be surviving here? Deeper into the forest I found a piece of bamboo stem which looked as if it had been shredded by an animal, as if damaged by feeding Broad-nosed Gentle-lemurs from the rainforest. I photographed and collected the evidence, excitedly wishing (albeit fleetingly) that I could share this news with someone.

The work so engrossed me that I forgot which way I had come into the jungle. All I could see was bamboo. I squeezed between the poles until sheer limestone barred the way. It would be easy to find the way back from here: I would just follow the canyon wall along until I got back to the river cave. Yet after fifteen minutes' scrambling, I found myself in a blind-ending canyon. I began to feel worried. I must have been going in the wrong direction, so turned round and rather hurriedly walked the other way. Twenty-five minutes later, the terrain was no more familiar and the vegetation was so thick that I still had no hope of getting my bearings. Why was I not carrying a compass? I cursed my stupidity and suddenly felt terribly frightened, incompetent and alone. What now? The others would not be coming here for several more days. I had no water and no matches to light a fire to show them where I was. I ran back and forth along the canyon wall, first convinced that one way was right, then the other. I tried to calm myself down. I would climb up out of the canyon so that I could orientate myself. This was an easy solution so why was I panicking? Fortunately the walls were not very high here and it was a simple climb even for someone as inept as me. At fifty feet above the canyon floor there was still too much vegetation to see where I was. I needed to climb up higher onto the *tsingy*. I had watched Crowned Lemurs scampering about up here, quite unperturbed by sharp limestone, harpoon burrs and thorny vegetation; I wished I had a quarter of their agility.

The surface of the limestone was made up of innumerable tiny spikes, so it was easy to get my boots to grip, but my hands got badly grazed again as I climbed. My leather gloves had fallen apart weeks ago. I found myself clinging on to a huge block which rocked threateningly. It was like this everywhere on the *tsingy* and I had become accustomed to the boulders which seemed so alarmingly unstable, but which were in fact securely perched. I had grown blasé: they were just too large to slip. That day, though, I jumped on to a block perhaps a yard long by two wide and found myself sliding on it down into a gully. I stood balancing, and in that strange, distant, slow-motion that life assumes when something frightening is happening, I wondered whether to stay with my sledge or to jump off. Either might have disastrous consequences. I must have hesitated only for a split second, then a small leap got me clear, unscathed except for a minor laceration – to the knee of my trousers.

The incident shook me up, for even a sprained ankle out here on my own would be unpleasant. I continued more carefully and eventually got high enough up to be able to see where I was. The view was unbelievable, especially after the claustrophobic bamboo forest. I could now see how I had got lost. Beneath me a blind-ending spur led off the main canyon which, from up here, was vivid green with bamboo straggling out of it. I *had* been going in the right direction when I first started trying to find the way home, but following the canyon wall had led me into a sheer-walled cul-de-sac. All I needed to do was descend, cross to the far side of the canyon and follow the other wall until the ground dropped away into the dry river valley where I had made my camp. Easy!

From this vantage point I could see across to the boulders outside the river cave. Above, lemurs were feeding amongst screw-palms and scrawny *tsingy* shrubs. Looking west was the section of the *Canyon Forestier* that we had struggled along for hours. In the foreground was the parched tangled low scrub and this merged into increasingly green forest. Then, on the horizon, a notch in the seemingly endless hostile *tsingy* marked the deepest, narrowest part of the canyon where we had marvelled at the strangler figs and swung on lianas. Whilst it was difficult to appreciate inside the forest that it was only a patchwork between the *tsingy*, I could see why we so often got lost in it. In places it was a maze of *tsingy* islands and blind-ending canyons and it was easy to forget that we were moving through tongues and pockets of forest, rather than the limitless tracts that they appeared to be.

Looking behind me, eastwards, the canyon continued into a patch of rich green forest where Flame Trees – the source of senna – and Hildegardia were decked in lavish crimson and orange blossoms. The Second River Cave irrigates this section of forest, too. The few trees growing on the *tsingy* around and above it, watered only by infrequent rains, were yellow and weedy. Even their leafless branches looked meagre, in stark contrast to the dark green canopy below. I could see beyond the edge of the massif to the expanse of red dusty desiccated savannah and to the towering volcanic ash-cones. The road linking Diégo to Ambilobé must have been only a few miles away. How strange to be able to see to the outside and yet be so remote from it. If I had an accident no one would know; people would continue travelling, crammed into minibuses, totally unaware of the inhospitable terrain that hemmed me in. I felt small, insignificant and a very long way from home. Then strange marks on the rock caught my attention and made me forget my isolation. Although the *tsingy* was absolutely dry, its surface had been rasped away by the tongues of snails. Then layers of algae and mosses grew in crevices and it seemed that when the rains come, the *tsingy* turns green. Aestivating snails then emerge to graze on the algal bloom. There were enormous numbers of large white discoid shells scattered everywhere. It seemed incredible that the baked desiccated limestone could ever grow enough algae to support such a substantial population of snails. I imagined hundreds of them awaking after a six-month sleep, unbolting their front doors and slithering out to feast on the algae.

I had not come up here to marvel at the ecology, though, and realised that I had forgotten the way down. Yet again I had failed to note my route. I scrambled onto a wide ledge, alarming a solitary male Crowned Lemur, then looked around to see how to descend the last sheer thirty feet. Eventually I resorted to embracing a tree which was growing close to the canyon wall and slid to the ground with an undignified slither and scrape. I landed, thoroughly scratched, with my shirt up around my neck and with my hair full of twigs and thorns. Back in camp, five minutes later, I felt thoroughly unfit to be leading this Royal Geographical Society sponsored expedition!

The third thing to go wrong that day was that the lemurs did not turn up. They had been able to get enough to drink from licking leaves after the previous night's rainstorm. I felt suddenly desolate and lonely without their company and contemplated packing up and returning to base camp. Then visits from my friends, the Coucal and the Pigmy Kingfisher and the annoying but reassuringly familiar Blankety-blank bird, made me feel less isolated and sloth made me delay my departure. Next day the lemurs were back to cheer me up and provide more information to swell my field notebooks. I was absolutely happy again.

The Crowned Lemur had never been photographed in the wild before and I thought that portraits of them framed in the cave entrance would be really stunning. I got close to where the lemurs passed on their way into the river cave and settled down, hidden by a large overhanging rock, with my camera poised a few feet from the habitual route of nearly half of the troops. Three young males began the descent to the cave entrance. When they rounded the corner which brought me into view, though, they exploded into a chorus of shrieks and fled up into the trees again. From this safe distance they stared at me anxiously, screaming, grunting and swinging their pendulum tails. I was acting like a predator and so they were treating me like one! I should have predicted this response, having observed the suspicion with which they had treated my water container. I had wedged it just inside the cave, just visible in a crack, and there it lurked motionless behaving just like a predator. My marauding behaviour had so surprised and upset this troop, that they were now too scared to come down at all. Rather than prevent the lemurs from drinking, I retreated, and spent the rest of the afternoon collecting more seeds for Kew.

☆

After a few more days alone, Sally and Paul arrived to replenish my supplies and check that I still knew what day it was. Paul teased me about not having a calendar of notches on a tree trunk. Sally had suffered on the walk; first the barbed grass had got her, then she had brushed against a leguminous climbing plant with pea-pod seeds which were covered in fine penetrating irritant hairs. Each of the hundreds of fibres stuck into her skin needed to be removed one by one. I listened sympathetically, and then expounded my new ecological theories and told of the adventures of the previous days. It was good to converse with someone other than the animals (I did not admit that I had been talking to them). Once they had bathed, I enjoyed seeing the delight on their faces as they watched my lemurs going about their daily antics. With confidence and morale boosted again by human company, I explored the surrounding forests with more enthusiasm, starting to map lemur territories. There was much less fruit here and the poorer food supply meant that troops needed to range further than those at base camp. We continued detailed behavioural observations, comparing notes, delighting in good views of newborn lemurs and enjoying the tranquillity of the glade by the cave waterhole.

We needed to collect yet more blind fish for the Malagasy National Museum in Tana, and for British taxonomists to describe and identify. We also wanted to take some alive so that biologists in London could study their specialised, energy-saving physiology. The lemur observations were once again punctuated by further trips to the end of the Second River Cave. At this point Sally announced: 'I've never been caving – may I go in?'

This have-a-go-at-anything approach was typical of Sally. She had responded to a request for a nutritionist scrawled on a notice at the London School of Hygiene, and had soon committed herself to a four-thousand-mile trip in a small outrigger boat of the kind that the first settlers might have used. The expedition was to prove that it would have been possible to navigate across the Indian Ocean from Indonesia to Madagascar two thousand years ago. She was the only female crew member in the company of eight men she hardly knew and, although taken on as nutritionist, to her horror, she ended up as cook. On arriving at Ankàrana she firmly announced that she could not cook, but nevertheless enriched our diet with some appetising new recipes; most popular was rice pudding made with coconut milk. The conditions, for most of their seven weeks afloat in the *Sarimanok*, were utterly miserable. They subsisted on half-cooked rice, were constantly hungry, wet, tired and often fearful. One of the team had died, another was taken desperately ill half-way, and there had been the constant threat of capsize. But Sally played down her adventurous spirit. When asked of her interests, she said she liked watching television.

The river cave was hardly the place to be introduced to caving. A careless splash would put out the carbide lamp and there were all those jagged rocks under the surface, but Sally was heading for the cave entrance even before I had finished trying to dissuade her. Cruising calmly in, she chattered enthusiastically about the beauty of the cave and disappeared around the corner. All was quiet except for the occasional slopping of water against the mudbanks. I sat on a boulder at the water's edge, straining to hear what she was doing, feeling anxious and already forgetting that I had taken worse risks myself. Her light reappeared twenty minutes later and, as she came close, all I could see were shiny white teeth and an extremely broad grin. The cold had not dampened her excitement: 'That was great!'

While I was at the Second River Cave most of the others had left base camp to start heading homewards; now the prospect of returning to a deserted camp did not appeal very much. Nor did I relish the thought of repeating the five hours' liana-bashing to get back. We stayed on together until the food had all but run out. I left the cooking pot, water container and the little remaining rice at the river cave campsite, promising myself a return trip in a few days' time. At last I was beginning to recognise individual lemurs and was slowly starting to make sense of the apparently chaotic troop hierarchy. One more trip would enable me to tidy my data into an ecological masterpiece – or at least an acceptable basic ecological description of the unstudied, endangered Crowned Lemur.

The return trip along the *Canyon Forestier* did not seem as long this time. We had started early and the gentle morning light made it easy to see where the lianas had been cut, and we were back under the forest canopy before it got too hot. Here Paul pointed out the pair of Collared Nightjars, a species supposedly confined to Madagascar's eastern rainforests but which were always in this spot. Weeks before Roo had noticed them camouflaged to look like the red-brown leaf-litter where they spent each day. Paul, impressed by such a close view of such rare and attractively marked birds, sneaked up on them with his fancy camera equipment and snapped off ten shots. When he had finished, Roo sauntered up much closer. The nightjars were so confident of their camouflage that they stayed and posed for him. He took a wonderful close-up portrait with his instamatic camera – a far better photo than Paul's!

# 15. A Sting in the Tail

*Ohatra ka tsy maintsy ho kekerim-biby aleo kakerin' ny tantely!*
If you must be bitten by something let it be by a bee:
at least the bee has given you honey!

Malagasy proverb

It was good to be back home at base camp with its comforts,
familiarity and a more varied menu. Dave Clarke, who had been
on his own for a few days now, was as pleased to see us as
we were him. He brought out for our admiration all the insects
he had collected, and proud-father-like he showed us the larvae,
camouflaged as bird droppings, that he had tenderly reared. At last
he had an appreciative audience for his latest creepy-crawly stories.
In his searches for butterflies and citrus leaves to feed the larvae, he
had visited Matsaborimanga and returned with new captives which
delighted him. They were compact black insects with yellow stripes
and he enthused about how much more attractive these were
than their American counterparts. These were endemic Madagascar
Hissing Cockroaches – not creepy-crawlies, he said, but distinguished
insects with character. They whistle when courting, and he squeezed
one to make it hiss in disapproval at being picked up. They were quite
amusing, I suppose.

I was too thirsty to respond much to his enthusiastic chatter.
Priorities were a drink, a bath and some cold boiled rice and sugar.
I sat down to guzzle a mugful of water when a troop of Sanford's
Lemurs caught my attention. They were sitting in a line along a
branch, spot-lighted by sun streaming through a hole in the canopy.
One of the females had a week-old infant on her back. I plunged my
hand into my bag for another film.

Suddenly I feel a sharp searing pain in my right index finger and
hear scuttling from inside my bag. A scorpion has drawn blood. I

squeeze hard and try to suck out the poison, while people gather round to see what has happened. I expected it to be more painful than this. Paul, veteran of two tropical expeditions, tells me I should take some pain killers: 'It'll hurt.' I think he is exaggerating, but follow his advice. I continue to suck my throbbing finger while Dave and Paul explore my bag for the culprit. I feel foolish and . . . what about my photograph? The lemurs are still there watching us.

My assailant's body is three inches long, but it looks bigger, sitting with its long tail and distended sting curled over it. It is like a diminutive tank: a formidable iron-clad of the leaf-litter. Dave says that the nastiest ones have small claws because they rely on their venom to kill their prey. This one has small claws. I don't need this kind of information now. The scorpion gets dropped into alcohol, a treatment which normally dispatches insects in seconds. But it responds to this noxious environment by sealing its spiracles and, for over an hour, it swims around in the alcohol, seemingly unaffected.

I should apply a tourniquet, but it's getting too painful now. I consider local anaesthetic, but an injection would sting horribly and I am too cowardly to inflict more pain. I start to feel strange and tell myself that it would be sensible to lie down. The puncture mark is no longer visible, but my finger now feels as if it has been hit with a large hammer. It is throbbing, swollen and red. Painful pins-and-needles are spreading into my forearm. It is still not too bad but it is getting worse minute by minute. Sweat starts to stream off me and I cannot find a comfortable position. People look concerned. Any movement makes my hand and arm more painful. The pain spreads up my arm as far as my armpit. My left hand and feet are tingling, too, and my back aches. The tingling must be because I am over-breathing. I chastise myself, mumbling that only neurotics hyperventilate. The others ask what I said. Silently, I concentrate on breathing slowly.

Trying to think about something else, I ask Paul why he doesn't take the lemur photo. 'You want that picture badly, don't you?' Half-heartedly, he snaps a photo. I feel bad. I kneel up, lie down, lie propped up, curl up. Take some morphine. The water to wash the tablets down feels like swallowing red hot tintacks. There is a lump in my throat. My nose and sinuses are congested and my eyes stream. Blowing my nose provokes a wave of severe pain in my face. My throat feels tight and I begin to worry that my airway is closing up. I have never even seen a tracheotomy performed. I vaguely know where to make the incision, but I do not fancy teaching someone how to cut into my throat while I am asphyxiating. Best not think about that. I wonder if there is any treatment. The books say that scorpion stings are only painful, not dangerous. The Chinese shopkeeper in Diégo-Suarez who sold us much of the tinned food for the expedition said that if anyone was stung we should crush the scorpion in a pestle and mortar and apply this to the sting site. When I suggest this, Paul, with remarkable and disarming faith in the local medical services and our abilities to reach them, says that having the scorpion would help doctors decide on the right treatment. I wish I had his confidence. The nearest doctor is a day away and even once I got to him, 'supportive therapy' would be the best I could expect. There was no antidote.

'I think I'll have the hydrocortisone. Has anyone ever given an injection?' No one has. Nervous hands drop the only needle into the leaf-litter. I don't care: an abscess from a dirty needle would be the least of my worries. I grab the ampoule and hypodermic and shakily draw up the hydrocortisone into the syringe. The air bubbles will not disperse and I feel like crying. People, looking worried and perplexed, are watching, so I don't, and gain a strange distant control of the situation. I tell myself what to do, as if teaching a medical student. People look strangely at me as I mouth instructions. Cleaning a patch of skin with an injection swab reveals my filthy state. Having just got back to base camp after a hard half-day's jungle-bashing, I need a long cool soak in our subterranean bathroom. I stab the little orange needle into my calf muscle, surprised that it does not hurt and wondering if anyone else has given an injection there before.

Another wave of pain grips my face. I wonder how much morphine I dare take: too much and I'll stop breathing. I have already swallowed six tablets – far more than I give even to terminally ill patients. I vaguely consider the risks and decide to take more. The pain is now severe and constant no matter what position I am in. The shakes make it worse. I am aware that I am whimpering but the sound is far away – like someone else. The others say I should drink, for the sweat continues to pour off me, but it is too painful to swallow, even my own saliva. They tower over me. I long for them to entertain me. Why can't they take my mind off this? Just talk to me! Their silent expressions tell me I look ghastly. I don't feel comforted. I wish they would make light of the sting and distract me from my pain but they can't think of anything to say, except that I should try to drink.

Hours drag by in agony from my arm, face, lower back. What is this doing to my kidneys? Slowly the morphine begins to work, or maybe the injection has helped. Perhaps it would have eased by now without these drugs. I can sit up: still in a lot of pain, but it is tolerable now. The worst is over. I am not going to die. I am calm now. The worst is really over. Compared to that previous agony, I am comfortable. As the pain eases, though, I become aware of another sensation – as if it is raining – and there are unpleasant cold feelings, like sitting in a puddle, wherever my skin touches anything. I am not over-breathing, but the painful pins-and-needles in my hands, feet and tongue persist.

I feel hungry. It is early evening and I have not eaten since a snatched breakfast before six. Sally squeezes out cool soothing coconut milk from grated flesh and offers it to me. Opening my salivating mouth to drink provokes a painful spasm of my chewing muscles and the red-hot pins-and-needles return when I swallow. I should not have sucked out the poison. I will eat tomorrow.

At last, as dusk gathers, I begin to feel as if I could drift off to sleep. It is going to be a long night. Sally offers her Walkman and a choice of Tina Turner or Mozart's *Requiem*. Christian touchingly offers his bed. A scorpion got him on the arm a week before and the swelling of his face has only just resolved. Afterwards, to avoid any further encounters, he built a sleeping platform out of saplings. I accept his bed, knowing I will never sleep in my hammock as I am. He struggles inexpertly into my hammock and is soon snoring. I long to be able to sleep.

Night falls. The pain returns, six hours after taking the first morphine. I take more. Appropriate as the *Requiem* seems – Paul later said that he thought I was going to die – it does not create the right atmosphere, particularly with the nightjars accompanying the soloists. It starts to rain, for the second time in two months. The rain on my arm is excruciating, scalding. Sally brings a huge piece of polythene. That hurts my arm, too, but I can prop it up so it does not touch my hypersensitive skin. I cannot sleep. It is an interminable miserable night. Even the lemurs, usually so entertaining, torment me by shrieking at the rain, upset by thunder, and dropping half-eaten fruits on me. I fall asleep around 4am, half an hour before first light, and snatch a little sleep before breakfast sounds wake me again. I feel better and am sure I will need no more morphine. But when I sit up I realise that I am sick, bleary eyed and still quite heavily sedated. I have a morphine hang-over. Sweet tea and travel-sickness pills help. I ache all over. I spend the rest of the day cat-napping when I can no longer fight off drugged sleep. And in my dozy, spaced-out state, I recall Princess Manarovika of Andrafiabé saying that scorpions never sting white people. Would that she had been right!

☆

Later, in Diégo-Suarez, Sally, Dave and I visited Jean. I tried to look pleased as Madame Radofilao offered *Bon-bon Anglais*. I sipped politely as I related my misadventure.

'No, Malagasy scorpion stings are not supposed to be fatal,' said Jean. 'It is the spiders here, not the scorpions which kill . . . though one of my students died after a scorpion sting. He was a large eighteen-year-old.'

'What happened?'

'He drank cold water.'

At that moment, Sally and Dave must have recalled how they had pressed me to drink. Our eyes met and I burst into uncontrolled hysterical laughter.

Back in England, I tried to find out how I should have treated myself. Some texts say that it is dangerous to administer morphine and steroids, while other experts actually recommend this treatment. Noone really seems to know. I found a reference to a child being saved by an injection of haemolymph – this scorpion equivalent of blood was thought to neutralise scorpion venom. Perhaps the Chinese grocer in Diégo had been right and a poultice made from my assailant would have been the best treatment; or maybe it would have made things worse. Lebanese doctors cauterise the sting site with lighted matches, while others recommend urinating on it! Apparently when Indonesian lizards get stung by scorpions, they plunge into the nearest cowpat and emerge revived. Perhaps even manure neutralises the toxin.

The scorpion which got me was *Grosphus palpator* – and it did provoke my heart to palpitate. Stings from close relatives of this species kill numerous adults in India each year. That fact alone is quite worrying, for there are not many animals which can kill a healthy full-grown person. Scorpion venom not only poisons the nervous system, but also forces the blood pressure so high that the lungs fill with fluid and people die of heart failure and asphyxia. The damage to the heart muscle shows up on ECG like a heart attack and takes several months to return to normal.

☆

My index finger had no feeling for a month and it still protests in cold weather. Two years later my two-finger typing is hampered by an uncomfortable sensation in one of them. But I felt reasonably well again thirty-six hours after the sting. Frustratingly, though, my arm and hand remained painful and useless for more than a week and there was still so much to do at Ankàrana. Jean had told me in passing of a cave containing skeletons of what seemed from his descriptions like extinct giant lemurs. Perhaps even bones of the Elephant Bird might be there. The remains were beyond a vertical drop sixty feet deep. I was the only member of the expedition remaining at Ankàrana who knew how to abseil, and although Paul was more than capable of learning, it would have been madness for a cripple and a novice to descend into the cave, especially as there would be no one to help if we got into trouble. The sting put paid to my planned return to the Second River Cave waterhole, too. I could not face struggling through that undergrowth with a sore arm. I had also developed a scorpion neurosis – paranoia almost – and found myself minutely searching my sleeping bag several times a night, so that going to sleep took an age of preparation.

A few days after I was stung I was awakened by something moving between the sheet liner and my sleeping bag. Nightmare! I tried to reach the little torch I kept clipped to my hammock, but it dropped out of reach. What should I do now? If I swung out of the hammock I would certainly get stung again. I called for help. Dave appeared with a torch and helped me out, and we searched the bedding. There was no sign of a scorpion, but a little mouse scampered away into the night. I had been woken before by a mouse climbing on my face and had been amused by its bravado. But this time I was not laughing: I was sick with fear and in a cold sweat.

As the wet season set in, the scorpions became more and more numerous. We suspended rucksacks, bags and shoes from nails on trees, but scorpions continued to get into our clothing and luggage. They appeared from everywhere. We obsessively searched for them, but even so Sally managed to annoy one while she was rummaging amongst the food baskets. It prodded her with the sharp end of its sting, but for some reason did not dispense any venom, only warning her to leave it alone. She was lucky.

I was growing very tired and increasingly had days when, awakened by the lemurs' pre-dawn travelling bout, I cursed them. I wanted to sleep longer, especially after nights disturbed by mosquitoes. They would home in on my face, whining infuriatingly, just as I drifted off to sleep. Slapping and swatting drove them away but then, just as sleep was beginning to envelop me again, they would be back. I buried my head in my sleeping bag, but that was too hot and I had to emerge to get bitten again. Gingerly, I rummaged in my washbag for something to relieve the itching. Nothing helped very much, but applying cream was a displacement activity: at least I felt as if I was doing something. The tube I found was cooling, and cured the itching immediately. I made a mental note to contact the drug company who had generously donated it, for they deserved a letter of glowing recommendation. Soothed at last, I drifted off to sleep, dreaming of cheese and crisp green apples. The following morning people looked so disapprovingly at me that I thought maybe I should brush my hair for a change. I had not looked in a mirror for nearly two months and had not exactly been careful about my appearance lately.

'Whatever happened to you?'

'Pardon?'

'What happened to your face?'

Someone found a mirror and showed me. My face was covered in toothpaste.

Bothered by insects and scorpions, we also had another reason for looking forward to the end of the expedition. Food was running out. All we had left now was rice, those disastrously indigestible little beans, a very sad and wrinkled pumpkin, garlic, sugar, coffee and a great deal of salt. By now we had bought up the entire stock of dried bananas from Matsaborimanga and even the unpopular Tutti-Frutti jam had finally run out. I dreamt of meals in the cordon bleu restaurants of Diégo: king prawns, crunchy salads, green beans and carrots, fresh lime juice, papayas, pineapples, and eyebrow-singeing banana *flambé*. Only Sally was unimpressed by the deprivation: food and conditions had been far worse on the Sarimanok expedition. My food fantasies faded for a few days after a brief unexpected visit by Benjamin and Patryck, French *professeurs* from Diégo. They arrived to find me hunched uncomfortably over my little MacArthur microscope – 'looking at poo again', as Roo disrespectfully described my research. The *professeurs* wanted to know what I was doing, so I told of the fascinating parasites I was finding under the microscope and of my theory to explain why lemurs carried such light worm infestations. Lemurs browse on ebony trees and since ebony is used locally as an anthelminthic, this might keep the lemurs worm-free, too. Benjamin asked if I had tried eating ebony leaves; then, to my amazement, he suggested instead that we share the steaks, cheese, cool beer, even wine they had brought. He talked enthusiastically of lobsters and swordfish *fumé* and then of his other passion: lemurs. Benjamin's bushy black beard and his obsession with lemurs had earned him the not entirely complimentary name of '*Babakoto*' from his pupils. He was a fanatical conservationist and had devoted every spare second of his eight years in Madagascar searching for lemurs; he knew Ankàrana well, yet he too was unaware that it was a reserve.

Despite the increasing discomforts, I tried to convince myself that this was a good time to be at Ankàrana. Rain stimulated great changes in the ecology. Now birds were singing their hearts out, insects were stridulating and chirping, even the lemurs seemed to be grunting more enthusiastically. Seemingly dead twigs and vines up on the *tsingy* were putting forth leaves, fruits and flowers. Wild figs sprouted succulent little red fruits which the Crowned Lemurs particularly relished after their spartan dry-season diet. The fig bushes provided the first real focus for squabbles between lemur troops. It was as if the lemurs had called a truce during the hard times of the dry season, but as food became abundant again, they could afford to waste energy arguing over it.

Early one morning I encountered a Crowned Lemur troop and managed to keep them in sight for a couple of hours. I made detailed notes on their behaviour, confidently anticipating the completion of the first ever unbroken day's observations on this species. They fed and browsed and dozed and groomed, then suddenly I realised that the lemurs had disappeared. Without alarm or obviously bounding away, they had evaporated into the forest. I cursed my concentration lapse. The lemurs were still not completely habituated to our presence. Failing to make contact with the troop again, I decided to return to camp for a cold rice lunch. An unfamiliar and desperate cry up in the canopy startled me. It sounded like a small rodent but it moved about the tree-tops as fast as a large bird. I hurried around camp trying to get in a position where I could see what it was through gaps in the leaves. The sound continued to move about, but eventually I saw, perched high on a thick branch a hundred feet above me, a large bird of prey. In other circumstances I would have called her handsome, with intelligent yellow eyes, sleek tawny wings and fine speckled breast, but the sight that met my eyes turned my stomach. Out of her mouth protruded the front half of a small mammal. Even with binoculars I could not make out whether it was a large rat or a tenrec. Most of the prey was either bitten off or half-way down the raptor's throat, but it still managed to scream piteously and struggled desperately with its free forefeet. The bird was unmoved and manoeuvered so that she could gulp the rat a little further down. Did any carnivore kill kindly? No wonder lemurs were anxious of shadows in the skies.

So small mammals were emerging from their aestivation. More butterflies appeared, both to amuse Dave and to increase his workload. Land crabs became active, and I was fascinated by the giant millepedes. They were nearly a foot long and as thick as a man's thumb. Impressive creatures, looking from a distance like highly polished snakes, they glided silently over the *tsingy*, managing vertical surfaces easily. Others, an inch broad and two inches long, rolled themselves into impenetrable balls when handled, just like British Pill Millepedes but ten times as large and more attractively marked. Both species browse on leaf-litter and other vegetable detritus and are completely harmless, although their slightly irritant defensive secretions make lemurs sneeze as they gobble them up.

I collected some millepedes and tied them into a plastic bag full of dead leaves, thinking they would make ideal exhibits in the vivarium at Tsimbazaza Zoo. Next morning, when I went to show them to Dave, they had gone, leaving only a neat half-inch hole in the plastic bag. He said it was a pity that they had escaped, for they were magnificent animals and Great Characters! He was not so fond of the eight-inch *Scolopendra* centipedes which now infested camp.

They must be the most ferocious fighting machines ever designed by nature or Man. They bite at one end, sting at the other, and each leg can inflict a nasty little wound – as Dave knew to his cost. He is Keeper of Insects at London Zoo, where he was once sent an unmarked box. The centipede inside, rather irate, ran up Dave's arm registering its indignation at every painful step.

☆

Simagaul arrived with his *chariot-aux-boeufs* for the last time. He asked for a third course of antibiotics to cure his VD, but I was unsure whether he had actually caught it again or only intended to. We stoked up the breakfast fire with the dining table, Christian's bed and all our rubbish. The men from Matsaborimanga were horrified at our intention to burn the remains of our clothes, ripped on the *tsingy*. My trousers were the only ones still with a seat, reflecting how much less intrepid I had been than the rest of the team. Even the white trousers that had made Paul look so dashing when he had had lunch with the British Ambassador in August, had metamorphosed into a pair of well ventilated, asymmetrical shorts. Simagaul was delighted with our cast-offs: filthy short-sleeved shirts which once had been long-sleeved, bits of trousers, saucepans, cutlery, buckets, water containers and baskets.

We loaded the cart with rucksacks and Simagaul's souvenirs and made our final walk through the forest of the *Canyon Grand*. I took one last sad long look at the Place-of-the-Rock, wondering if ever I would return. Armand guided us out across the savannah to a junction of two dirt tracks, about eight miles from camp, where a *taxi-brousse* passed around 11am each day. He picked some custard apples, and ate them with us before he departed. It had been a good expedition. We had achieved a great deal and had had very few arguments. I sat in the shade, so sad to be leaving, but musing greedily on the culinary delights awaiting us in Diégo. It would not take long to replace the stone of fat I had lost during my first two and a half months in Madagascar. I planned the tasks I would tackle once back in town. First was to see whether the freight had arrived.

A sparkling new Mercedes lorry came by and we flagged it down. Sally and I were invited to sit with the driver, while Dave had to ride on the timber in the back. Big profits were being made in timber if dealers could afford to buy such expensive lorries. I asked where the planks were destined. The driver did not want to talk about his work and asked what we were doing in such a remote place. Lemurs did not mean much to him, but on hearing I was a doctor, he started to tell me in great and boring detail about various symptoms that troubled him. He had stomach trouble when he ate rich foods and an invisible rash on his arms. After so many weeks treating the uncomplaining Antankarana, his symptoms did not impress me. Most of the population of Madagascar would have loved to have been able to complain of rich foods giving them indigestion. I tried to buy his attention to my questions about our forest by promising some special English cream for his 'rash'. Whenever I asked about where the trees had come from and whom he worked for, though, his previously excellent grasp of the French language suddenly failed him. On much pressing, he finally told me that the planks were destined for a Roman Catholic girls' school in Diégo.

Dave was thoroughly scorched by the time we reached town and children danced along behind him singing, 'Mena bé! Mena bé!' (Very Red! Very Red!).

We showered and lunched in style at the *Hotel Valiha*, grateful that the menu was far from traditional. I ordered Devilled Crab and a huge salad, followed by *crêpe surprise*. Dessert was not quite the surprise I had anticipated, though. The *crêpe* was filled with the loathsome Tutti-Frutti jam.

The freight shipment containing all our essential equipment had arrived at the Trans-7 office a few days before, so I attempted to start the long process of shipping most of the cargo back home again. As far as I know it is still in Madagascar.

We celebrated our last night in Diégo back at the *Nouvelle Hotel* nightclub, this time with Benjamin. Our inept attempts to copy the sedate local dance style made us very thirsty; the *rhum* and coconut milk punch slipped down too easily and made the night whizz by. Next morning, I realised that the *punch au coco* was not as innocuous as it had tasted. My head was pounding and my stomach was out of control on the flight south and I almost missed a last glimpse of Ankàrana as we flew over. It looked deceptively green; the few shrubs now growing on the limestone gave the impression of luxuriant vegetation. The green must have matched my complexion. Slumped back in the seat for the rest of the flight, I wondered distractedly whether I would need to use that little paper bag that Air Mad so indelicately labelled *sac vomitoire*.

☆

The rest of the team were long gone by the time we arrived in Tana in October, but Maggie and Anne were waiting for us there. We had reports to write, more people to meet, specimens to distribute and preparations to make for the medical projects. Dave showed us the insect exhibit that he had put together in Tsimbazaza Zoo. It was now impressively stocked with spectacular invertebrates and the chamaeleons and Day Geckos we had brought back from Ankàrana.

Word of our discoveries at Ankàrana preceded us, so as soon as Dr Césaire Rabenoro heard that we were back in Tana, he insisted that I give what he described as an *exposé* about our work there. To me this conjured up a turn in naughty French underwear. I was almost as alarmed when I realised he wanted me to lecture to the *Académie Malgache*. How could I talk to a group of distinguished biologists about the fauna of their own country in broken French? Reading the alarm in my eyes, Dr Rabenoro explained that English was one of the *Académie*'s three official languages and that his colleagues needed English language practice: I should lecture in English.

The day came for the talk. Forty key academics sat around a long leather-covered table ready to take notes; their interested faces looked expectantly at me: the ambience was formidable. This was almost as bad as facing another scorpion attack. There was a complex ritual-etiquette to these meetings. When Martine had presented her palaeontological work the week before, she initially spent a full ten minutes saying how honoured she was to be talking to the *Académie*, how fortunate she was to have been able to do the work, how grateful she was to me for inviting her on the expedition, how the whole thing would have been impossible without the support of her *chef du service* and funding from Duke University; she thanked everyone imaginable and, much to my embarrassment, made a dozen unnecessary references to Dr Jane Wilson. Martine went on to give an impressive paper on the importance of the subfossil finds from Ankàrana and how they contributed to the understanding of Madagascar's ecology before the great wave of extinctions precipitated by Man's arrival. After her talk, someone gave a long and effusive speech on how the

*Service du Paléontologie* had come of age and taken its place amongst the academic departments of the world. I would never be able to match this excessive style, and was sure that my reserve might make me seem rude.

Dr Rabenoro gave a long flowery introduction in Malagasy. Since I could follow very little of what was said, I smiled benignly, presumably creating the impression of having the intellect of a Mesite. As his oration continued, my mind drifted back to all those meetings at the beginning of the expedition and especially to the one with Dr Randrianasolo who had mistaken us for a high-powered, internationally-funded academic team. For all our inexperience, amateurism and lack of money, we had achieved much and completed the most detailed study yet of any Malagasy reserve. Even the reserves and parks which were easily accessible had not received such attention by so many specialists. Later, largely through Phil's efforts the following year, wardens were employed to patrol the reserve which now attracts interest from both biologists and tourists. Suddenly I felt rather proud of our expedition and pulled myself together, determined to convince my audience of the value of our work and the need to conserve Ankàrana.

Maggie read a *résumé* in French and then I began. I spent only a minute on my opening preamble, thanking everyone and saying how wonderful I thought Madagascar. The academics sat attentively, looking puzzled, for in my anxiety I gabbled too fast to be comprehensible. I was grateful for my linguistic advantage, since I hoped it might make them overlook my lack of manners. I rambled enthusiastically about Ankàrana's uniqueness, wealth and beauty. To my surprise, half an hour of questions followed. Apparently I had convinced them that Ankàrana was indeed an ecological wonderland. When Dr Rabenoro summed up he said that next time I came to Madagascar I should take members of the *Académie* to see Ankàrana! I surveyed my smartly-dressed, well-fed, middle-aged audience and hoped that I would not really be expected to lead such a rash expedition.

By the end of December the expedition's commitments had been fulfilled and the reports were all written. A bevy of Malagasy friends came to the airport to see me off. Monsieur Abraham of Madagascar Airtours whisked me past desks for health checks, police checks, currency checks, and straight to the customs post.

'*Manao ahoana tompoko!*' I greeted the *douanier*. He looked delighted.

'How long have you been in Madagascar that you speak Malagasy so well?' he asked in French. He delved into the top of my bulging rucksack and pulled out a plastic bag containing some specimens. 'What are *these*?'

I handed him my hard-earned inch-thick pile of permits entitling me to export specimens and souvenirs; each was headed the Crocodile Caves of Ankàrana Expedition.

'Are these crocodiles?'

'No, they're bats – *chauves-souris* – *ramanvy!*'

Confused, he referred to my papers. On top was a permit to export a fresh pineapple.

'Ah, they are for eating?' He tossed the bats away, wiped his hands and dismissed me with revulsion and no more than a superficial luggage search.

Next came the security check. The officer found twenty French francs in my purse. 'You have not declared this,' he remarked, slipping it into his pocket. After six months enjoying Malagasy hospitality, such petty corruption by an underpaid government servant could not sour my affection for Madagascar. Yet it set me thinking about corruption on a bigger scale. How easily Ankàrana's forests could disappear: felled to line the already full pockets of some avaricious official or unscrupulous businessman.

# Updated Postscript

In June 1988, we heard from Patryck, one of the French *professeurs*. The Kharma Sawmill Company was logging the rich, crucial *Canyon Grand*, a refuge for Aye-aye, and where we had recorded a forest packed with amongst the highest density of primates on earth. I received the news with the same incredulity and bitterness as when a good friend was raped by a stranger. I imagined my placid, defenceless lemurs first panicking, then bewildered as their forest home was ravaged. Then, with their dry-season larder gone, August would see them starving.

I didn't expect to hear of the one-eyed Abyssinian again and never imagined his greed could push the Crowned Lemur to the very brink of extinction. George Kharma arranged the logging, but Prince Tsimiharo III and even officials of the *Direction des Eaux et Forêts* were rumoured to be enjoying the proceeds of the timber sales. The caterpillar-tractor and chainsaws were withdrawn after acrimonious lobbying by conservationists, by which time one third of the *Canyon Grand* had been felled and bare cliffs could be seen. The exploitation continued for the rest of 1988: villagers cut rare *pallisandre* trees (*Dalbergia* spp.) by hand and took them out on bullock carts. Kharma explained that he had only needed the timber to reconstruct the bridge at Ambody Pont, so that locals no longer needed to risk crocodiles by wading across the river. He did not mention that the bridge also allowed more efficient removal of logs from the reserve.

Kharma's wanton act provoked such fiery criticism that plans to protect the region were rushed through. In February 1989 the Malagasy government (MPAEF) employed six guards, trained by the World Wide Fund for Nature (WWF). They travel on mountain bikes, working in pairs for increased security; two are stationed in the north (at Anivorano Avaratra), two in the west (Matsiboramanga) and two in the east (Mahamasina). By now two more should be working in the south.

Patrick Marks and Hilary Bradt who visited in November 1992 and 1994 respectively, sent me heartening accounts of the state of the forests since the guards started work. Our old base camp (now known as the *Camp des Anglais*) is still a wonderful place to see lemurs and Patrick even spotted the Fossa that we had frequently heard there but never seen; the Mesites are still scrabbling around in the same brainless way – their survival is a sure sign that the canopy, in this part of the forest, at least, is intact. And shrieking Lepilemurs still disturb the slumbers of human intruders to the Lost World. Closer to the savannah, the forest is regenerating. As it recovers it contributes yet more diversity which is the key to Ankàrana's incredible ecological riches.

JMW, July 1995

# Appendix 1

*Lemurs at Ankàrana – subfossils and living species
recorded up to 1995*

Since Martine's work at Ankàrana in 1986, there have been a series of palaeontological
expeditions which have discovered that an array of lemur species once lived there. A
list follows of all species known both from subfossil evidence and from our sightings of
living animals.

| Species | | Current Status at Ankàrana | Conservation Status[1] |
|---|---|---|---|
| **Common Name** | **Scientific Name** | | |
| | *Pachylemur* sp. | – | extinct |
| | *Megaladapis* cf. *madagascariensis/grandidieri* | – | extinct |
| | *Mesopropithecus* sp. | – | extinct |
| | *Palaeopropithecus* cf. *ingens* | – | extinct |
| | *Archaeolemur* cf. *edwardsi* | – | extinct |
| Sloth Lemur | *Babakotia radofilai* | – | extinct |
| Indri | *Indri indri* | locally extinct | endangered |
| Broad-nosed Gentle Lemur | *Hapalemur simus* | locally extinct | endangered |
| Grey Gentle Lemur | *Hapalemur griseus* (maybe *occidentalis*) | scarce | vulnerable |
| Sanford's Lemur | *Eulemur fulvus sanfordi* | common | vulnerable |
| Crowned Lemur | *Eulemur coronatus* | common | endangered |
| Sportive Lemur | *Lepilemur septentrionalis* | common | vulnerable |
| Mouse Lemur | *Microcebus* sp. (maybe *rufus*) | common | abundant |
| Fat-tailed Dwarf Lemur | *Cheirogaleus* sp. (maybe *medius*) | scarce | rare |
| Fork-marked Lemur | *Phaner furcifer* | scarce | rare |
| Woolly Lemur | *Avahi laniger* | scarce | vulnerable |
| Perrier's Sifaka | *Propithecus diadema perrieri* | very scarce | endangered |
| Aye-aye | *Daubentonia madagascariensis* | rarely seen | endangered |

[1]conservation classifications are defined (by IUCN) as follows: extinct (no longer
existing anywhere on earth); endangered (in danger of extinction); vulnerable (likely
to become endangered in near future); rare (small global population but not yet
vulnerable or endangered); abundant (not presently threatened). See also C. Harcourt
and J. Thornback, *Lemurs of Madagascar* IUCN, 1990.

# Appendix 2

*Members of the Crocodile Caves of Ankàrana Expedition, 1986*

## British scientists at Ankàrana

| Name | Background | Responsibilities |
| --- | --- | --- |
| Phil Chapman | Education officer, French speaker | Zoology (especially birds), photographer. Co-leader |
| Dave Checkley | Medical researcher | Exploration and logistics |
| Dave Clarke | Keeper, London Zoo insect house | Insects and reptiles; breeding swallow-tailed butterflies |
| Sally Crook | Entomology researcher | General zoology |
| Anne Denning | Doctor, French speaker | Clinics, lemur surveys |
| Simon Fowler | Entomology researcher | Photography, entomology |
| Ben Gaskell | Zoologist | Bats |
| Sheila Hurd | Computer analyst, French language graduate | Exploration, expedition secretary |
| Maggie Hutchings | Doctor, French speaker | Clinics, lemur surveys |
| Nick Lear | A-level student | Zoology |
| Mick McHale | Outwardbound instructor, zoology graduate | Zoology (especially cave biology and bats) |
| Paul Stewart | Ecology undergraduate | Ecology (especially crocodiles, lemurs, mesites), photography |
| Richard (Roo) Walters | Electronics engineer, French speaker | Cave exploration, surveys and maps, scientific report editor |

| Jane Wilson | Doctor,<br>biology graduate | Zoology (especially lemurs),<br>parasitology.<br>Co-leader |

## Malagasy collaborators at Ankàrana

| Name | Background | Responsibilities |
| --- | --- | --- |
| Jean Radofilao | Mathematics lecturer | Cave exploration and surveys |
| Jean-Elie Randriamsy | Curator of insects | Entomology and ornithology |
| Guy-Suzon Ramangason | Botany lecturer | Botany |
| Raobivelonoro Ralaiarison-Raharizelina | *Chef de Service*, Department of Palaeontology | Palaeontology |
| Martine Vuillaume -Randriamanantena | Palaeontology lecturer and researcher | Palaeontology |

## Team at Morondava

Sally Crook    Nutritionist, parasitologist
Ann Denning    Doctor
Simon Howarth    Irrigation and public health engineer
Maggie Hutchings    Doctor
Ermone Ranaivoson    Parasitologist at the *Institut Pasteur de Madagascar*
Marco Ravoajanahary    Linguist and organiser
Jane Wilson    Doctor, parasitologist

## Members of the Southampton University Madagascar Expedition, 1981

André Adamson    Leader, undergraduate ecologist
Mike Boase    Undergraduate archaeologist
Catherine Howarth    Undergraduate ecologist
Liz Sparke    English graduate
Mary Styles (née Wilson)    Medical student
Jane Wilson    Medical student

# Appendix 3

*Selected Bibliography*

Anon, *A Glance at Madagascar*. Tout pour l'école, Antananarivo, 1973.

Attenborough, David, *Zoo Quest to Madagascar*. Lutterworth Press and Pan, London, 1961.

Battistini, R and Richard-Vindard, G (editors), 'Biogeography and ecology in Madagascar' in *Monographiae Biologicae*, Volume 21. Junk, The Hague, 1972.

Bradt, Hilary, *Guide to Madagascar*. Bradt Publications, 1988.

Bradt, Hilary, *Madagascar*. Aston Publications, 1988.

Brown, Mervyn, *Madagascar Rediscovered*. Damien Tunnacliffe, London, 1978.

Horn, Alfred Aloysius, *Trader Horn in Madagascar: the waters of Africa*. Jonathan Cape, London, 1929.

Jolly, Alison, *A world like our own – man and nature in Madagascar*. Yale University Press, New Haven/London, 1980.

Jolly, Alison, 'On the edge of survival' in *National Geographic* **174** (2) 132–61, August 1988.

Jolly, A, Oberlé, P and Albignac, R (editors), *Madagascar* (Key environments series). Pergamon Press, Oxford, 1984.

Meier, B, Albignac, R, Peyriéas, A, Rumpler, Y and Wright, P, 'A new species of *Hapalemur* from south-east Madagascar' in *Folia primatologica* **48**, 211–15, 1987.

Oberlé, Philippe (editor), *Madagascar, un sanctuaire de la nature*. Lechevalier, Paris, 1981.

Petter, JJ, Albignac, R and Rumpler, Y, *Faune de Madagascar* series, **44**: *Mammifères, Lémuriens*. ORSTOM/CNRS, Paris, 1977.

Shaw, George A, *Madagascar and France*. The Religious Tract Society, London, 1885.

# Appendix 4

*Scientific Publications Resulting from the Expeditions*

ECOLOGICAL PAPERS

Past and Present Lemur Fauna at Ankàrana, N. Madagascar. *Primate Conservation* in press, 1995

*Glossogobius ankaranensis*, a new species of blind cave goby from Madagascar. *aqua: Journal of Ichthyology and Aquatic Biology* 1994, **1** (3) 25–28

*Troglobius coprophagus*, a new genus and species of cave-dwelling collembolan from Madagascar with notes on its ecology. *International Journal of Speleology* 1990 **19** 67–73

Ecology and conservation of the Crowned Lemur, *Lemur coronatus*, at Ankàrana, Madagascar with notes on Sanford's Lemur, other sympatrics and subfossil lemurs. *Folia primatologica* 1989 **52** 1–26

Survey and management proposals for a tropical deciduous forest reserve at Ankàrana in northern Madagascar. *Biological Conservation* 1989 **47** 297–313

Ankàrana: a rediscovered reserve in northern Madagascar. *Oryx* 1988 **22** 163–171

Clear-felling of more Lemur Forest in Madagascar. *Primate Eye* 1988 **36** 21–22

Lemurs and Forest Conservation at Ankàrana, N. Madagascar. *Primate Eye* 1987 **32** 30–31

The Crocodile Caves of Ankàrana, Madagascar. *Oryx 1987* **21** 43–47

The Crocodile Caves of Ankàrana: Expedition to northern Madagascar 1986. *Cave Science* 1987 **14** 107–119

Population ecology of Ring-tailed Lemur and White Sifaka in Madagascar. *Folia primatologica* 1986 **47** 39–48

Ecology of the Crocodile Caves of Madagascar. *Cave Science* 1985 **12** (4) 135–138

Freshwater shrimp genera *Caridina* and *Parisia* of Madagascar with descriptions of four new species. *Journal of Natural History* 1984, **18** 567–90

MEDICAL PAPERS

Wells worms and water in western Madagascar. *Journal of Tropical Medicine & Hygiene* 1988 **91** 255–264

A study of Bilharzia and intestinal worms in children from Morondava. *Archives Institut Pasteur de Madagascar* 1987 **52** 105–116

FILM

*The Wilds of Madagascar*. National Geographic film and video.

# Glossary

Malagasy and French words are in *italics* and scientific names in **bold**.

*aide sanitaire*: health worker

*alo-alo*: carved wooden posts used to decorate tombs of the Mahafaly tribe. Often these feature events in the life of the deceased and are topped by carvings of zebu horns.

Antandroy: 'People-of-the-Thorns' – a nomadic tribe living in the arid south of Madagascar around Ambivombé. They live very simply, wear few clothes and subsist mostly on millet, maize and cassava. Like the Mahafaly, they build substantial tombs for their Ancestors.

Antankarana: 'People-of-the-Rock' – a tribe inhabiting northern Madagascar around Antsiranana, Ambilobé and Ankàrana.

Antanosy: 'People-of-the-Island' – people of the south, principally around Fort Dauphin

*Babakoto*: Indri, **Indri indri**, the largest (tailless) surviving lemur

*bé*: big

*brèdes*: green leafy vegetable

*car-brousse*: a full-sized bus (usually), providing a public transport service into *la brousse*, 'the bush'

*chariot-aux-boeufs*: bullock cart

*fady*: complex system of taboo in Madagascar

*famadihana*: '*retournement des morts*'; exhumation to honour The Ancestors

*fanorona*: Malagasy board game which resembles draughts. Like draughts, a player wins when he has taken all his opponent's pieces. Moves are made along the lines of a complex grid of squares and diagonal lines.

*fiadànana*: peace

*fòkon' òlona*: council of elders or responsible people who have jurisdiction over a community which traditionally has a common ancestor, often comprises two or three villages, and is known as a *fokontany*. *Olona* means people and *tany* means earth or land.

*grotte:* cave

*Hauts Plateaux*: high plateau of central Madagascar

*hotely*: roadside shack selling basic rice meals and tea to travellers; the European kind of hotel is called *hotely misy fandriambahiny* – literally, a hotel with beds.

*Imerina*: part of the island of Madagascar inhabited by the Mérina tribe; the central high plateau

*lamba mena*: shroud; literally, red cloth

*lamba oany*: rectangle of brightly printed cotton material worn like a Malay sorong

*Madagasikara*: Madagascar

Mahafaly: tribe of about 120,000 people who inhabit the south-west desert around Ampanihy and Ejeda. The name means 'Those-who-make-taboos'.

*maki*: Malagasy word for several Lemur species, including the Ring-tail

*manao ahoana tompoko*: respectful greeting

*mena*: red

*Mérina*: the dominant and most numerous of Madagascar's eighteen tribes. They inhabit the *Hauts Plateaux* around Tana, which is also known as Imerina.

*misaotra*: thank you

*mofo 'gasy*: *mofo* (pronounced moof) means bread, and *gasy* is short for Malagasy. This is a sort of greasy doughnut.

*mpanandro*: wise man who advises on auspicious days and on *famadihana*

*nosy*: island

*omby*: zebu, ox, hump-backed cattle

*raiketa*: the racquet-shaped 'cactus' or prickly pear, **Opuntia dillenii**

*Ramanavy*: insectivorous bats

*rano*: water

*ranovola*: literally, golden water, but actually the tea-like drink traditionally served with a rice meal and made by boiling water with burnt rice

*ravenàla*: **Ravenala madagascariensis**, the endemic Madagascar Traveller's Palm or Traveller's Tree

Sakalava: 'People-of-the-Long-Valleys' – once the largest and most powerful of the Malagasy tribes, they practised human sacrifice up to the middle of the last century. Traditionally the Sakalava keep cattle and the number of cattle owned by a family determines its wealth and status.

screw-palm or screw-pine: substantial palm-like shrubs of the **Pandanus** genus; Madagascar has seventy endemic species.

*sifàka*: lemurs of the **Propithecus** genus, named after their alarm call

*taxi-brousse*: bush taxi

*taxi-bé*: literally, big taxi; a large car, usually a Peugeot 505, running a regular 'bus service'; a communal taxi

*tsi* or *tsy*: no or not having; so Tsimafana means Not Hot or a cool place

*tsingy*: spiky limestone scenery in Madagascar

*valiha*: cylindrical stringed musical instrument made from a piece of bamboo often nearly a metre long

*vazaha*: foreigner, usually meaning European but sometimes used to mean Malagasy of another tribe

*veloma tompoko*: goodbye

*zaza*: child (Tsimbazaza means forbidden to children.)

*zebu*: the ox or hump-backed cattle; these are different from the grey water buffaloes familiar to those who have travelled in Asia.

*zoma*: Friday or a market which occurs on Fridays. The word is a corruption of the Arabic for Friday.

# Acknowledgements

Kind people, too numerous to mention all of them here, helped with the expeditions. They include: David and Lucy Andriamparison, Jean DeHeaulme, R D Hyde, Steve Kingsley, Benjamin LeNormand, Mr Abraham and staff of Madagascar Airtours, Mme Voangy Rakotonirina, Dr Hilarion Rakotovololona, Mme le Dr Berthe Rakotosaminanana, Mme le Dr Rakotovoa, Mme Suzanne Ramanantoandro, Dr Georges Randrianasolo, Mme le Dr Vololomboahangy Ravaoalimalala, Marco Ravoajanahary, Valerie and Phillipe Traquis, Patryck Vaucoulon, Miss Susan White, Dr Jim Williams, Alex Bourke, Hilary Bradt, Dr Andy Cairns, Mrs Thelma Clinton-Carter, Dr Lee Durrell, Dr Peter Edwards, Dr A T R Fuller, Eric Gordon, J E Hill, Dr John Horton, Dr Catherine Howarth, the late and much missed Dr G T Jefferson, Martin Jenkins, Dr Alison Jolly, Howard Jones, Dr Tim Mead, John Middleton, Peter Moore, Harry Pearman, Dr Jon Pollock, Dr Rory Putman, Dr Alison Richard, Mike Salisbury, Sir Peter Scott, Dr Vaughan Southgate and colleagues, Miss Winifred White, Jill and David Wilson. Others are mentioned in the book; companies which generously supported us are acknowledged in our scientific publications.

The budget for the 1981 expedition totalled £4,141.48 and that for the 1986 project, £15,268.44. This was raised through personal contributions and from grants from the British Ecological Society, British Museum, W A Cadbury Charitable Trust, Duke of Edinburgh Trust, Fauna and Flora Preservation Society, French Protestant Church of London, Gilchrist Educational Trust, Ghar Parau Foundation, John Spedan Lewis Trust, Mammal Society, Royal Geographical Society, Royal Society of Tropical Medicine and Hygiene, Scientific Exploration Society, Sir Samuel Scott of Yews, Smith Kline and French, Sports Council, Twenty-seven Foundation, University of Southampton and Westcroft Trust. The Winston Churchill Memorial Trust deserves special mention; they supported the 1981 expedition through a grant to Mary Styles née Wilson and also funded my first expedition in 1976 and thereby began my travelling career.

I am grateful to those who provided information while I was writing, marooned in Asia far from libraries. Among them are: Reverend Jim

Hardyman, Joseph Wilson, Dr Mary Styles, Hilary Bradt, Paul Stewart, Dr Boudewyn Peters and Winifred White.

Joseph Wilson (my Dad), Jill Sutcliffe, Alaric Wyatt and others generously gave time suggesting improvements to the manuscript. Jane Tewson revived my confidence when I thought I would never find a publisher. My greatest debt of all is to Simon Howarth for his quiet support during the labour pains of both expeditions and for criticism of the book in all its innumerable drafts; without his encouragement it would never have been finished.

The poem on page v is by 'Dox', whose real name is Jean Verdi Salomon Razakandrainy; it was published in Labatut, F and Raharinarivonirina, R, *Madagascar, étude historique*. Nathan-Madagascar, Tananarive, 1969. The translation of the poem which starts Chapter 14 is from *The Wandering Scholars*, published by Constable & Co Ltd, 1927.

The Scorpion Story at the beginning of Chapter 15 was first published in the Christmas 1987 issue of the British Medical Journal.

Royalties from this book will go to the Jersey Wildlife Preservation Trust to be spent on species rescue and other conservation projects in Madagascar.